MORRIS CARR
800 W. 1ST St. LA.
6265000

Clark Guidebooks

I

VIEW OF SAN IGNACIO

From a cliff looking southwest. See text page 138.

Lower California Guidebook

A Descriptive Traveler's Guide

with Twenty Detail Maps and Key Map
Illustrations, Bibliography and Index

by
PETER GERHARD
and
HOWARD E. GULICK

Fourth edition
With revision notes

THE ARTHUR H. CLARK COMPANY
GLENDALE, CALIFORNIA   1967

CONTENTS

		PAGE
PREFACE		7

INTRODUCTION

The Land	15
The People	18
Fiestas	20
History	23
Immigration and Customs Regulations	27
Money	29
Weights and Measures	30
Places to Stay	31
Health Conditions — Food and Drink	32
Means of Transportation	34
Roads	34
Railways	36
Air Travel	36
Travel by Sea	37
Bus Lines	38
Hunting and Fishing	40
Plants	46
Books about Baja California	52

ROUTE DESCRIPTIONS

Route 1. Tijuana to Mexicali	57
Route 2. Mexicali to San Felipe and on to Laguna Chapala	75
Route 3. Tijuana to Ensenada	87
Route 4. Ensenada to San Felipe	93
Route 5. Ensenada to Santa Rosalía	103
Route 6. Santa Rosalía to La Paz	149
Route 7. Excursions near La Paz	173
Route 8. La Paz to San José del Cabo, via Santiago	175
Route 9. San José del Cabo to La Paz, via Todos Santos	187
Route 10. Places reached by sea	195

MAP SECTION	213
INDEX	233

MAPS

Tijuana city map 56

Mexicali city map 71

Ensenada city map 91

La Paz city map 171

Route maps, numbers 1 to 16 . . . . 215 to 230

Folding key map 231

ILLUSTRATIONS

View of San Ignacio . . . . *Frontispiece*

Bridge across the Colorado River 99

Meadow in the Sierra San Pedro Mártir 100

Vegetation of the Northern Desert 117

Barren Peak of El Matomí 117

Palm Canyon leading to Santa María Mission 118

Mountain Ranch of San Gregorio 127

Mission Church of San Borja 127

Fishing Village and Cannery at Turtle Bay 128

Road through the Vizcaíno Desert 128

Mining town of Santa Rosalía 145

Turtle Camp on Laguna San Ignacio 145

Burros on the Road near Concepción Bay 146

Road along the Cliff on Concepción Bay 146

Mission Church at San Javier 163

Children of Comondú 163

La Purísima Canyon 164

La Presa Ranch, north of La Paz 164

Cowboys of the South in Leather Trappings 181
    Photograph by E. F. Dugeau

Malecón, or Sea-walk, at La Paz 181

Cape San Lucas 182

Sugar Mill at Todos Santos 182

PREFACE TO THE FOURTH EDITION

During the last two hundred years a great deal has been written about Lower California. One of the first books published (in 1771) was entitled "An Account of the American Peninsula of California, with an Appendix about False Accounts." By the end of the 18th century, with each new author attempting to correct the errors of his predecessors, the world had a fairly accurate picture of the geography of the peninsula and the tragic history of its native tribes and its heroic missionaries.

More recently Lower California has been re-explored by scholars specializing in different branches of science, and their findings have been and are still being published, with the result that many details which were previously undisclosed or forgotten have been brought to light.

In spite of all this, Lower California for some reason has become endowed in recent years with an aura of mystery, and much misinformation has been published about it. The present authors have attempted in this book once more to set the record straight and to present a useful and detailed description of the peninsula, with the sort of factual information that a traveler would want to have. And since facts are sometimes tiresome, they have included a few of the more romantic and generally pseudo-historical legends (always identifying them as such), although it is their opinion that history in this case is romantic and interesting enough to satisfy anyone.

Unless there is a note to the contrary, every route described in this book has been traveled by one or both of the authors and every place mentioned has been visited by them. Historical information was gleaned from published and manuscript sources in numerous libraries, archives, and private collections in California, Mexico, France, and Spain.

Both the second and third editions were considerably revised. The authors had continued to travel in Baja California, and in 1961 re-traveled practically all the main roads from the border to the cape, making appropriate corrections and additions to the routes, enlarging the chapter on plants, and revising other details.

In 1962, realizing that the opportunity would probably not again present itself to do the field work necessary to write a completely revised edition, the authors expected that the revised text of the third edition would serve the Baja California enthusiasts for a number of years, even after changes were made in the roads, and as new ranches appeared and new villages sprang up. Therefore it contained frequent references to the dates of much of the then-current information.

Now, more than five years later, the *Lower California Guidebook* is still serving the Baja California traveler, and the demand for it is continuing. Since changes come slowly on the peninsula, the information in the 1962 and 1964 editions is still basically accurate as to road descriptions; and the historic, socio-economic, and recreational information continues to have the same value.

Though the authors have not continued their intensive travel on the peninsula, they have frequently visited Baja California both by motor vehicle and commercial airline. Also, through other travelers and published information, they have been able to keep abreast of changes which are occurring to the roads, settlements, and means of transportation.

The following is offered as a supplement to acquaint the reader of this fourth edition with some of the principal developments and changes which have taken place since the preparation of the 1962-64 edition. For the convenience of the reader, the subjects mentioned here are referred to in the text, and are included in the index.

PAGE 38 — TRAVEL BY SEA

The single most important change in traveling conditions in the southern part of Baja California was brought about by the ferryboat "La Paz" which, since late 1965, now plies the 270 miles of sea between La Paz and Mazatlán, Sinaloa, on the Mexican mainland. This 350-foot motorship has the capacity to carry 114 automobiles (or an equivalent length in other vehicles). Its 370-passenger capacity consists of 220 reclining chairs plus cabin accommodations for 150 passengers.

The per-person fare for salon class passengers (reclining chair) is $4.00 (U.S.) For sleeping accommodations there is tourist class at $16.00 (U.S.), cabin class at $28.00 (U.S.), and two special suites at $50.00 (U.S.).

Rates for vehicles commence with $30.00 (U.S.) for an auto up to 14-ft. length, and there is a graduated scale for longer autos and auto-trailer combinations. For example, an auto with trailer from 23 ft. to 39 ft. 3 in. in overall length costs $96.00 (U.S.).

The ship has a restaurant, cafeteria, bar, and two lounges. Two round trips are made weekly. Departures from Mazatlán are made Saturday and Tuesday at 5 p.m., with arrivals in La Paz at 9 a.m. the next day. Departures from La Paz are on Sunday and Thursday at 5 p.m., with arrivals in Mazatlán at 9 a.m. the next day.

The "La Paz" is proving to be a very popular means of reaching southern Baja California, and travelers must expect some difficulty in obtaining passage during Easter Week or Christmas Week. Reservation requests may be made in La Paz at Calle Ezquerro No. 9; in Mazatlán at Prolongación Calle Carnaval (Muelles Fiscales); or in Mexico City at Insurgentes Sur 214, second floor.

PAGE 52 — BOOKS ABOUT BAJA CALIFORNIA — Additional interesting and informative books, which have appeared since 1962, have been inserted in the bibliography.

PAGE 59 — TIJUANA (last paragraph)

In 1967 some of the water shortage problem had been temporarily alleviated by two years of good rains which again put some water in the lake behind Rodríguez Dam. The pipeline from La Misión was in service. Plans for an aqueduct from the Colorado River had been discarded in favor of a scheme to desalt ocean water. In late 1966 an announcement was made of a contract to build a desalting plant to operate in connection with the steam electric generating plant at Rosarito.

TIJUANA TO MEXICALI

PAGE 66, M.69.2. In 1967 the "Café de las Delicias de Acapulco" had become "El Canelo" store. A better place to branch off on this side road to Laguna Hanson was now about 1.5 mi. before reaching this store.

M.98.7. In 1967 the junction for turning on the branch to Laguna Salada was about a mile west of this former turnoff.

MEXICALI TO SAN FELIPE AND BEYOND

PAGE 78, M.31.0, Riíto. The road continuing on to Santa Clara (El Golfo) is now paved.

PAGE 79, M.55.4. In 1966 this track over the salt flats was no longer usable, and VUELTA LA CURVINA had ceased to exist.

PAGE 80, M.72.7, (12.0), 34.5. The road between Arroyo Jaquejel and Arroyo Jamau was reported badly washed out and completely impassable about 1964.

PAGE 83, M.197.2. On the Gulf shore opposite EL HUERFANITO Island there was a small fishing camp for tourists in 1966. Boats were advertised for rent.

PAGE 85, M.232.1. At PUERTO DE SAN FRANCISQUITO a small scale tourist accommodation was being developed in 1966.

TIJUANA TO ENSENADA

PAGE 87. A "freeway" under construction from Tijuana to Ensenada was not yet completed in early 1967. This road will head west to PLAYAS DE TIJUANA (see M.5.1) and follow approximately the route described on this page down the coast, just by-passing ROSARITO. It will be a toll road, and the older road will be kept open as well.

PAGE 88. Where the present highway leaves the coast to go inland past LA MISIÓN, the "freeway" route continues down the coast, past SALINA BEACH.

PAGE 89, M.56.3. The "freeway" rejoins the present highway at "San Miguel Village," and from here the road to Ensenada in 1967 was a divided highway. Though not yet open, in early 1967 it was evident the new road will enter Ensenada via the coast instead of cutting back inland.

PAGE 90, ENSENADA, *Hotels.* By 1966 the historic and palatial Riviera Pacífico hotel was closed and partially dismantled.

ENSENADA TO SAN FELIPE

PAGE 93, M.0.0. In 1966 the road toward Ojos Negros was paved for 10 miles out of Ensenada, and this followed a slightly altered route, missing the picturesque PIEDRAS GORDAS region.

ENSENADA TO SANTA ROSALIA

PAGE 103-104, M.10.5, MANEADERO. The paved branch to the right continues for a distance of 13.1 mi. from Maneadero. It ends at a cove on the open sea side of the Punta Banda peninsula. This is a popular parking spot, as a walk of 100 yards to the right leads to a vantage spot to see LA BUFADORA, a spectacular "blow hole." Air trapped in a small cave is compressed by wave action, and as the wave recedes the pressure blows water high in the air.

PAGE 105, M.46.1. A change in the road here has caused some mileage changes. This road joins that down from San Vicente 9.1 mi. from the highway and reaches the sea at EJIDO ERÉNDIRA after 11.0 mi. The rest of the mileages would be similarly affected.

PAGE 105, M.53.2. The same change in the road mentioned above causes the road down the canyon to join the road from M.46.1 at 8.6 mi. from San Vicente and reach Ejido Eréndira after 10.4 mi.

PAGE 106, M.71.9. The highway surface beyond the end of the pavement at this point has greatly deteriorated in recent years. Once ready for pavement for the next 50 miles, it had a fine foundation and roadbed. Due to heavy traffic and neglect of the surface, by 1967 it was full of chuckholes and very rocky. This was particularly bad through the Valle de San Quintín (p. 110).

PAGE 110, M.121.4. The "main highway" beyond this point, whose roadbed was never properly compacted, is in very bad shape. In early 1967 it was advisable to branch to the left at this point on the old road described, going via SAN SIMÓN and SANTA MARÍA. After 7.6 mi. this branch rejoins the main highway at M.128.5 on the main highway.

PAGE 113. The road leaves El Rosario de Arriba as described. Just before turning to cross to the south side of the valley (M.160.7) it passes through RANCHO LA ESTRELLITA, commenced about 1960 by the late Sr. Santiago Espinosa, pioneer resident of the El Rosario area.

PAGE 120, M.216.5. At this junction to San Simón is the SONORA CAFÉ. Gasoline and meals were available in 1966.

M.235.0. At the crossing of Arroyo de Cataviñacito is the small RANCHO CATAVIÑACITO, inhabited in 1966.

M.238.7. Leaving SAN LUIS the main-traveled road in 1966 angled to the right from the road described in the guide, completely by-passing SANTA INÉS.

PAGE 122, M.246.7. In 1966 SAN IGNACITO was uninhabited, and its former buildings in a state of destruction.

M.249.9, JARAGUAY. In 1966 gasoline and meals were available, but the little bath house was in ruins.

M.259.6, EL PEDREGOSO. In 1966 the one-time cattle ranch and windmill had completely disappeared, with only a clearing to mark its location.

PAGE 124. At M.32.4, 1.6 mi. from the turnoff from the Los Angeles Bay road, a little traveled road goes left up a narrow valley. In 1963 tracks could be followed 5.9 mi. to where some vertical cliffs (to the right) contain a number of small Indian petroglyphs.

M.33.5. In 1963 the branch through AGUA DE HIGUERA was the main traveled road, which returned to join the road described in the guide. There was a cattle camp near the waterhole.

PAGE 124.   At M.45.1 a branch road to the right by-passed SAN BORJA completely, reaching SAN IGNACITO (p. 125, M.58.6) after 9.2 mi.

PAGE 126.   The junction described at 7.3 mi. beyond Punta Prieta is often missed, and travelers desiring to take the left branch here (see also p. 133, M.322.9) often miss the turn, and either end up at BACHANDRES or continue down the valley to the coast as described on p. 126. A good idea of where to turn to get on the left branch is obtained by looking to the left; the road may be seen climbing the hills to the left of the valley.

PAGE 133, M.322.9.   See the above paragraph for a hint on locating this junction among the many branch roads in this region.

M.339.3, ROSARITO.   It was reported in 1966 that most of the traffic was taking the road to the right here and joining the "coastal route" as mentioned. The marsh below Rosarito was now by-passed by a new dry road. Much of this traffic continued on to GUERRERO NEGRO as described on pp. 126-129 (M.38.2 to M.88.6). Those who desire to take this right branch at Rosarito, yet continue directly to El Arco, are advised to take the left branch at LOMA AMARILLA (p. 129, M.46.5) and rejoin the "main road" at M.358.6 as described on p. 219.

PAGE 137, M.440.7, EL TABLÓN.   In the mountains due east of here, near CERRO SAN FRANCISCO (see Map 10) is the tiny hamlet of SAN FRANCISCO, located very near the crest of the mountains. In deep canyons of this region are the spectacular Indian paintings, a major archaeological find, described by Erle Stanley Gardner in his *The Hidden Heart of Baja* (see herein page 53). This area may be reached by pack animal from El Tablón.

SANTA ROSALIA TO LA PAZ

PAGE 151, M.29.0.   It was reported in 1966 that this road to the left (or perhaps another branching off near here) leads to a newly built fishing resort for fly-in tourists, located at BAHÍA SANTA INÉS.

PAGE 152.   In 1966 it was reported that a new road was being traveled which branches right from the main road at a junction about 18 miles below El Coyote (i.e. about M.80). This road goes southerly, crosses some mountains, and rejoins the main road about 3 miles before it reaches the fork where the Comondú and La Purísima roads branch (p. 157, M.107.9). This new road shortens the distance to Comondú or La Purísima by about 10 miles. To go to Loreto keep left at this junction and follow the road described in the guide.

PAGE 154, Loreto, *Hotels.* A new resort for tourists, the Hotel Oasis, is located on the beach below the center of town.

PAGE 166, M.218.0. In April 1961 the paved road out of La Paz reached this point, 136 mi. from La Paz. In 1966 it was reported that this pavement extended only about 100 miles out of La Paz. The rest of the paving had been destroyed by washouts due to heavy rainstorms.

EXCURSIONS NEAR LA PAZ

PAGE 173, Bahía Pichilingue. In 1965 a paved road was completed to this bay, and the distance was made considerably less than shown in the guide. It is at Pichilingue that the terminal for the ferryboat "La Paz" is located.

LA PAZ TO SAN JOSE DEL CABO VIA SANTIAGO

PAGE 175. Now that convenient auto ferry service to La Paz from Mazatlán is available, the tourist traffic on the "loop" from La Paz to San José del Cabo, Cabo San Lucas, and return via Todos Santos, has considerably increased. The roads in the area have been improved and realigned. In late 1966 it was reported that the section out of La Paz toward El Triunfo was about to be paved. Along this route, as far as Cabo San Lucas, a number of tourist resort hotels have been established in recent years.

SAN JOSE DEL CABO TO LA PAZ VIA TODOS SANTOS

PAGE 187, M.15.3, Puerto Chileno. At this cove there is now a large deluxe tourist hotel and fishing resort, called Hotel Cabo San Lucas.

M.23.8, San Lucas. On the San Lucas Bay, very close to the cape, is a tourist hotel and resort, the Hacienda Cabo San Lucas. This and the more elaborate, similarly named "Hotel" at Puerto Chileno, as well as Hotel La Palmilla (M.5.0) are primarily patronized by the fly-in trade.

THE LAND

Baja California (Lower California), Mexico, is a rugged, mountainous peninsula running southeast from the state of California (which was once known as Alta, or Upper, California), and separated from the rest of Mexico by the Colorado River and the Gulf of California. It has an area of 53,280 square miles, about the size of the state of Florida. The peninsula is about 800 miles long (more than 1,000 miles by road) and from 30 to 145 miles wide. The highest mountains are in the north, rising more than 10,000 feet above sea level. Along both coasts, but particularly on the Gulf side, are many barren islands.

Most of Baja California is desert country with very little rainfall. The climate in the northernmost part is similar to that of Southern California, with winter rains along the Pacific, fairly heavy precipitation (with some snow) in the mountains, and practically no rain, with great extremes of temperature, on the desert east of the mountains. Going south from Tijuana to Rosario the climate gradually becomes dryer and warmer, although the winters are rather cold because of fog and strong winds along the coast. The central part, from Rosario to La Paz, is the dryest of all, a true desert with great forests of strange desert plants. In this region sometimes several years go by without a drop of rain. Beginning near San Ignacio and extending south of Comondú is a vast area covered with lava flows, the result of a fairly recent volcanic upheaval. The tip of the peninsula south of La Paz, being partly within the Tropic Zone, has a climate and vegetation all its own, with summer rains and tropical hurricanes. By and large the air and water temperatures on the Pacific side are considerably lower than those on the Gulf side.

The population of Baja California is concentrated in several favored areas, leaving the greater part of the peninsula almost uninhabited. The most densely populated section is the fertile Mexicali Valley, where many thousands of colonists from central Mexico have settled within the last fifty years. The Pacific coast from the border south to San Quintín is another region of fairly dense population, also because of favorable conditions for agriculture. The whole central section, from San Quintín 600 miles south to La Paz, is without inhabitants except in scattered oases and mining settlements, and in the recently-developed agricultural area north of Magdalena Bay. The Cape Region south of La Paz is better watered and supports a relatively dense population. According to the 1960 census there were 604,346 people in the whole peninsula, 85% of whom lived in the north close to the border. The following are the principal cities with 1960 population figures (provisional estimates):

Mexicali	172,554
Tijuana	151,939
Ensenada	42,770
La Paz	23,324
Tecate	7,074
Santa Rosalía	5,361

Most of the inhabitants of Baja California are farmers and cattlemen, with smaller groups engaged in fishing and mining. Cotton, grapes, olives, chile, and beans are the principal crops in the north. The south also produces wheat, cotton, winter vegetables, sugar cane, dates, and a variety of subsistence crops. Industry is pretty well confined to the border area, which has several fish canneries, breweries, cotton gins, etc. In the south, La Paz has vegetable packing plants, cotton mills and a tannery.

There are sharp regional differences within Baja California. The northern part, because of its proximity to the United States, is much more "Americanized" than the south. American products are sold, hotels and restaurants are replicas of those north of the border, and the cost of living is only slightly less than in Southern California. Mexicali has more in common with neighboring towns in the Imperial Valley than with any other city in Mexico. In recent years Tijuana and Ensenada have become in outward appearance more and more like the resort towns of Southern California, with motels, service stations and modern markets on all sides.

It is not until one leaves this border area and gets off on the unimproved roads that he begins to appreciate the great contrast between Upper and Lower California. The influence of the United States is still felt in the southern part of the peninsula, but it is secondary to the influence of mainland Mexico. Getting away from the larger towns, Baja California is a primitive land of cattle ranches and small isolated subsistence farming communities. The back roads are definitely not for the fastidious tourist. South of Ensenada the motorist will find few good hotels and practically no restaurants, very few shower baths, and in most places no plumbing or electricity at all. In other words, he will have to "rough it."

Beginning at San Ignacio the road passes through a series of beautiful oasis villages with a character all their own. Little whitewashed adobe houses are hidden in vast groves of date palms and fruit trees, presenting a vivid contrast to the surrounding desert. Here the people live isolated from the rest of the world in a sort of Shangri-La atmosphere.

La Paz, near the southern end of the peninsula, is a growing tourist center but still retains the character of a sleepy Mexican port. Some of the best deep-sea fishing in the world is found in the warm Gulf waters near here. The southern tip of Baja California is more typically Mexican and tropical than any other part.

In many ways Baja California today is like the "Wild West" of the United States seventy-five or a hundred years ago. It is a frontier region, largely undeveloped, with great future possibilities. Communications are primitive, and the horse, pack mule, and burro still play an important role in getting from one place to another. All of this is changing, particularly in the region along the northern border, but much of Baja California will always remain primitive and beautiful. This is probably its chief attraction to the sportsman and tourist who can travel in a few hours from the smog and noise of Los Angeles to a different world, a completely foreign country of great charm, beauty and serenity.

THE PEOPLE

The original Indian inhabitants of Baja California were wiped out in a series of epidemics during the 18th century, leaving the peninsula almost deserted until the arrival of mestizo (mixed Spaniard and Indian) immigrants from across the Gulf in the 19th century. Descendants of these mestizo farmers and cattle ranchers today make up the bulk of the population in the southern part of the peninsula. Generally speaking, they are friendly and hospitable, scrupulously honest, not too addicted to hard work, better educated than the average Mexican, intensely patriotic, and fond of music and fiestas. Like most Mexicans they are easily angered but quick to forgive, strongly individualistic and proud, completely unperturbed by physical hardship, with little resistance to alcohol, and with a constant and overwhelming interest in members of the opposite sex. The men love to fight when inebriated, but as they go unarmed no one is seriously hurt. They have a provincial distrust of foreigners, but are willing to accept a stranger on his individual merits. In the more isolated places the traveler meets with a disinterested hospitality sometimes carried to embarrassing extremes, where the host gives up his bed, his meager food supply, and anything else he may have to offer, and proudly refuses to accept payment. In these circumstances a good article of exchange is a supply of .22 cartridges, often more welcome than money.

Mexican children, who are adored by their parents, are as a rule much better behaved than American children. They are also more resourceful and are taught to make themselves useful at an early age. The traveler on the back roads might take along a supply of candy and inexpensive toys, but *he should never distribute money* to the children.

The border cities of Mexicali, Tijuana and Ensenada, particularly the first two, have in recent years become inundated with thousands of migrant farm workers and certain undesirable elements from central Mexico. Here there is a serious problem of unemployment, poverty, delinquency and vice, and the traveler should be as wary as if he were in one of the slum areas of the United States.

Spanish, with certain regional differences, is spoken throughout Baja California. Obviously a knowledge of Spanish is a tremendous advantage to the traveler, and it is strongly recommended that he learn at least some of the more usual phrases. Ignorance of the language is not, however, an insurmountable obstacle, since English-speaking people are found in most of the larger places.

Roman Catholicism is the traditional and predominant religion in Baja California. Most Mexicans, even though they may not be particularly devout Catholics, are extremely sensitive about their religion, and travelers of other beliefs should of course show the proper respect when visiting churches, shrines, etc. Ladies particularly should be modestly dressed and wear some covering on their heads. Women in shorts or slacks are apt to create a bad impression, except in the principal tourist centers in the north where the residents have become accustomed to them.

Mexicans find it hard to understand the average tourist's curiosity toward the more sordid and unattractive side of life, and the traveler is cautioned against taking photographs of poverty-stricken people, "quaint" scenes, etc., at least without first securing the consent of the persons concerned.

FIESTAS

As a rule, holidays are celebrated somewhat more vehemently in Mexico than in the United States. In the larger cities, public ceremonies accompanied by speeches, parades, and fireworks characterize the principal patriotic anniversaries. Perhaps of more interest to the visitor are the local religious festivals in the smaller towns. In the isolated and long-abandoned missions it is customary for the ranchers from hundreds of miles around to assemble on the saint's day and celebrate with dances, barbecues, and large quantities of beer and tequila.

The most important fiestas in Baja California are as follows:

[VARIABLE DATE] *Carnaval.* The pre-Lenten Carnival, equivalent to Mardi Gras in New Orleans, begins the weekend before Ash Wednesday. The only places where this fiesta is taken seriously are Ensenada and La Paz. The custom is to fill egg-shells with confetti and throw them at passers-by. There are usually a series of dances and parties where costumes and masks are worn.

[VARIABLE DATE] *Pascua* (Easter). Lent *(Cuaresma)* is more or less strictly observed by the predominantly Catholic population of the peninsula. On Palm Sunday *(Domingo de Ramos)* decorations of palm leaves are sold outside the churches, where the usual services are held. Everyone has a long holiday from Holy Thursday *(Jueves Santo)* through Easter Sunday *(Domingo de Pascua).*

[MAY 1] *Primero de Mayo.* International Labor Day. In the larger towns there is a workers' parade organized by the labor unions *(sindicatos).*

[MAY 5] *Cinco de Mayo.* Battle of Puebla Day. The anniversary of the defeat of the French invading army by Mexican forces outside Puebla, in 1863. There are parades and patriotic speeches in the larger towns.

[JUNE 21] *San Luis Gonzaga.* Local fiesta at the tiny oasis and former mission of San Luis Gonzaga (see pp. 166-67).

[JULY 25] *Santiago Apóstol.* Another local religious holiday, celebrated at Santiago, south of La Paz.

[JULY 31] *San Ignacio Loyola*. Saint's day in the old mission town of San Ignacio.

[SEPTEMBER 4] *Santa Rosalía*. This religious holiday is celebrated both in the mining town of that name and the old mission town of Mulegé. Fireworks, religious services, and general festivities.

[SEPTEMBER 8] *La Virgen de Loreto*. On this date the people of Loreto, the first permanent mission of California, celebrate the birthday of their patroness. Each day beginning August 30 an image of the Virgin is solemnly carried to a different house in the village and returned to the church. On September 8, in the afternoon, the Virgin is placed in a decorated car surrounded by children dressed as angels, and by the most beautiful girls of Loreto. The procession winds through the streets to the accompaniment of gay music.

[SEPTEMBER 16] *Dieciseis de Septiembre*. Mexican Independence Day. This is an important holiday everywhere in Mexico. The celebration actually begins in the evening of the 15th. In the larger towns the chief civil authority (the *Gobernador*, in Mexicali and La Paz) appears at 11 o'clock on the balcony of the Government Palace, waves the National Flag, and gives the traditional *Grito de Dolores* (the ceremony originated in 1810 in the town of Dolores Hidalgo, Guanajuato, where Padre Miguel Hidalgo first proclaimed Mexico's independence from Spain). Festivities continue through the 16th, accompanied by a parade of troops, fireworks, etc.

[OCTOBER 10] *San Francisco de Borja*. Local fiesta in the old mission of San Borja (see pp. 124-25). Ranchers come in from the surrounding country to celebrate with fireworks, firewater, and music.

[NOVEMBER 15] *Santa Gertrudis*. Another local religious holiday at the mission of Santa Gertrudis (see pp. 136-37).

[NOVEMBER 20] *Día de la Revolución*. A national holiday commemorating the Mexican Revolution which began in 1910, ousting the dictator Porfirio Díaz.

[DECEMBER 3] *San Javier*. The saint's day of the old mission of that name near Loreto. A colorful local fiesta attended by ranchers from many miles around.

[DECEMBER 12] *Nuestra Señora de Guadalupe*. Day of the Virgin of Guadalupe, Patroness of Mexico and Latin America. An important religious anniversary.

[DECEMBER 25] *Navidad*. The Christmas season is the occasion for many family parties. Perhaps the most characteristic Christmas custom in Mexico is the *Posadas:* groups of carolers go to the houses of their friends and serenade them with the traditional songs, representing the wanderings of Mary and Joseph trying to find a place to spend the night in Bethlehem. Finally they are admitted to the house and regaled with the usual Christmas cheer. Everyone goes to Mass on Christmas Eve, and festivities continue through the following day, in fact until New Year's Day *(Año Nuevo).* Mexican children receive their presents on Twelfth Day (January 6) from the Three Kings *(Los Reyes Magos),* instead of Santa Claus.

There are many other fiestas which locally may be more important than the above. Every day is the day of some saint, and since nearly everyone and every place is named for a saint there is always a celebration somewhere. Children's parties always include a *piñata,* a thin clay pot or pasteboard container suspended from the roof, filled with candy and presents. The children (and sometimes the adults) are blindfolded and take turns trying to break the *piñata* with a pole.

HISTORY

When the Spaniards discovered Baja California the peninsula was inhabited by about 70,000 Indians, divided into many tribes speaking different languages and having little contact with one another. With the possible exception of the inhabitants of Tierra del Fuego, these were the most primitive people in America in historical times. They had no agriculture (excepting the tribes around the Colorado River delta), and lived from hunting, fishing, and gathering wild plants. The men went entirely naked, while the women usually wore a diminutive apron. Only a few tribes had even the flimsiest shelters made of stones and branches carelessly piled together. For the most part they lived under the open sky, wandering from one water hole to another in search of food. Their weapons consisted of a crude bow-and-arrow and wooden spears propelled by a throwing-stick. Some of the coastal tribes had clumsy rafts, and fishing spears and nets, but generally they preferred to catch fish by the easy method of trapping them in tidal pools.

Because of the long periods of drought and the inadequacy of their weapons, the Indians were always on the verge of starving. They ate practically anything they could find, including all kinds of insects, grubs, and reptiles, but principally wild plants in the form of seeds, roots, and fruits. When they were lucky enough to kill a deer or other animal, the custom among some tribes was to tie a string to a piece of the meat, chew, swallow, and pull the morsel back, then hand it to the next man who repeated the process until there was nothing left. In the summer and fall the southern tribes gorged themselves on *pitahayas*, a cactus fruit with a delicious red pulp filled with tiny seeds. When the *pitahayas* were all gone the Indians gathered up their stools to recover the seeds, which were then ground into a meal and eaten again. During the *pitahaya* season family ties were forgotten and whole tribes mixed together in a general orgy.

These then were the people first seen by Europeans in late 1533 or early 1534. Hernán Cortés, the conqueror of Mexico, sent out an expedition from Tehuantepec to explore the coast to the north. One of the ships was commanded by Diego de Becerra, who was killed by the pilot, Fortún Ximénez. The mutineers sailed across the Gulf and landed in La Paz Bay, where most of them were in turn killed by the Indians.

Cortés himself went in 1535 to the same bay, which he named Santa Cruz, and founded a colony which lasted a year or more.

It was about this time that California got its name. In a medieval Spanish romance, *Las Sergas de Esplandián*, mention is made of a fabulous island of California "on the right hand of the Indies, very close to the terrestrial paradise," inhabited by a tribe of Amazons. This seemed to the *conquistadores* to be about the right location for the "island" they had just discovered, so they applied all of the wonderful legends of their day to the barren peninsula. Serious accounts were sent to the king of Spain describing a lake filled with pearls, and mountains of pure silver somewhere in the interior, guarded by a beautiful Amazon queen who lured men to their destruction. For many years there was a learned dispute as to whether California was an island or a peninsula. As late as the 18th century many people held that there was a passage from the upper Gulf to the North Pacific.

Cortés found pearls in La Paz Bay, and for centuries afterward the coast was visited by Spanish pearling expeditions. There were several attempts on the part of the viceroys to colonize Baja California, notably the expeditions of Sebastián Vizcaíno (1596-1603), Francisco de Ortega (1632-36), Porter Casanate (1648-49) and Atondo y Antillón (1683-85). Atondo was accompanied by the renowned Jesuit missionary-explorer Padre Eusebio Francisco Kino. All of these attempts failed because of inadequate preparation, the scarcity of good sites for agriculture, and the difficulty in getting supplies across the stormy Gulf.

Finally the Jesuits, led by Padre Juan María Salvatierra, founded the first permanent Spanish settlement in California, at Loreto, in 1697. During the next seventy years Salvatierra and his successors explored most of the peninsula and founded twenty missions. The missionaries were appalled by the poverty and primitive living conditions of the Indians, and did what they could to introduce their charges to an orderly Christian life. The Indians were collected into mission settlements, by force when necessary, and taught to recite the catechism, wear clothes, build houses and churches, and till the soil. Each mission consisted of a central village *(cabecera)* where the missionary and one or two soldiers lived, and a number of outlying visiting stations *(pueblos de visita)*. Soon after the first mission was founded the Indians began to be decimated by epidemic diseases introduced by the Spaniards. The native population of the area colonized by the Jesuits dropped from an original 40,000 to 7,000 in 1768. Some of this loss occurred during the suppression of a serious revolt of the southern tribes in 1734-36.

In 1768, as a result of political machinations in the court of Madrid, the Jesuits were expelled from Baja California and all Spanish dominions. They were replaced in the Californias by Franciscan friars led by Junípero Serra. For seventy years the Jesuit order had been in control of the peninsula, and it was generally believed that they had accumulated vast wealth in pearls and precious metals. When José de Gálvez, *visitador general* and personal representative of the king, arrived in California in 1768 he was much disappointed not to find any great treasure. A legend arose that the Jesuits had hidden their pearls and gold in a "lost mission," still being sought by treasure hunters.

The Franciscans founded one more mission to the north of the Jesuit territory, San Fernando, before going on to colonize Upper California (the present State of California). In 1773 Serra turned Baja California over to the Dominicans, who founded nine more missions in the north. Following is a list of all the missions in the peninsula, with an indication of how the sites can be reached at the present time.

MISSION	ORDER	FOUNDED	ABAN-DONED [1]	TYPE OF CHURCH	HOW REACHED
Loreto	Jesuit	1697	1822	Stone, rebuilt	Auto, Rte. 6
San Javier	Jesuit	1699	1817	Stone	Auto, Rte. 6
Ligüí	Jesuit	1705	1721	No ruins	Auto, Rte. 6
Mulegé	Jesuit	1705	1828	Stone	Auto, Rte. 6
Comondú	Jesuit	1708	1827	Stone ruins	Auto, Rte. 6
La Purísima	Jesuit	1719	1822	Stone ruins	Auto, Rte. 6
La Paz	Jesuit	1720	1749	No ruins	Auto, Rte. 6
Guadalupe [del Sur]	Jesuit	1720	1795	Stone foundation	Trail, Rte. 6
Dolores	Jesuit	1721	1740	Adobe ruins	Trail, Rte. 6 or Sea, Rte. 10
Santiago	Jesuit	1724	1795	No ruins	Auto, Rte. 8
San Ignacio	Jesuit	1728	1840	Stone	Auto, Rte. 5
San José del Cabo	Jesuit	1730	1840	No ruins	Auto, Rte. 8
San Miguel [del Sur]	Jesuit	1730	1737	No ruins	Auto, Rte. 6
Todos Santos	Jesuit	1734	1854	Adobe, rebuilt	Auto, Rte. 9
San Luis Gonzaga	Jesuit	1737	1768	Stone	Auto, Rte. 6
La Pasión	Jesuit	1737	1768	Stone ruins	Trail, Rte. 6
Santa Gertrudis	Jesuit	1752	1822	Stone	Auto, Rte. 5
San Borja	Jesuit	1762	1818	Stone	Auto, Rte. 5
Calamajué	Jesuit	1766	1767	Adobe ruins	Auto, Rte. 5
Santa María	Jesuit	1767	1769	Adobe ruins	Auto, Rte. 5
San Fernando	Fran.	1769	1818	Adobe ruins	Auto, Rte. 5
El Rosario	Domin.	1774	1832	Adobe ruins	Auto, Rte. 5
Santo Domingo	Domin.	1775	1839	Adobe ruins	Auto, Rte. 5
San Vicente	Domin.	1780	1833	Adobe ruins	Auto, Rte. 5
San Miguel de la Frontera	Domin.	1787	1834	Adobe ruins	Auto, Rte. 3

[1] Usually indicates the date of departure of the last resident missionary.

Mission	Order	Founded	Aban-doned [1]	Type of Church	How Reached
Santo Tomás	Domin.	1791	1849	Adobe ruins	Auto, Rte. 5
San Pedro Mártir	Domin.	1794	1806	Adobe ruins	Trail, Rte. 5
Santa Catalina	Domin.	1797	1840	Adobe ruins	Auto, Rte. 4
Descanso	Domin.	1814	1834	No ruins	Auto, Rte. 3
Guadalupe [del Norte]	Domin.	1834	1840	No ruins	Auto, Rte. 1

It should be noted that the mission churches still to be seen were generally built some years after the founding date of the missions, to replace earlier buildings. For example, the stone churches at San Ignacio, Santa Gertrudis, and San Borja were built by the Dominicans in 1786, 1796, and 1801, to replace the older Jesuit adobe churches.

The Indian population continued to decrease from disease during the Dominican period, and the survivors were absorbed by the mestizo element which gradually drifted into the peninsula after Mexican Independence in 1821. By 1850 the southern tribes had completely disappeared, while not much more than a thousand Indians remained in the north. Today a few hundred California Indians still live in the Colorado delta area and in the mountains above Ensenada.

During the Mexican War (1846-48) Baja California was occupied by American troops in La Paz and San José del Cabo. There was a considerable amount of resistance on the part of the local residents, and battles were fought in Mulegé, La Paz, San José, and Todos Santos. The commander of the American fleet issued a proclamation stating that the peninsula had been annexed to the United States, but the peace treaty returned it to Mexico. A few years later, in 1853, the American soldier of fortune, William Walker, invaded Baja California and proclaimed himself president of a new "republic," but he was ejected early the following year. Numerous other attempts were made by Americans to get control of the peninsula, notably by land companies in the 1860's, and by an army of "socialist" filibusters who invaded the northern part in 1911.

In 1887 Baja California was divided into two federal districts, with capitals at La Paz and Ensenada (later moved to Mexicali). Since then the southern half (Territorio Sur) has progressed relatively little, while the northern part has greatly increased in importance. The main reason for the prosperity of the north was the opening of the Imperial Valley to irrigation in 1902, since which time many thousands of farmers from central Mexico have settled in the vicinity of Mexicali. In 1952 the Northern Territory was made a state (Estado de Baja California) with an elected governor, legislature, etc. The southern half remains a federal territory (Territorio Sur de Baja California), with its governor and other officials appointed from Mexico City.

IMMIGRATION AND CUSTOMS
REGULATIONS

Mexico welcomes tourists as one of her biggest sources of revenue, and makes things as easy and pleasant for them as possible. No formality at all is required of United States citizens who wish to visit the border towns and as far south as Ensenada or the San Felipe area for a 72-hour stay.* For longer visits or to go further south it is necessary to have a Tourist Card *(Tarjeta de Turista)*, which can be obtained at any Mexican consulate (there are consulates at Los Angeles, San Diego and Calexico), at airline offices, and at many travel agencies. The only requirements are some proof of nationality and a fee of three dollars. This card should be presented at the Mexican immigration office at the border, (or at Maneadero, 10 mi. below Ensenada, in the case of travelers going south on the highway). Travelers leaving Tijuana or Mexicali by plane should present their cards to the immigration authorities at the airport. Upon leaving Mexico the cards are surrendered to the same authorities at the border. It is against the law for the holder of a Tourist Card to work or go into business in Mexico. The card is good for a visit of six months, and if the tourist wishes to remain longer he must return to the border before the expiration date and obtain a new Tourist Card. Another type of card costing five dollars permits the traveler to enter and leave Mexico as often as he wishes during a 6-month period.

The requirements for a foreigner who wishes to live permanently in Mexico, or engage in business there, are somewhat more complicated. Information about the necessary formalities can be obtained at any Mexican consulate.

All of Baja California is a free zone, meaning that foreign-made articles (with some exceptions) are imported free of duty. Besides the obvious advantage in keeping prices down, this arrangement permits the motorist to bring in his car without posting a bond. Automobile insurance issued by American companies is generally not recognized by Mexican authorities, and it is advisable to take out a policy with a Mexican company at the border (there are also agents of Mexican

---

* In Feb. 1962 requirement of a permit ($0.50 Dls., good for 5 days) was instituted for visits to San Felipe.

insurance companies in Los Angeles). Policies are available by the day. American and other foreign driver's licenses are accepted in Baja California unless the motorist becomes a resident, in which case he should obtain a Mexican driver's license.

The allowances made by United States Customs on articles purchased by tourists in Mexico were considerably reduced in 1961. A customs declaration is required, and it is advisable to keep receipts for any expensive items. Tourists may bring in $10.00 worth of goods duty-free if they have been in Mexico less than 24 hours and $100.00 worth after a 24-hour visit. A pamphlet with the latest regulations can be obtained at the American custom-houses at the border. There is a local law of the State of California prohibiting the importation from Mexico of plants and alcoholic liquors.

MONEY

American currency is generally accepted in the border towns, but it is advantageous if the traveler is planning to stay more than a day or two to convert at least some of his money to Mexican currency. The present rate of exchange in the banks is 12.50 Mexican pesos for one American dollar, in other words the peso is worth eight cents of a dollar. There are coins of 5, 10, 20, 25, 50 centavos, and one peso; banknotes of 1, 5, 10, 20, 50, 100, 500, and 1000 pesos. It is difficult to change the higher denomination bills, particularly in the smaller towns. Traveler's checks are accepted in the larger cities, but are unknown in the smaller places. Personal and other checks are accepted in the banks for collection, which generally involves a delay of ten to twelve days. There are banks in Mexicali, Tijuana, Tecate, Ensenada, Santa Rosalía, La Paz, and San José del Cabo.

Tipping is not customary except in the more plush American-type hotels and restaurants. Taxi drivers do not expect a tip. It is best to come to an agreement with the driver as to the fare before hiring a taxi. The old Latin custom of bargaining prevails here, as well as in most of the stores.

Generally speaking, the cost of living in Baja California is low compared to the United States, although somewhat higher than in central Mexico. There has been the usual inflation since the last devaluation of the peso, but the traveler with a dollar income can live for a small fraction of what it would cost at home, particularly if he can get along without expensive imported items. Prices are much higher in the border towns than in the southern part of the peninsula. It is not necessarily true that Americans are taken advantage of; it is just that they are freer with their money and less skillful at bargaining than most Latins.

WEIGHTS AND MEASURES

The metric system is used in Baja California, as well as a few obsolete Spanish units. English equivalents are given below:

1 *metro* (meter) — 3.28 feet
1 *kilómetro* (kilometer) — .621 mile
1 *litro* (liter) — 1.057 quarts (.264 gallon)
1 *kilo* (kilogram) — 2.2046 pounds

In many places gasoline is sold by the *lata* (5 gallon can).

The ranchers occasionally use the old term *legua* (league) in estimating distances. Theoretically a *legua* is the distance which can be traveled on muleback in one hour (*hora*, 2½ to 3 miles), but the traveler will not be far off if he doubles this distance (5 to 6 miles) in converting ranchers' estimates.

PLACES TO STAY

Hotels in Lower California can be divided into three categories. First there is the luxurious resort, patronized almost exclusively by Americans who drive to Ensenada or fly down to the south. These resorts are like little islands cut off from the rest of the country. Everyone speaks English, and the food and atmosphere, and often the décor, are similar to what one would expect to find in the United States. Prices are usually quoted in dollars and are not low even by American standards. The more pretentious places are listed in the text as I-A. Category I-B indicates a somewhat less luxurious establishment with slightly lower rates.

The second group of hotels is the "commercial" or Mexican resort type. As a rule the clientele is both Mexican and American and the food and atmosphere Mexican-international. The rooms are usually clean, each with a private bath. These are listed as II-A or II-B, depending on the relative price of the accommodations.

Finally there is the small and completely Mexican hotel, patronized almost exclusively by Mexicans. Included in this category is what is called a *casa de huéspedes* (guest house). This is the sort of place one finds in the smaller towns, but they also exist in the cities. Meals may or may not be served. When they are, the food is simple, at some places very good and at others almost inedible. The beds or cots are usually clean, but the plumbing is more often primitive or nonexistent, with only one shower bath and privy for the use of all the guests. English is rarely spoken. These are listed as class III.

RATES

Following are the approximate price ranges in each category in April, 1961. Rates are generally higher in the north along the border.

I-A $15 to 25 Dls. per day per person, meals included.

I-B $8 to 16 Dls. per day per person, meals included.

II-A 80 to 150 pesos per person, meals included.
30 to 70 pesos, room without meals.

II-B 50 to 80 pesos per person, meals included.
10 to 30 pesos, room without meals.

III 25 to 50 pesos per person, meals included.
5 to 15 pesos, bed or room without meals.

HEALTH CONDITIONS – FOOD AND DRINK

Baja California is by no means an unhealthy country, in fact health conditions are generally good. The traveler should, however, take the precaution of drinking only bottled or boiled water (an excellent substitute is beer) and avoiding uncooked vegetables and questionable-looking fruits, milk, cheese, etc. A bottle of Halazone tablets for purifying water is a useful item to take along, and if one wishes to be prepared for anything he can pack a small bottle of Terramycin or some other dysentery cure. Malaria formerly was a problem in the southern part of the peninsula, but the anopheles mosquito has now been destroyed. It is always advisable, and sometimes required by the authorities, to carry a valid (less than three years old) smallpox vaccination certificate.

The eating habits of Mexicans are really not too far removed from those of Americans, and the change to "Mexican food" should not be a difficult one for the average tourist unless he is unusually squeamish. There are several hotels and restaurants in Baja California catering almost exclusively to American tourists which serve food imported from the States, prepared American-style. In the border towns even such un-Mexican delicacies as hamburgers, hot dogs, etc., are available. In most restaurants in the larger towns there is a selection of steaks, poultry, fish, eggs, and cooked vegetables. Salads should generally be avoided by the unacclimated tourist.

Mexican popular dishes *(antojitos mexicanos)* such as enchiladas, tacos, tamales, mole, chiles rellenos, etc., if properly prepared, can be delicious. Beans *(frijoles)* mashed and fried are eaten by Mexicans at every meal, often as a last course in place of dessert. Bread is available only in the cities; elsewhere its place is taken by *tortillas,* thin flat cakes made of wheat flour (in the south corn meal is often used). Contrary to popular belief, Mexican food is not usually served highly spiced, rather the seasoning is a matter of individual option. Often there is a jar of hot sauce or a dish of chile peppers on the table which can be used at one's discretion.

Sea food is plentiful in most places, ranging from abalone, lobster, and shrimp in the north to *callo* clams and swordfish steak in La Paz.

The giant sea turtle *(caguama)* is prepared as a huge piquant stew for special occasions in lieu of barbecue, but most tourists prefer it served as "turtle steaks."

Getting away from the larger towns, the food becomes much more simple, even scarce, and the traveler on the back roads would be wise to take along a supply of canned or dried foods. Coffee is available even at the poorest ranches, where it is offered as a hospitable gesture to visitors. There are a number of ranches along the main road where travelers can obtain a substantial meal usually consisting of flour tortillas, fried beans, *machaca* (a sort of hash prepared from dried meat), and coffee. Eggs are often available, and occasionally fresh beef or venison. In places the ranchers' diet is often confined to tortillas and goat cheese, the latter prepared under highly unsanitary conditions.

Many kinds of fresh fruits are grown and become available in the summer and fall, including oranges, apricots, figs, pomegranates, mangos, grapes, watermelons, avocados, dates, bananas, and sugar cane. Better than any of these is the juicy pulp of the *pitahaya*, a cactus fruit which grows wild all over the southern part of the peninsula, ripening from July to September. There are two kinds, *dulce* and *agria* (sweet and sour), both of which are delicious.

Mexican beer *(cerveza)*, somewhat stronger than American beer, is uniformly good and is an excellent substitute for water when the latter is scarce or polluted. The Mexicali and Tecate brands, brewed in Baja California, are available in cans, while Carta Blanca and those from central Mexico (Dos Equis, Bohemia, Pacífico, etc.) come only in bottles. Excellent wines (Terrasola, Santo Tomás) are made in Baja California and sold all over Mexico. Another beverage, *Crema de Damiana,* is made from a plant found south of La Paz and is supposed to have aphrodisiac properties. Stronger Mexican liquors include rum, tequila, and mescal, the last two made, by somewhat different distilling processes, from the juice of two varieties of century plant *(maguey)*.

MEANS OF TRANSPORTATION

Until a few years ago the only way of getting about in Baja California was by pack animal or boat. Vast areas can still be reached only by these primitive means, but most of the important places are now accessible to automobiles. The only railways are a few short lines near the border, in the north. Passenger-carrying ships connect the principal ports, but service is irregular and accommodations are limited. A few key points are served by airlines. Perhaps the most comfortable way to get around is by private plane (there are many landing fields, both natural and man-made, scattered throughout the peninsula), or yacht.

ROADS

There are good paved roads connecting Tijuana and Mexicali, Tijuana and Ensenada, Tecate and Ensenada, and Mexicali and San Felipe. These are all near the border in the north. The pavement south of Ensenada extends at the present time (1961) for 72 miles, after which there is a well-graded surface for another 51 miles. Similarly, north of La Paz the highway is paved for 136 miles, with grading extending for an additional 53 miles. The rest of the peninsular roads with few exceptions are extremely rough natural tracks winding through the desert and mountains. Even the main transpeninsular "highway" beyond the end of the graded portion is not to be recommended to any but the hardiest motorist. Plenty of water and extra gasoline should always be carried, and no one should attempt the trip without at least a rudimentary knowledge of mechanics and some of the more essential spare parts. Garages, service stations, even supplies of gasoline are few and far between. Passing drivers are generally very helpful to motorists in distress, but they should not be relied on to any great extent.

In recent years there have been recurring reports of a plan to build a paved highway through the peninsula. It is unlikely that this will be done in the near future. Even if the part now graded were to be paved, there would still remain some 575 miles (by present routing) to be graded and paved, and no provision has been made in the latest federal budget to do so.

The motorist accustomed to the countless signposts of United States highways may find the roads of Baja California rather confusing. Frequently he will come to a fork in the road, with no sign indicating which branch he should take. It is some comfort to know that whichever fork is chosen is probably as good as the other and they will come together again within a short distance, although it is preferable to follow the branch which has a greater number of *recent* wheel tracks. In the northern part of the peninsula there are still a few road signs put up by the Automobile Club of Southern California some years ago, but most of these have been removed or rendered illegible and others are on old sections of the road which are no longer passable. The motorist should be able to avoid taking any serious wrong turns by checking his mileages with those given below in the route descriptions, and by always following what appears to be the better traveled road.

Because of the low speed at which one must drive and the scarcity of traffic, there is little likelihood of a serious accident on the desert roads. However, the very fact that one hardly expects to meet another car adds to the possibility of a head-on collision on rises and blind curves. A harrowing experience is meeting another vehicle on a long, loose sandy stretch, where the accepted practice is for both drivers to step on the throttle; when the cars are only a few lengths apart each swerves away to pass, keeping the left wheels in the right track, and then continues on his way. It is far preferable to try to foresee such an encounter and get off on a hard shoulder, or even to back up a considerable distance to allow the other car to pass.

A special problem is the "washboard" surface which occurs on heavily traveled roads which have been once graded and then allowed to deteriorate into evenly spaced bumps separated by shallow ruts. To avoid back-breaking vibration, most drivers maintain high speeds on such a surface, with danger of a serious accident in case it becomes necessary to brake suddenly. It is much safer to proceed at a crawl, taking each bump carefully.

On the rare occasions when rains occur, flash floods are apt to come down from the surrounding mountains and make the unimproved roads impassable. Completely dry arroyos become sizeable rivers within a few minutes, making it necessary to wait, sometimes for several days, until the water subsides. Camp should never be made in an arroyo bottom if there are any signs of rain in the vicinity.

The best type of vehicle for these desert roads is a four-wheel-drive with normal tread and a high center, such as a weapons carrier or command car. Extra low speeds and front-wheel traction are especially useful in getting through muddy places after a rain. However, late model low-center passenger cars, lightly loaded, are frequently taken by careful professional drivers down the main road from Ensenada for delivery in La Paz. A Jeep is good and can go anywhere, but the standard model is somewhat at a disadvantage on the loose sandy stretches where its narrow tread does not fit into the ruts. Some of the older model high center cars of the 1930's and before are still used by the local ranchers and are particularly suited to these roads.

In most of the smaller places gasoline, when available, is sold from 50-gallon drums and transferred by means of five-gallon cans and hose-syphons. When so dispensed it is apt to contain dirt or water, and it is advisable to strain it through a chamois or piece of felt.

RAILWAYS

There is only one passenger-carrying railway in the peninsula. The Ferrocarril Sonora — Baja California, was completed in 1948 between Mexicali and Benjamín Hill, Sonora, making it possible for the first time to travel by land from central Mexico to Baja California without passing through the United States. It leaves Mexicali from the southeast, crosses the rich farming area west of the Colorado River, and reaches the Gulf of California at Puerto Peñasco, Sonora, a commercial fishing and tourist port of growing importance. Then it goes inland past the old towns of Caborca and Pitiquito and joins the main line of the Ferrocarril del Pacífico (formerly Southern Pacific Railway of Mexico) at Benjamín Hill. Most of the route is through a barren, sandy desert. It takes about 15 hours to make the run of 333 miles. There is a through sleeping car daily between Mexicali and Mexico City, a trip of 2½ days if the train is on time.

AIR TRAVEL

Two major Mexican air lines operate commercial passenger service to points in Baja California (Trans-Mar de Cortés, s.a., the pioneer air line of the peninsula, was taken over by Aeronaves de México in March, 1962). The planes are comfortable DC-3's or larger, manned by competent Mexican pilots, with good service and an excellent safety record. Furthermore, air travel in Mexico is economical, costing considerably less than in the United States. Routing and schedules are subject to frequent change. The following air lines and routes were being operated in March 1962.

AERONAVES DE MÉXICO, s.a.

Ticket office in Tijuana: Av. Revolución and Calle 2a.

TIJUANA direct to LA PAZ, continuing to MAZATLÁN and MEXICO CITY and return (3 times a week, DC-6).

TIJUANA-HERMOSILLO-GUAYMAS-CULIACÁN and return (3 times a

week). Connection in Guaymas with flight below for Santa Rosalía, Loreto, and La Paz.

EL PASO-CHIHUAHUA-GUAYMAS-SANTA ROSALÍA-LORETO-LA PAZ and return (3 times a week).

TIJUANA-MEXICALI-NOGALES and return (3 times a week).

MAZATLÁN to LA PAZ and return (2 times a week).

TIJUANA-GUADALAJARA-MEXICO CITY and return (daily).

MEXICANA DE AVIACION
Ticket office in Mexicali: Av. Reforma and Calle México.

MEXICALI-HERMOSILLO-MAZATLÁN-GUADALAJARA-MEXICO CITY and return (daily).

In recent years Baja California has become increasingly popular among people owning light airplanes, who can fly down for a weekend of fishing, hunting, etc., at remote spots which otherwise could be reached only by a long and arduous automobile trip. Besides the landing strips mentioned in the text, there are many dry lakes, salt flats, hard sand beaches, and other places which can be used by light aircraft. Aviation gas is generally available at Tijuana, Ensenada, Mexicali, San Felipe, Hamilton Ranch, Los Angeles Bay, Santa Rosalía, Mulegé, and La Paz, and sometimes at Isla Cedros, Guerrero Negro, Bahía Tortugas, Loreto, El Crucero, Las Cruces, and La Palmilla (near San José del Cabo). Emergency gas and water should always be carried. This kind of travel should be attempted only by experienced pilots with thoroughly reliable aircraft. Aerial charts at 1:1,000,000 are sold by the U.S. Coast and Geodetic Survey, Washington, D.C. Information as to the necessary government formalities can be obtained at any Mexican consulate.

TRAVEL BY SEA

Passenger service on the few commercial ships which call at ports in Baja California is an unpredictable thing, dependent on the whims of the shipowners, cargo requirements, weather, and a number of other factors. Accommodations are far from luxurious, the food is generally poor, and the ships are small, crowded, and slow. If, in spite of these warnings, the reader is still determined to travel by sea, he is strongly advised to do so in the spring or early summer. During the winter months northerly gales, and in the fall tropical hurricanes from the south, are apt to make navigation quite uncomfortable and even dangerous in any but the most seaworthy vessels.

Yachtsmen are referred to the last section of this book, "Places reached by sea."

There are plans to inaugurate a regular car ferry service across the

Gulf from La Paz to mainland Mexico, but it may be some time before this happens. Meanwhile it is possible to send cars across on most of the existing vessels. (See Preface page 8 for 1967 information.)

Servicios Marítimos de México, s.a., operates one ship every ten days more or less in each direction between Ensenada, La Paz, and Mazatlán or Topolobampo. Offices are at Ryerson 101 in Ensenada, and Lerdo y Comercio in La Paz. The passenger fares, including berth and meals, are 325 pesos from Ensenada to La Paz, 116 pesos from La Paz to Mazatlán, and 70 pesos from La Paz to Topolobampo. Automobiles are carried for about 750 pesos between Ensenada and La Paz, and 400 pesos between La Paz and the mainland. WARNING: Stevedores' fees for loading or unloading a vehicle may, under certain conditions, equal or even surpass freight charges. All such fees are doubled after 6 p.m. and on Sundays or holidays.

Servicios Terminales del Pacífico, s.a., has a weekly sailing from La Paz to Mazatlán and return, with occasional service from La Paz to Ensenada and south to Acapulco. Passenger and automobile fares are the same as in the last paragraph. The office is on Calle Esquerro, La Paz.

La Perla de la Paz (Ruffo Brothers) has three ships with weekly service between La Paz and Mazatlán or Topolobampo with the same rates as above. Only one of them, however, takes cabin passengers. Deck passage (meals included) costs 70 pesos to Mazatlán. Automobiles are carried.

Sucesores de Jorge Von Borstel, La Paz, have sailings weekly between La Paz, Loreto, Isla del Carmen, and Guaymas on the little "Arturo." The still smaller "Blanco" runs twice a week between La Paz and Topolobampo, taking 16 hours to cross the Gulf. The "Raúl" goes from Santa Rosalía to Guaymas and return twice weekly (fare, including berth and meals, 110 pesos).

BUS LINES

Passenger buses (*camiones, autobuses*) connect the principal border cities and are a comfortable, rapid, and cheap means of transportation.

Two companies, Autotransportes Tres Estrellas de Oro ("Three Gold Stars") and Transportes Norte de Sonora, operate large buses between Tijuana and Mexico City via Mexicali. Some of these are operated on irregular schedules which depend upon the traffic. There are from three to five departures a day. Other buses, also operated by these companies, go as far as Guadalajara. Both first and second class services are available.

The border towns of the north are served by the Autobuses Amarillos

(Yellow Buses) and Autobuses Verdes (Green Buses). Between Tijuana and Mexicali the former line has eleven trips a day each way, and the latter has nine trips. Between Tijuana and Ensenada they operate ten and seven trips a day each way, respectively. These same lines make several trips daily from Mexicali to San Luis, Sonora, and return. The Autobuses Amarillos also have three trips daily each way from Tecate to Ensenada via Guadalupe.

The complex of *ejidos* and *colonias* of the Mexicali Valley is served by several bus lines radiating out of Mexicali. Their routes overlap considerably. Some of these lines are: Líneas de Auto Transportes José E. Montejo (to K-57, Algodones, and along the San Luis highway); Líneas de Auto Transportes de Servicio Mixto del Valle de Mexicali (to K-57 and Ejido Hermosillo); and Líneas Katia (to Algodones and K-57).

The Cooperativa Maya makes two trips daily from Mexicali to San Felipe and return.

South of Ensenada the Autobuses Amarillos and the Autobuses Verdes operate buses on alternate days as far as San Quintín Valley, and the former sends one weekly on to El Rosario. From here to San Ignacio there is no public transportation, and even postal service is lacking. Travelers can, however, arrange to ride on private trucks, which make the run to Santa Rosalía in four or five days or to La Paz in six or seven. Passengers should carry bed rolls and canteens and be prepared to eat at ranches along the road. This is an uncomfortable way to travel, but a good way to get acquainted with the country.

Between San Ignacio and Santa Rosalía the mail truck *(el correo)*, running about twice a week, carries a few passengers.

Another mail truck, which carries a limited number of passengers, goes once a week from Santa Rosalía to La Paz and return, stopping at Mulegé, Loreto, Comondú, and numerous intermediate places. It is a trip of two or three days each way. Still another mail truck runs between Comondú and La Purísima once a week.

Autotransportes "Aguila" has a number of passenger lines in the south, leaving from the Malecón in La Paz. There is a daily bus to Santo Domingo, on the highway north (6½ hours each way); a station wagon daily between La Paz and Los Planes (2 hours); and another daily service via El Triunfo and Santiago to San José del Cabo (8 hours). A rival company also has daily service both ways between La Paz and San José del Cabo, and the mail truck carries passengers between San José del Cabo and San Lucas.

Another bus line makes 3 round trips a week between La Paz and Todos Santos.

HUNTING AND FISHING

Baja California has much to attract the sportsman. Both big and small game are relatively unexploited in its rugged mountains, and the fresh and salt water ponds at the mouths of its dry rivers are stopping-off places for millions of game birds. Most of all, the waters of the Gulf of California and, to a lesser extent, the Pacific are generally conceded to be one of the finest deep sea fishing areas in the world.

Hunting and fishing laws in Mexico are somewhat more lenient than in the United States. Generally, open seasons are longer and bag limits larger in Baja California than they are north of the border. Since the restrictions change from time to time, it is best to get the latest information from a Mexican consulate, the Mexican Hunting and Fishing Association in Los Angeles, or the Secretaría de Agricultura y Ganadería office in Mexicali or Tijuana. The killing of bighorn sheep, pronghorn antelope, and Cedros Island deer is illegal; most other species are in little danger of extinction. Nonresidents may purchase hunting permits at the border, after first obtaining a gun permit from the military authorities. Residents of Mexico must belong to a recognized Mexican hunting club in order to secure permits.

Every sportsman who returns from Baja California has his favorite hunting and fishing spots. As might be expected the best hunting grounds are those farthest removed from the settled areas, but since the main road passes through some of the wildest country imaginable it can hardly be said that game is inaccessible. Plenty of game, even big game, can be shot from your car if you do not feel up to a long pack trip. The local ranchers, who are skilled hunters themselves, are usually very helpful in guiding a visitor to the best places for his chosen sport. Fishing is excellent everywhere but is better in the Gulf than on the Pacific side, and generally improves toward the southern end of the peninsula. For the less energetic sportsman interested only in getting together an easy meal, both coasts are lined with tremendous quantities of shellfish, clams, oysters, abalones (Pacific only), crabs, and lobster.

The following list gives the sportsman a general idea of what he can expect to find in Baja California (Spanish names in parentheses):

BIG GAME

DEER *(Venado)*. Deer are found everywhere, even near settled areas, and are extraordinarily abundant throughout the peninsula in the more isolated ranges and on brush-covered mountainsides and plains. They are also found on the islands of Cedros and San José. During the war, when ammunition was scarce, there were so many deer that they became a pest to farmers. Their meat, a delicious venison, is highly prized by the ranchers who make it into jerky *(carne seca)* by drying it in the sun.

MOUNTAIN LION *(León; puma)*. This timid cat, sometimes reaching a length of 4½ feet and weighing 160 pounds, is generally not seen during the daytime but can be found wherever there are cattle or other large game. It is particularly abundant in the Cape Region mountains south of La Paz.

WILDCAT; BOBCAT; LYNX *(Gato montés; lince)*. The wildcat, not too abundant, is found all over the peninsula but particularly in places where there is thick underbrush. It sometimes reaches a length of 2½ feet, and eats rabbits, rodents, and occasionally birds.

MOUNTAIN SHEEP; BIGHORN SHEEP *(Borrego; incorrectly, berrendo)*. Now protected by the Mexican Government after a period of indiscriminate slaughter, this handsome animal is reported to be holding its own. It is found in many of the isolated, extremely dry desert ranges along the Gulf, from north of San Felipe to just north of La Paz, and on the east slope of the San Pedro Mártir mountains.

PRONGHORN ANTELOPE *(Berrendo; antílope)*. Vast herds of this graceful animal used to roam over most of the peninsula. Recently, because of the imminence of extinction, killing of it has been made illegal. At present it is found on the Vizcaíno Desert and (at least until recent years) northwest of San Felipe, mostly in open plains country. It is very fast and timid.

FOX *(Zorra)*. The gray fox, which feeds on rodents and small mammals, is found nearly everywhere. The smaller kit fox lives in the central desert and is more rarely seen.

COYOTE; PRAIRIE WOLF *(Coyote)*. The bark of coyotes at night can be heard practically anywhere in the peninsula. Frequently curiosity and hunger overcome their shyness and they can be seen prowling around campfires at night. After a protracted dry spell coyotes and skunks *(zorrillas)* sometimes become rabid.

WILD GOAT *(Cabra; chivo)*. There are a great many goats in the southern part of the peninsula which may appear to be wild, but usually a goatherd somewhere in the vicinity will claim them. Ownerless goats live on the islands of Cedros, Guadalupe, Cerralvo, San José, and San Marcos. Their meat is quite good.

WILD PIG *(Jabalí)*. These pigs, which feed on acorns in the Cape Region mountains south of La Paz, have been erroneously described as wild boars. Actually they are the descendants of domesticated pigs.

We have not mentioned the largest mammals of all, the whales and the elephant seals. The California gray whale can be seen practically anywhere along the Pacific coast and has its principal calving grounds at Scammon's Lagoon (Laguna Ojo de Liebre), Laguna de San Ignacio, and Bahía Magdalena. Another large species of whale, the finback whale, inhabits the constricted "Midriff" area of the Gulf. The elephant seal ("sea elephant"), protected by law, is found principally on Guadalupe Island (see p. 196), with herds also on the San Benito Islands.

SMALL GAME

JACK RABBIT *(Liebre)*. The most numerous and widely distributed game, found everywhere. The best time to hunt *liebres* is at dusk. Their meat is generally good. A special type of black jack rabbit is found only on Espíritu Santo Island.

BADGER *(Tejón)*. This nocturnal animal is fairly abundant on the dry, cactus-covered plains of the peninsula. Killing it is prohibited by law.

RACCOON *(Mapache)*. The small raccoon population lives in well-watered places and stream bottoms. They are good eating, but there is no sport in hunting them since there are no hounds trained for this purpose in Mexico.

RING-TAILED CAT *(Babisuri; cacomixtle)*. A nocturnal relative of the raccoon, with a black and white striped tail longer than its body, the *babisuri* lives in great numbers in the rocky cliffs near date palm groves. It is also found on Espíritu Santo and San José Islands.

Other small game includes cottontail rabbits *(conejos)*, squirrels *(ardillas)*, and several kinds of chipmunks, gophers, kangaroo rats, etc. To feed on the above there are countless rattlesnakes *(víboras)*. Lizards are plentiful, but there are no poisonous varieties.

BIRDS

Game birds, both resident and migratory, are plentiful. Quail are so thick in some places that it is considered more sporting to shoot them with a .22. The migratory birds are generally found from fall to spring in ponds and *esteros* along the beach, particularly on the Pacific side. Only the principal varieties are named below:

QUAIL *(Codorniz; chacuaca).* Coveys of quail are found everywhere. They are most numerous in the Cape Region (south of La Paz) from January to March, and in the foothills above Tijuana and Ensenada in the autumn.

DOVE; PIGEON *(Paloma).* Several varieties of dove are found distributed throughout the peninsula. They are particularly abundant near cultivated areas. The farmers are usually very glad to give a sportsman permission to shoot in their fields.

GOOSE; BLACK BRANT *(Ganso).* This bird is found from fall to early spring in lagoons and salt water ponds along the Pacific coast.

DUCK *(Pato).* Great numbers of ducks (mallard, pintail, teal, baldpate, gadwall, scaup, scoter, merganser, bufflehead, and others) winter in coastal ponds and bays especially on the Pacific side. They are also found in fresh water marshes, and in the sloughs of the Colorado delta.

RING-NECKED PHEASANT *(Faisán chino).* An introduction from China, this fine game bird is found in quantity in the irrigated farmlands southeast of Mexicali.

CHUKAR PARTRIDGE *(Perdiz).* Coveys of chukars live in the Sierra Juárez and perhaps by now have spread to the San Pedro Mártir range. They are extremely difficult to shoot.

FISH

The waters around Baja California abound with many kinds of fish. Sportsmen regard the Gulf of California as two fishing areas separated by the "Midriff," which is the constricted area from Tiburón Island to Angel de la Guarda Island. The following list of the more important fish was supplied by Mr. Raymond Cannon, author of *How to Fish the Pacific Coast* (Lane Pub. Co., Menlo Park, 1953).

BARRACUDA. 3 species. Pacific Coast and throughout Gulf.

BASSES *(cabrilla).* 36 species, including:
JEWFISH *(mero).* Central and north end of Gulf.
BLACK SEA BASS *(garropa).* Pacific Coast and throughout Gulf.
GROUPERS *(garropa, cabrilla, pinto).* 4 species. Pacific south from Cedros Island and throughout Gulf.
CABRILLA. 3 species. Same range as groupers.
SAND BASS *(pinto).* Pacific north from Magdalena Bay.
GOLD SPOTTED BASS. Throughout Gulf in deep water.

BROWN SPOTTED BASS *(pinto)*. Throughout Gulf and Pacific in shallow water.

KELP BASS. Pacific, north from Punta Abreojos.

BONEFISH. Throughout Gulf and Pacific, shallow backwaters.

CROAKERS *(roncador)*. 34 species, including:
CORBINAS. 3 species. Pacific and Gulf, in surf.
CORVINAS. 5 species. Pacific south from Cedros Is.; throughout Gulf.
YELLOWFIN CROAKER. 4 species. Pacific and Gulf.
WHITE SEABASS. North of Magdalena Bay; central and upper Gulf.
TOTUAVA. Central and north end of Gulf.

DOLPHINFISH *(dorado)*. 2 species. Pacific and Gulf.

FLATFISHES *(Lenguado)*. 20 species, including:
HALIBUT. 2 species. Pacific, and central and upper Gulf.
SANDDABS. 5 species. Pacific and Gulf.
FLOUNDERS. 2 species. Pacific and Gulf.
SOLES. 2 species. Gulf.

GRUNTS *(mojarrón, roncador)*. 23 species. Pacific and Gulf.

JACKS. 28 species, including:
AMBERJACK. Throughout Gulf up to Midriff.
(CALIFORNIA) YELLOWTAIL *(jurel)*. Pacific and Gulf up to Bahía San Luis Gonzaga.
MAZATLÁN YELLOWTAIL. Gulf up to Midriff.
JACK CREVALLE. South from Madgalena Bay. Gulf up to Midriff.
POMPANOS. 4 species. Throughout Gulf.
ROOSTERFISH *(pez gallo)*. Throughout Gulf up to Midriff.

MANTA RAY *(manta raya)*. Throughout Gulf. Pacific north to Magdalena Bay.

MARLIN. Pacific and throughout Gulf.

MULLET *(lisa)*. 6 species. Brackish and backwaters, Pacific and throughout Gulf.

OPALEYE. 2 species. Pacific and throughout Gulf.

SAILFISH *(pez vela)*. Throughout Gulf.

SHARKS *(tiburón)*. 26 species, including:
MAKO and HAMMERHEAD. Pacific and throughout Gulf.

SKIPJACKS *(barrilete)*. 2 species. Pacific and throughout Gulf up to Midriff.

SNAPPERS *(pargo)*. 9 species. Pacific south from Sebastián Vizcaíno Bay and throughout Gulf.

SNOOK *(robalo)*. Magdalena Bay, and Gulf north to Mulegé.

SPANISH MACKEREL. 4 species, including:

MONTEREY SPANISH MACKEREL. Gulf, north from Loreto.

SIERRA. South end of Gulf and Pacific to Cedros Is.

BONITO. 2 species. Throughout Gulf and Pacific.

SWORDFISH *(pez espada)*. Pacific and Gulf up to Midriff.

TUNAS *(atún, albacora)*. 3 species.

ALBACORE and BLUEFIN TUNA. Pacific north to Cedros and Guadalupe Islands.

YELLOWFIN TUNA. Pacific south of Magdalena Bay and throughout Gulf up to Midriff.

WRASSES. 13 species, including:

SHEEPHEAD. Pacific and Gulf up to Midriff.

PLANTS

Baja California may be divided roughly into five regions as to vegetation. Four of these, in the extreme north, are continuations of similar regions in California, and may be designated as "Pacific slope," "piñon-juniper woodland," "coniferous forest," and "desert." The desert region extends to the south and comprises most of the area of the peninsula. The fifth region contains the "arid tropical" vegetation of the Cape region. It extends northward spottily in the higher mountains almost to San Ignacio. Within each region are variations which depend upon altitude, latitude, type of soil, proximity to the sea, etc.

In the Pacific slope area the hills are covered with chaparral (brush) growth, including CHAMISO DE VARA PRIETA (Chamise, *Adenostoma fasciculatum*); CHAMISO DE VARA COLORADA (Ribbon bush, *Adenostoma sparsifolium*); LENTISCO (Sumac, *Rhus laurina*); LECHUGUILLA (Spanish bayonet, *Yucca Whipplei*). In the canyons and valleys are found ENCINO (Coast Live Oak, *Quercus agrifolia*); and ALISO (Sycamore, *Platanus racemosa*).

The piñon-juniper woodland is arid semi-desert country, usually on the Pacific drainage, from 3,000 to 5,000 ft. elevation and is characterized by PIÑÓN (Piñon-pine, *Pinus monophylla* and *P. quadrifolia*) and HUATA (California Juniper, *Juniperus californica*). Accompanying these are DÁTIL (Mojave Yucca, *Yucca schidigera*); CHAMISO BLANCO (Sagebrush, *Artemisia tridentata*); ENCINILLO (Scrub Oak, *Quercus dumosa*); and CANUTILLO (Desert tea, *Ephedra californica*).

The coniferous forest area is above 5,000 ft. elevation. At lower limits are forests of PINO PONDEROSA (Yellow Pine, *Pinus ponderosa*); while at higher elevations are found Incense Cedar *(Libocedrus decurrens);* White Fir *(Abies concolor);* and Sugar Pine *(Pinus Lambertiana);* as well as Quaking Aspen *(Populus tremuloides).*

The desert area, east of the mountain ranges, has, in its northern part, the same plants as the southern California desert. The characteristic plant is the ever-present GOBERNADORA (Creosote bush, *Larrea divaricata*). The trees are largely of the pea family: MEZQUITE *(Prosopis juliflora);* PALO VERDE *(Cercidium microphyllum);* PALO FIERRO (Ironwood, *Olneya tesota*); PALO CHINO or UÑA DE GATO (Cat claw, *Acacia Greggii*); and PALO TRISTE (Smoke tree, *Dalea spinosa*). Along watercourses and at springs are found ÁLAMO (Cottonwood, *Populus Fremontii*); and the introduced PINO SALADO (Tamarisk, species of *Tamarix*). Cacti are not very numerous in the north, the most common being several kinds of CHOLLA (see below), NOPAL (flat-stemmed *Opuntia*), and BIZNAGA (see below). Other thorny plants include OCOTILLO *(Fouquieria splendens)* and MAGUEY (see below).

As one travels south the first three types of vegetation are left behind, and the desert extends from coast to coast except where interrupted by mountains. Beginning near El Rosario on the Pacific side and before reaching San Felipe on the Gulf side, the traveler begins to encounter new species not found in California. The plants in the following list are especially characteristic of the desert and of the arid tropical regions of Baja California.

Plants are listed here according to the common name in most frequent use, but the traveler will find many local regional variations.

This list has been prepared with the cooperation of Miss Annetta Carter of the staff of the University of California Herbarium, Department of Botany, Berkeley.

BIZNAGA *(Ferocactus acanthodes)*. This "barrel cactus" grows to a height of over five feet in the central part of the peninsula. Said to be a source of water for the thirsty desert traveler, but its tough interlaced spines defy anything but a heavy sharp tool.

CANDELILLA *(Pedilanthus macrocarpus)*. Consists of almost leafless gray-green stems 1 to 3 feet high, with a thick milky sap. Very common on the central plains where it is sometimes used for making wax for candles.

CARDÓN *(Pachycereus Pringlei)*. The giant cactus, resembling the saguaro of Arizona, occurs as far north as San Felipe. Two other species, CARDÓN PELÓN *(P. calvus)*, distinguished by its lack of spines, and CARDÓN BARBÓN *(P. pecten-aboriginum)* with abundant comb-like spines, occur in the south.

CHIRINOLA *(Machaerocereus eruca)*. The "creeping devil," a thick-stemmed cactus which grows prostrate. Found on the Magdalena Plain.

CHOLLA. This name is applied to several species of *Opuntia* with cylindrical branches. Characteristic of the central and southern portions of the peninsula is *Opuntia cholla* which is very green, with widely spaced spines. The joints are easily detached from the plants.

CIRIO *(Idria columnaris)*. A slender tree with usually unbranched columnar trunks and short, pencil-like horizontal branches which quickly produce leaves after a rain. The yellow flowers are produced in a "plume" at the tip of the trunk. Seen along the road from below El Rosario almost to El Arco. These weird trees grow only in Baja California and in Sonora near Puerto Libertad.

CIRUELO *(Cyrtocarpa edulis)*. Spreading, heavy-limbed, gray-barked trees, especially abundant on the plains south of La Paz. The edible fruits ripen in summer.

COPAL *(Bursera Hindsiana)*. A small tree with reddish brown twigs and trunks and usually simple leaves 1 to 1½ in. long, which grows near the Gulf coast. In its aromatic properties and its appearance when leafless, it is very similar to the TOROTE.

COPALQUÍN *(Pachycormus discolor)*. Elephant tree (sometimes called TOROTE, a name usually applied to *Bursera microphylla;* see below). Low spreading tree with thick, tortuous trunks and pinnate leaves (distinguished from the similar-appearing *B. microphylla* by lobed leaflets and lack of strong aroma). Coming from the north they are first seen on the hills south of San Agustín. Along the windswept coast southwest of Punta Prieta (Map 7), and at its southern limit near Magdalena Bay the large trunks are prostrate.

DAMIANA *(Turnera diffusa)*. Shrub 1 to 2 feet high with aromatic foliage and yellow flowers up to one inch in diameter. Abundant on plateaus and lower slopes of mountains south of La Paz. A liqueur flavored with it and a tea made from the dried twigs and leaves are said to have aphrodisiac and medicinal properties.

DATILILLO *(Yucca valida)*. This tree yucca is abundant on the arid Pacific slope from Punta Prieta southward. It bears huge clusters of creamy yellow flowers.

DIPÚA, DIPUGA, DIPÚO, DIPUGO *(Cercidium microphyllum)*. This palo verde, found in desert areas of most of the peninsula, is a spreading tree with green trunks and stems; leaves develop after rains. The younger branches are cut for fodder (see PALO BREA).

ENCINO *(Quercus Brandegeei)*. The large, narrow-leaved oak common along arroyos on the east side of the Cape Region mountains. Its acorns are sold in the markets.

FRUTILLA (Species of *Lycium*). Low, many-branched shrub with sharp spines, often forming thickets. The small but showy red or orange fruits, usually maturing in the spring, are edible but insipid.

GARAMBULLO *(Lophocereus Schottii)*. The thick-ribbed stems of this cactus are tipped with coarse, hair-like spines. Found only on the Gulf side in the north, but southward it is frequent on sandy plains.

Güérivo *(Populus Brandegeei)*. A straight-trunked, whitish-gray barked tree sometimes reaching a height of 70 feet, found in the higher canyons of the Cape Region, as well as west of Puerto Escondido and near Guadalupe mission (see p. 150). Its hard wood is used for making furniture.

Hierba de la flecha *(Sapium biloculare)*. Many-branched shrub occurring in the foothills and along arroyos from San Ignacio southward. Used as fish and arrow poison; sleeping in its shade, or exposure to smoke from the burning wood is said to cause sore eyes.

Lomboy *(Jatropha cinerea)*. The limber branches of this shrub bear broad heart-shaped leaves up to 3 inches in length. The astringent copious dark sap is reputed to have medicinal properties. Common on the plains near Punta Prieta and southward.

Maguey, mescal (several species of *Agave*). The century plant. The thick, toothed, sharp-pointed leaves form a rosette. The Indians roasted the heart for food. The typical species of the north: *A. deserti* in the desert and *A. Shawii* along the Pacific coast, give way to several other species of varying size farther south.

Mangle *(Rhizophora mangle)*. The mangrove. Shrubs 8 to 10 feet high with dark green leaves. They grow in shallow tidal waters on stilt-like stems and form impenetrable thickets. Abundant in Concepción and Magdalena bays.

Mariola *(Solanum Hindsianum)*. A much-branched shrub up to 5 feet high, with gray-green leaves, slender spines, and showy pale lavender to deep violet flowers. San Quintín south to San José del Cabo.

Matacora *(Jatropha cuneata)*. Shrub 2 to 4 feet high whose usually leafless slender branches fan out from the base. Peeled stems were used in basketmaking and the astringent juice is claimed to have medicinal qualities. Common on gravelly slopes in the southern half of the peninsula.

Mirasol *(Heliopsis rubra)*. A showy annual or short-lived perennial 2 to 2½ feet high with deep green leaves and yellow sunflower-like flowers. Abundant after rains along arroyos south of El Arco to Cabo San Lucas.

Palma. The California fan palm *(Washingtonia filifera)* is found in many canyons on the east side of the Sierra Juárez and Sierra San Pedro Mártir. Often occurring with it is the Palma Ceniza *(Erythea armata)* or blue fan palm. In the Southern Territory is found the slender trunked *Erythea Brandegeei* whose fan fronds are used for thatching roofs.

PALO DE ARCO *(Tecoma stans).* Shrub with abundant slender stems, willow-like leaves and large, trumpet-shaped yellow flowers. The straight stems are used to make woven fences, walls of houses, and crates for *panocha.* Along arroyos and on plains from Loreto southward.

PALO BLANCO *(Lysilóma candida).* Tree with a slender, white-barked trunk which branches to form a feathery, broad crown. Flowers yellow and acacia-like. Seen along the road from near Santa Rosalía southward. The bark is employed in tanning.

PALO BREA *(Cercidium praecox).* A palo verde with stout sharp spines which has a flat-topped, spreading shape where it occurs on exposed volcanic mesas. From north of San Ignacio southward. Two other *Cercidiums* in the mountains near Loreto are known as PALO VERDE *(C. peninsulare) and* PALO ESTRIBO *(C. sonorae).* All of these, as well as the DIPÚA, resemble each other in having green trunks and branches and, in late spring, bearing a mass of yellow flowers.

PALO SAN JUAN *(Forchammeria Watsonii).* Trees with thick, straight trunks and a dense, rounded crown of dark narrow leaves. Occasional on open plains from Mulegé southward.

PALO ZORRILLO *(Cassia emarginata).* Slender tree up to 25 feet tall whose clusters of yellow flowers appear before the leaves and whose slim pods are up to a foot long. It is plentiful on the plateaus south of La Paz.

PALVADÁN, PALO ADÁN *(Fouquieria peninsularis).* A tree-like close relative of the OCOTILLO, occurring southward from the central portion of the peninsula. Its slender spined branches, leafless most of the year, bear small clusters of red flowers near the tips.

PEGAPEGA *(Sympetaleia aurea).* An annual forming a dense rounded clump of deep green, shiny leaves surmounted by a mass of dark orange (occasionally yellow) flowers. Following rains it is abundant on shaded cliffs. The name is also used for other related plants with leaves which adhere to one's clothes.

PITAHAYA AGRIA *(Machaerocereus gummosus).* This cactus with sprawling or erect branches 2 to 3 inches in diameter is common throughout the peninsula. The somewhat acid fruit is edible and refreshing.

PITAHAYA DULCE *(Lemaireocereus Thurberi).* This "organ pipe" cactus is common in the southern half of the peninsula. Its fruits, which ripen in summer, are highly prized (see p. 23).

SAN MIGUEL *(Antigonon leptopus).* A showy, red-flowered vine forming dense masses in arroyos following late summer rains.

TOROTE, TOROTE COLORADO *(Bursera microphylla)*. A low spreading tree with reddish brown twigs and thick trunk. The pinnate leaves with tiny leaflets and the small reddish fruit have a strong "piney" aroma. It occurs sparingly in California, where it is called "elephant tree," and along the northern Gulf coast. Abundant from Punta Prieta southward.

VINORAMA *(Acacia farnesiana)*. A spreading thorny shrub with finely divided pinnate leaves; covered in the spring with flowers which appear like fluffy yellow balls. Abundant along arroyos in the southern part. In many regions (including the Sierra Giganta, where another species, *A. Brandegeana,* is called VINORAMA) this is called HUISACHE.

ZALATE *(Ficus Palmeri)*. Large broad-leaved trees with white-barked thick trunks and roots. The latter creep grotesquely over boulders and hang down canyon walls. The fruit of these wild fig trees is edible but dry and uninteresting. Also called HIGUERA.

BOOKS ABOUT BAJA CALIFORNIA

Unfortunately for the American reader, some of the best books about Baja California are either in Spanish or long out of print. The following brief bibliography is confined to works in English which are relatively easy to obtain by purchase or from the larger public libraries.

ASCHMANN, Homer, *The Central Desert of Baja California.* Ibero-Americana: 42 (Berkeley and Los Angeles, 1959).
A good study in historical geography and ecology covering the region from San Fernando to San Ignacio.

BAEGERT, J. J., *Observations in Lower California* (Berkeley and Los Angeles, 1952).
One of the few first-hand accounts of the missions, written by a German Jesuit who was at San Luis Gonzaga from 1751 to 1768. It is particularly interesting for the description of the Indians.

BANCROFT, Griffing, *The Flight of the Least Petrel* (New York, 1932).
A popular account of a cruise along both coasts of Baja California. An excellent general description of the peninsula.

BANCROFT, H. H., *History of the North Mexican States and Texas,* 2 vols. (San Francisco, 1884-89).
A monumental collection of historical data.

BEAL, Carl H., *Reconnaissance of the Geology and Oil Possibilities of Baja California, Mexico.* Geological Society of America Memoir 31 (New York, 1948).
Result of a field study made in 1921.

BUSH, Wesley A., *Paradise to Leeward—Cruising the West Coast of Mexico* (New York, 1954).
Some good pointers for yachtsmen going to Baja California and farther south. A worthwhile supplement to the H. O. *Sailing Directions.*

CANNON, Ray and the *Sunset* Editors, *The Sea of Cortez* (Menlo Park, Calif., 1966).
A profusely illustrated description of the land and sea, fishing, wildlife and travel conditions in Baja California as well as the Mexican mainland coast.

CLAVIGERO, F. J., *The History of (Lower) California* (Stanford University, 1937).
A good general account of the Jesuit missions, originally published in Italian in 1789.

DUNNE, P. M., *Black Robes in Lower California* (Berkeley and Los Angeles, 1952).
Written for the general public, a well-documented history of the Jesuit mission period.

ENGELHARDT, Zephyrin, *The Missions and Missionaries of California*, Vol. I (Santa Barbara, 1929).
Another exhaustive historical study, particularly valuable for its information on the later Dominican years in the missions.

FIERRO BLANCO, Antonio de, *The Journey of the Flame* (New York, 1933). Reprinted (Boston, 1955) under the author's true name Walter Nordhoff.
An historical novel, probably the best popular book written about Baja California. The author, an Englishman, spent most of his life in the peninsula and collected many romantic legends which are included in his story.

GARDNER, Erle Stanley, *Hunting the Desert Whale* (New York, 1960).
An account of a trip to Scammon's Lagoon to photograph gray whales in their calving place.

GARDNER, Erle Stanley, *Hovering over Baja* (New York, 1961).
Exploration of desert canyons by helicopter and motor scooter.

GARDNER, Erle Stanley, *The Hidden Heart of Baja* (New York, 1962).
An account of the discovery and exploration by helicopter of the spectacular Indian caves in Baja California.

HANCOCK, Ralph, and others, *Baja California* (Los Angeles, 1953).
This book has some good tips on hunting and fishing and general information. An account of the travels of a group of sportsmen, well illustrated.

KRUTCH, Joseph Wood, *The Forgotten Peninsula: a Naturalist in Baja California* (New York, 1961).
The author works descriptions of the plant and animal life into a travelogue.

MEIGS, Peveril, *The Dominican Mission Frontier of Lower California* (Berkeley, 1935).
A serious study in historical geography of the northwest corner of the peninsula, as far down as El Rosario.

MURRAY, Spencer, and Ralph Poole, *Cruising the Sea of Cortez* (Palm Desert, Calif., 1963).
A detailed story of a cruise the length of the Gulf in a small inboard cruiser. It contains much guide material and information useful to small boat travelers.

NELSON, E. W., *Lower California and its Natural Resources* (Washington, 1922).
The best geographical description of Baja California yet written. It is the report of an official United States expedition which traveled through the peninsula on horseback in 1905-06.

NORTH, Arthur W., *Camp and Camino in Lower California* (New York, 1910).
Another horseback trip in 1905-06. A good account.

SHREVE, Forrest, *Vegetation of the Sonoran Desert*. Carnegie Institution Publication 591 (Washington, 1951).
A scholarly work with photographs and distribution maps. More than half of the book is concerned with vegetation in Lower California.

STEINBECK, John, and Ricketts, E. F., *Sea of Cortez* (New York, 1941).
The account of an expedition to the Gulf coast of the peninsula. The narrative part of the book has been published in a cheaper edition: Steinbeck, John, *The Log from the Sea of Cortez* (New York, 1951).

Sunset Discovery Trips in Mexico (Menlo Park, Calif., 1955).
Pages 78 to 95 deal with Baja California. Brief but graphic descriptions of the northern and southern extremities of the peninsula.

TIMBERMAN, O. W., *Mexico's Diamond in the Rough* (Los Angeles, 1959).
Experiences of a man and wife traveling about the peninsula.

U.S. NAVY, Hydrographic Office, H.O. Pub. No. 26 (formerly No. 84), *Sailing Directions for the West Coast of Mexico and Central America* (Washington, 1951. Change No. 6, 1960).
An indispensable reference book for the yachtsman in Baja California waters. In looseleaf form; changes issued periodically.

WORTMAN, Bill and Orv, *Bouncing Down to Baja* (Los Angeles, 1954).
The account of a jeep trip down the peninsula and return through Sonora.

Automobile Routes

The following route studies are arranged in order of geographical progression from north to south, as are the accompanying maps. In general the column farthest to the left shows the total distance in miles on the main road from the beginning of the route. Figures in the second column indicate the distance from the place mentioned immediately above. Mileages on side roads are given usually in the third column. In the second column, partial mileage figures shown in parentheses are side road mileages. Mileage figures on the unimproved roads are subject to slight differences, as there is often a choice between two or more somewhat parallel tracks, and new tracks are constantly being opened.

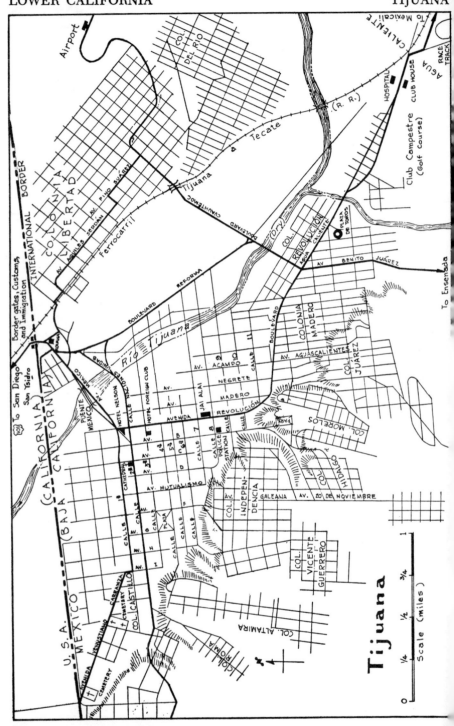

Tijuana

ROUTE 1

TIJUANA TO MEXICALI

This is a paved highway (MEXICO 2) across the mountains. There is a gradual climb eastward through the vineyards and border town of Tecate to the Sierra Juárez, then a spectacular drop with many hairpin curves down to the desert floor and Mexicali.

TIJUANA. Elevation: 125 ft. Population: 151,939 in 1960.

Climate: Cold in winter (average temperature, Nov.-Apr. 57.5° F.; coldest months, Dec. to Mar.); almost perfect in summer (average temperature, May-Oct. 66.4° F.; warmest months, July and Aug.). Average annual rainfall: 12.4 in., nearly all from Dec. to Apr. There is a constant breeze off the Pacific. During the summer fogs very often set in at night, generally lifting early in the morning.

Communications: Land telegraph and telephone to Ensenada and Mexicali, connecting with lines in the United States. Radio telegraph and telephone to La Paz, Mexico City, and other points in the interior. Air mail and also air passenger service between Tijuana and Los Angeles, Mexicali, Nogales, Hermosillo, Guaymas, La Paz, and other points. The airport, with paved runways long enough for the largest propeller planes, is just below the border 2 miles northeast of town.

There are several local bus lines within Tijuana. Buses run between Tijuana and Mexicali via Tecate and between Tijuana and Ensenada. Also buses connect Tijuana with Mexico City (see page 38). Passengers to points in the United States must cross the border on foot and continue by bus from San Ysidro, California to San Diego.

Tijuana has a great many taxicabs, stationed at the border crossing and at almost any corner along Avenida Revolución. Fares are best agreed upon prior to entering a cab.

Hotels: There are many good hotels and motels. In the center of town are the Nelson, Caesar's, and the León (motel). On the road to Ensenada are many motels, including La Sierra and Tropicana. The Travel-Inn is located across the street from the race track. Most are I-A in price range.

Restaurants: Caprí (Av. Revolución 366); La Casita (116 4th); Guillermo's (123 7th); and many others. There are also restaurants in most of the leading hotels and motels.

Banks: Banco Nacional de México; Banco de Baja California; Banco Mercantil; Banco Comercial de la República; Banco Mexicano de Occidente. United States currency is generally used in Tijuana, but it is a good place to change to pesos if one is going south. The banks offer the best rate of exchange. Traveler's checks are accepted upon proper identification.

Hospitals: There is a large municipal hospital, in addition to several private clinics.

There is an American consulate in Tijuana (Agua Caliente Blvd. and Fresnillo). Tourist cards for travel to the interior can be purchased at the Mexican Immigration Office at the border or at Mexican consulates in the United States.

The Tijuana Tourist Bureau (Comité Municipal de Turismo de Tijuana) maintains a booth on Revolución between 3rd and 4th St. for the assistance of tourists. Friendly English-speaking employees give information and advice.

The principal gateway to Baja California and the liveliest port of entry in Mexico, Tijuana is just below the border, 16 miles south of San Diego and 5 miles from the Pacific. Until a few years ago a sprawling, dreary collection of grim bars and brothels, it has recently been transformed into a modern commercial center with attractive public buildings, first-rate restaurants and hotels, and residential sections which would do credit to any city. Because much of the town's prosperity depends on the hordes of Americans who descend daily from the nearby populated centers of Southern California, tourist attractions still play an important and conspicuous part in the city's life. Nor have the more sordid forms of vice been entirely eradicated, as any solitary male will discover if he walks down Avenida Revolución, the main street, at night. But Tijuana is becoming more respectable all the time, legitimate businesses are taking the place of "rackets," and the atmosphere of the place is undergoing a subtle but definite change.

Tijuana, long referred to as Tia Juana, first came into existence as a ranch about 1830. By the end of the century it had developed into a small border town with a customhouse and a population of 240. In 1911 Tijuana was occupied for a few weeks by a force of "socialist" filibusters from the United States who attempted to set up an independent republic. The invaders were driven across the border by Mexican forces on June 22, which is celebrated as a local holiday. Growth was slow until the 1920's, when prohibition in the United States caused Tijuana to open up as a rip-roaring border town. A race track and gambling casino were inaugurated in 1929 at Agua Caliente which, together with other more sinful attractions, resulted in a deluge of weekend tourists from north of the border and gave Tijuana the reputation of being one of the wickedest towns in the world. A heavy blow to the town's prosperity was the closing of Agua Caliente in 1935, when the Mexican anti-gambling law was enforced. Two years later the race track was reopened, but most other forms of gambling are still illegal.

Avenida Revolución is the center of the "Mexican curio" business and the night life. Bars are two or three to the block, and after dark a myriad of neon signs invites the tourist to visit the numerous night clubs, and the palatial Jai Alai (*Frontón*, a Basque game) stadium. The shops are largely filled with items manufactured specially for the tourist trade and sold at high prices. Some stores have a good selection of leather and silver work, but it is difficult to get a bargain by Mexican standards, although prices are generally lower than in the United States. Savings can be effected on some European goods (cameras, watches, etc.) which are brought to Baja California free of customs duties.

On Saturdays and Sundays the horse races at Agua Caliente (Hipódromo de Tijuana) 1½ miles east of town, are the main attraction. The former gambling casino is now used as an industrial school and headquarters of the Mexican Pacific Military Region. The Club Campestre at Agua Caliente is a private club with a golf course open to public play. Other amusements include dog racing (Wednesday through Sunday nights) and cockfights (the latter illegal and held under rather furtive conditions). During the season (May through part of September) there are bullfights on Sunday. These alternate between the Plaza Monumental (near the sea 5 mi. west of town, see page 87) and the smaller but centrally located Toreo de Tijuana. Some of the best bullfighters in the world can be seen in Tijuana.

The rapid growth of Tijuana has caused serious civic problems in recent years. Expansion together with years of drought have caused a severe water shortage, and the lake at Rodríguez Dam, the principal source of supply for the city, was dry in 1961. A pipe line under construction in 1961 was to bring water 40 miles from wells in the valley of La Misión. Plans were being prepared for an aqueduct to bring a greater supply from the Colorado River some 160 miles to the east. Also in 1961 construction was commenced on a steam-electric generating plant (ultimate capacity 225,000 kw) located at Rosarito, to serve the entire northern part of the state, and in the same year a new municipal outfall sewer system was under construction. (See Preface page 9 for further 1967 information.)

The road to Mexicali is a continuation of the main street, Avenida Revolución (MEXICO 2):

Mi. from Tijuana	Partial Mileage	
0.0	0.0	TIJUANA. Junction with coast road to Ensenada.
1.7	1.7	AGUA CALIENTE, race track (see above). The road follows up the left bank of Arroyo Tijuana, through a rural suburban area.
9.0	7.3	PRESA RODRÍGUEZ. A concrete dam across the arroyo, 1,935 ft. wide and 250 ft. high, which, when full, forms a lake four miles long. The dam, finished in 1937, was built to protect Tijuana from floods and provide water for the city and for irrigating 10,000 acres. With the drought of recent years the lake has dried up. When there is water this is a favorite fishing, camping, and holiday spot. There are outboards for rent, stores, restaurants, etc.
11.0	2.0	Side road left under railway, the old road to Tecate via MATANUCO (2.5 mi., a community of scattered farms) and VALLE REDONDO (9.3 mi., a similar farming community).
14.0	3.0	EL FLORIDO. Palatial ranch belonging to former President Miguel Alemán. Olives and fruit are the crops.
22.9	8.9	EL GANDUL. Ranch where olives, grapes and hogs are raised. Side road left to Valle Redondo.
24.3	1.4	Branch road right, the old road south to Ensenada via Guadalupe:

	Mi. from main road	
(2.8)	2.8	EL CARRIZO. Ranch. The road crosses a low divide and emerges into the broad Valle de las Palmas, a succession of ranches and cultivated fields.
(9.4)	12.2	VALLE DE LAS PALMAS. Community center and schoolhouse.
(0.3)	12.5	Road joins the new Tecate-Ensenada highway 17.9 mi. from Tecate (see p. 61).

25.6	1.3	Side road in from left, from VALLE REDONDO (4.7 mi.). The highway passes little farms with vineyards, olive groves and orchards as Tecate is approached.
27.4	1.8	LA PUERTA. Elev. 1,590 ft. A health resort.
30.8	3.4	TECATE. Elev. 1,690 ft. Pop. 7,074 in 1960. Climate: pleasant in summer, cold in winter. Communications: Telegraph; tele-

phone; railway. Passenger buses between Tijuana and Mexicali stop here.

An attractively situated town in a broad valley surrounded by low mountains. It is immediately south of the international border with customs and immigration offices on both sides. The border gate is open from 8 a.m. to 6 p.m. (Beginning Dec. 1, 1961, the gate was to be kept open until midnight). On the California side a road leads to San Diego and another connects with the main highway (U.S. Route 80) between San Diego and the Imperial Valley. There are a number of stores, restaurants, service stations, a bank (Banco del Pacífico), etc. Travelers can stay at San Carlos motel (I-B), Hotel Tecate (II-A, above the bank), Hotel México (II-A). One of the largest breweries in Mexico (Cervecería Tecate) makes Tecate and Carta Blanca beer. Tecate and the surrounding country produce large quantities of grapes, olives, and grains.

In the early 1830's the region around Tecate was obtained from the Mexican government by a Juan Bandini. The ranches in the vicinity were subjected to Indian raids until toward the end of the 19th century. The town came into existence in the early 1880's with the opening of a general store, gradually evolving into the farming community that it is today.

The highway from Tecate to Ensenada (MEXICO 3) was completed and paved in 1961. It goes south from the center of Tecate over low hills into a valley of little ranches and vineyards:

Mi. from Tijuana	Partial Mileage	Mi. from Tecate	
(4.7)	4.7		GUADALUPE DE TANAMÁ, vineyard at right, one of the largest of several in this valley of TANAMÁ. A few miles further the highway climbs out of the valley over a pass in the rocky hills and down into the broad Valle de las Palmas.
(13.2)	17.9		One of several roads branching right to community center of VALLE DE LAS PALMAS, 0.3 mi. The road down the valley leads back via El Carrizo to M. 24.3 on the Tijuana-Tecate highway (see p. 60). The highway swings east and climbs out of the valley to cross a high ridge.
(4.6)	22.5		A side road left to RANCHO VIEJO, a large vineyard and modern winery and distillery.
(7.4)	29.9		A road left in a valley called EL TESTERAZO. This goes via La Ciénega to join the Las Juntas-Nejí road at 5.0 miles or 10.4 miles from the Tecate-Mexicali highway (see p. 63).
(4.9)	34.8		ESPIGA DE ORO, ranch left, in another valley called VALLECITOS. A road going past this ranch continues east

Mi. from Tijuana	Partial Mileage	Mi. from Tecate	

to Santa Clara (5.4 mi.), a farming settlement founded by American Negroes some years ago. In 1953 two families remained. The road continues to La Hiedra, 8.7 mi. from highway.

(5.0) 39.8 Side road left to El Burro (1.0), ranch. This continues to Valle Seco, ranch, not visited by authors, and a poor road is reported to continue to Real del Castillo (see p. 94). The highway goes down Cañón del Burro with its groves of live oaks.

(5.8) 45.6 Here the road comes out in the broad valley of the Guadalupe River. A side road goes left up the valley to end in the canyon after 6.2 mi. Agua Caliente, hot springs, is 0.8 mi. beyond on a foot trail.

(2.1) 47.7 At a left curve in the highway a side branch straight ahead goes to Guadalupe (center 1.0 mi.). Elev. 1,132. An agricultural colony along the banks of Guadalupe River. The principal crops are wheat, olives, and grapes for making wine. There is a store and post office.

Many of the farmers at Guadalupe are of Russian origin, members of a religious sect known as Malakán. The founders of the colony left Russia at the turn of the century in search of religious freedom, settling here in 1905. The older colonists speak Russian, disapprove of tobacco, wear long beards, and bathe in Russian-style steam houses. The group is dying out, as many of the young men have moved away to Ensenada and the United States.

The last mission to be established in California, Nuestra Señora de Guadalupe, was founded here in 1834 by the Dominican Padre Caballero. The leveled off area once occupied by the mission buildings is all that remains, on the north edge of the arroyo. The mission was abandoned in 1840, after an Indian raid. There are still a few Indian families living in the vicinity.

This branch road continues through the farming area, and at 3.8 mi. from the highway a farm road right leads to the hills through Agua Escondida and La Zorra to Descanso on the coast (see p. 88).

At 4.1 mi. is the center of Ejido Porvenir, a farming colony. From here a good road goes left past the Olivares Mexicanos (6.1 mi. from highway), a large olive orchard, to rejoin the highway at M. 54.8, 8.7 mi. after leaving highway.

The road straight ahead through Ejido Porvenir crosses the Guadalupe River (here usually dry) at 8.2 mi., and at 10.6 mi. from the highway joins an improved road. Going to the right on this leads 4.8 mi. to the Tijuana-Ensenada highway at M. 49.1 (see p. 89); going to the left leads 2.6 mi. to M. 57.2 on the Tecate-Ensenada highway.

At M. 47.7 the paved highway curves left and crosses the (usually dry) river on a bridge, then continues on the left side of the valley.

Mi. from Tijuana	Partial Mileage	Mi. from Tecate	

(7.1) 54.8 The road from Ejido Porvenir via Olivares Mexicanos joins from the right (see above).

(2.4) 57.2 An improved road right goes 7.4 mi. to reach the Tijuana-Ensenada highway at M. 49.1. After 2.6 mi. a branch right leads to El Porvenir (see above).

Mi. from Tijuana	Partial Mileage	Mi. from Tecate	
	(1.6)	58.8	SAN ANTONIO. An old village in a pleasant setting of live oaks. Almost a "ghost town" in the late 1940's, it is now known as VILLA JUÁREZ, and many new houses are appearing (1961). A road left here goes to the population center. The highway crosses some hills to a coastal valley.
	(6.6)	65.4	Junction with the Tijuana-Ensenada highway at M. 57.6 (see p. 89), just north of El Sauzal.

From Tecate, the main highway to Mexicali continues toward the mountains:

35.4	4.6	SAN JOSÉ. Cattle ranch.	
41.3	5.9	SAN VALENTÍN. Large vineyard and winery.	
42.5	1.2	EL ENCINAL. Ranch left in a grove of live oaks.	
45.6	3.1	A branch road right leads to the former through road to the south which is now (1961) fenced off below LAS JUNTAS (DE VALENCIA), 2.5 mi.	
47.4	1.8	A branch road right goes south and climbs into the mountains, eventually reaching the valley of Ojos Negros east of Ensenada.	

Mi. from M. 47.4			
(2.9)	2.9	The road turns right. Straight ahead leads to JACOMÚN, 1.8 mi., cattle ranch.	
(1.1)	4.0	LAS JUNTAS (DE SANTANA). Cattle ranch across meadow about half a mile to right.	
(1.0)	5.0	A road right (not entirely traveled by authors) goes to LAS CORNELIAS, ranch, ca. 4.5 mi. Beyond here in 1954 the road joined that in from Nejí after 1.3 mi. and continued past the Indian rancherias of LOS COCHES (5.0 mi.) and EL PLATERO (7.6 mi.), and LA CIÉNEGA, ranch (13.9 mi). At 19.0 mi. from Las Cornelias this joins the Tecate-Ensenada highway in the Testerazo Valley at M. 29.9 (see p. 61).	
(5.4)	10.4	NEJÍ. Cattle ranch, once an important Indian rancheria, in a valley at an elevation of ca. 3,000 ft. The Indians from this place, led by their chief Jatñil, destroyed the mission of Guadalupe in 1840. A little traveled old road right goes 4.9 mi. to join the road via La Ciénega (described above) to the Tecate-Ensenada highway.	
(7.7)	18.1	EL COMPADRE. Cattle ranch. The road continues south over a pass and comes out in a long valley about 4,000 ft. high. Groups of pine trees are seen for the first time.	
(5.3)	23.4	LA HECHICERA. Cattle ranch. House off road to right at edge of valley. Also a dam and pond, a large white house on a hill, and an airstrip.	

Mi. from Tijuana	Partial Mileage	Mi. from M. 47.4	
	(5.0)	28.4	SAN FAUSTINO. Ranch at the edge of a meadow, which becomes a small lake after heavy rains.
	(1.3)	29.7	Road forks. Left branch is a bypass, rejoining other branch after 5.9 mi. Right branch is followed here.
	(4.8)	34.5	SAN JUAN DE DIOS. Cattle ranch.
	(2.5)	37.0	The bypass road comes in from left.
	(1.3)	38.3	A road branching left connects (after 14.0 mi.) with the road between Los Gavilanes and San Pedro (see page 65). After 3.2 mi. on this road a branch right goes south 2.7 mi. to CASAS VERDES, ranch.
	(0.7)	39.0	Another road in from left, a branch of that mentioned immediately above.
	(4.5)	43.5	ROSA DE CASTILLA. Several houses. Here is a tungsten mine (El Fenómeno), no longer worked. The deposit is estimated to contain 700,000 tons of ore. During the last World War this mine was producing about 2½% of the world's tungsten supply.
	(7.6)	51.1	Road fork. The left branch goes 0.9 mi. to LA HUERTA, a rancheria consisting of about a dozen families of native Indians, located in a little cove at the edge of the mountains. In spite of "Mexicanization," some of the old customs have been preserved and the Indian language is still spoken in addition to Spanish. The chief receives an annual subsidy from the Mexican government. The survival of this and other small groups of Indians in the north is probably due to the fact that their ancestors were never subdued and reduced to mission life by the Spaniards. Beyond La Huerta, 2.1 mi. from the fork this branch joins the Ojos Negros-Laguna Hanson road near Encino Solo (see p. 94). Keep to right at M. 51.1 for Ojos Negros.
	(2.4)	53.5	Junction with Ojos Negros-Laguna Hanson road, 8.2 mi. east of M. 26.6 on the Ensenada-San Felipe road (see p. 94).

The main highway to Mexicali continues climbing gradually:

53.6	6.2	MARÍA EUGENIA, ranch.
54.3	0.7	Side road left, joins an old road to La Rumorosa (see below). JACUMÉ (10 mi. from the main highway), is a farming community near the international border, across from Jacumba, California (there is no road across the border).

Mi. from Tijuana	Partial Mileage	
57.1	2.8	LA HECHICERA. Ranch, gas station.
61.3	4.2	EL CÓNDOR. Gas station and cafe. A road branches right, running along the top of Sierra Juárez to Laguna Hanson and beyond.

	Mi. from Cóndor	
(1.3)	1.3	Crossing of an old road from Tecate to La Rumorosa, now little used, and probably closed west of here.
(1.9)	3.2	JAPÁ. Cattle ranch in a little valley. The road climbs into higher country.
(7.6)	10.8	TRES POZOS. Group of small ranches.
(1.8)	12.6	EL MEZQUITE. Large old house, not inhabited in 1961. The road continues across a plateau covered with piñon pines, with many shallow excavations and mounds, evidence of former mining activity.
(4.5)	17.1	A side road in from left rear is from the Tijuana-Mexicali highway at M. 69.2, near La Rumorosa (16.6 mi., see p. 66).
(0.5)	17.6	A less traveled road branching left goes to EL PROGRESO (3.9 mi., near the head of EL TAJO, the largest canyon of the Sierra Juárez, which drops easterly into the Laguna Salada basin) and LA MILLA (5.2 mi.), abandoned mining areas, and after 8.1 mi. rejoins this main road at M. 22.7 (see below).

(1.5)   19.1   Road forks. Main road goes left. The right branch is the older route. At 2.3 mi. on it from this junction a side road branches right to JASAY, ranch (0.4 mi., uninhabited in 1961) and beyond. At 3.8 mi. is MARGARITA, a tungsten mine. At 5.4 mi. is LOS GAVILANES, an extensive mining center with many ruined buildings off to left of road, not being worked in 1961. A less traveled road branches right at 11.0 mi. and goes 14.0 mi. to join the Nejí-La Huerta road (see page 64). SAN PEDRO (11.5 mi., cattle ranch, uninhabited in 1961) is near the beginning of the pine covered plateau, and the road joins the newer route (at M. 30.2, see below) 14.8 mi. from the junction.

The left branch at M. 19.1 continues through a somewhat wooded area.

Partial Mileage	Mi. from Cóndor	
(3.6)	22.7	A road left goes 2.9 mi. to La Milla and 4.2 mi. to El Progreso (see above).
(0.7)	23.4	EL TOPO, cattle ranch off road to right in a clearing. Shortly beyond the road climbs to a higher, rougher area.
(6.8)	30.2	Older road in from right from Los Gavilanes (see above). The road continues along the high plateau (elev. 5,000-5,500 ft.) of Sierra Juárez, winding through forests of ponderosa pines and past little meadows.

Mi. from Tijuana	Partial Mileage	Mi. from Cóndor	
	(9.7)	39.9	LAGUNA HANSON. Elev. 5,500 ft. A large depression, surrounded by huge granite boulders and pine trees. In rainy seasons this fills with water and becomes a lake. It was named after an American rancher who was murdered near here.

The road continues southwest to join the Ensenada-San Felipe road near Ojos Negros (see pp. 94-95).

The main highway climbs gradually higher into the mountains through scattered growths of piñon pine. Extensive forests of piñon have been burned off.

69.2	7.9		Branch road right to join the road just described. It branches off just west of "Café de las Delicias de Acapulco." (See also Preface page 9.)

		Mi. from Delicias	
	(2.4)	2.4	Road forks. Right branch is older road. Down this 0.9 mi. a branch right is an old road to Tecate. Left branch is best.
	(1.8)	4.2	A road left to a lime products plant.
	(1.8)	6.0	The older road rejoins from right.
	(1.0)	7.0	A branch right goes 0.5 mi. to RANCHO ESCONDIDO.
	(9.6)	16.6	Junction with road in from right from El Cóndor (see above).

70.5	1.3	LA RUMOROSA (Alaska). Elev. 4,370 ft. Here the old road from Tecate comes in from the left. This village, near the top of Sierra Juárez, is a favorite summer resort of the residents of Mexicali. There are several stores, gasoline pumps, motels, post office, etc. Nearby are a government insane asylum and a tuberculosis hospital.

One mile beyond La Rumorosa the highway begins a well-graded and spectacular descent of the abrupt east slope of the mountains. The cool highlands are left behind, and the bare rocky canyons drop swiftly to the desert floor. In the distance can be seen the expanse of Laguna Salada.

98.7   28.2   Branch road right (see Preface page 9) across LAGUNA SALADA, a 30-mile-long dry lake slightly below sea level. The road has branches leading to the edge of the Sierra Juárez and of the Sierra de los Cucapás. It turns into an impassable quagmire after a heavy rain. When large quantities of water are released into the lower Colorado River, floodwaters sometimes come around the south end of the Sierra de los Cucapás and form a vast sheet of water on the east side of Laguna Salada to within a few miles of the highway. (This occurred in 1958).

It is possible that at one time Laguna Salada was an arm of the sea, and there is a story that one of the early Spanish explorers sailed into the upper Gulf in search of the mythical "Straits of Anian," a passage thought to exist between the Atlantic and Pacific oceans. The ship was supposed to have run aground some place in Laguna Salada, with a great treasure in pearls aboard, and subsequently buried under drifting sands.

There are many interesting side trips on the Laguna Salada road and along the east base of the Sierra Juárez.

Mi. from M. 98.7	Partial Mileage	
0.0	0.0	The side road goes south, then turns west on the bed of the former highway.
1.2	1.2	A fork. Straight ahead leads to a road along the base of the Sierra Juárez.

	Mi. from M. 1.2	
(1.4)	1.4	Turn left (south) from old highway.
(8.2)	9.6	A lime kiln at left is called CALERA CONCEPCIÓN. Below here the road runs near base of Sierra Juárez.
(6.8)	16.4	A road in from left is M. 6.6 on the Laguna Salada road (see below), 10.2 mi. from here.
(0.3)	16.7	A road right goes to near CANTÚ PALMS, two groups of fan palms on the mountain slope.
(6.9)	23.6	CAÑÓN EL TAJO is at right, the largest of the canyons in Sierra Juárez (see page 65). Here a sandy road goes 1.2 mi. toward it. Groves of palms (both *Washingtonia* and *Erythea*) and water begin ca. 4 mi. beyond.
(4.7)	28.3	A poor road right goes up CAÑÓN EL CARRIZO 2.3 mi. to a spring and palm grove.
(1.2)	29.5	A junction. CAÑÓN DE GUADALUPE is to right 3.4 mi. This point is more easily reached via POZO DEMARA (see below).

The left branch at fork of M. 1.2 is the Laguna Salada road.

1.4	0.2	Begin flat surface of Laguna Salada. Side roads branch left and right. Take center tracks.
6.6	5.2	Fork in road; go straight ahead (left branch). The right branch goes 10.2 mi. to join the road skirting the base of Sierra Juárez at M. 16.4 (see above).

Mi. from M. 98.7	Partial Mileage	
15.7	9.1	A road left crosses the dry lake and joins the east side road (6.9 mi.).
16.8	1.1	Road forks. Right branch goes to Guadalupe Canyon.

	Mi. from M. 16.8	
(9.8)	9.8	Pozo Demara, abandoned ranch and well. Road heads toward the mountains.
(5.2)	15.0	A junction. This is M. 29.5 on the road along base of Sierra Juárez (see above). Turn left.
(3.4)	18.4	Cañón de Guadalupe (Agua Caliente). A hot spring among groves of fan palms. As in several of the canyons of this region, there are both *Washingtonia* and *Erythea* (blue) palms. Rustic bathing facilities. Fee charged for camping.

Left fork at M. 16.8 continues down the Laguna Salada, then leaves it toward the south end.

32.0	15.2	Pozo Cenizo, abandoned well 1.1 mi. past edge of Laguna Salada. A fair road continues south.
48.1	16.1	A road branches right. It crosses Arroyo Santa Isabel (4.7 mi.) and enters Cañón el Palomar, to end at a ranch in a palm grove (11.9 mi. from turnoff).
62.6	14.5	Road forks. Take right branch.
66.6	4.0	An extremely dim track goes left across a sandy wash. After 0.6 mi. another dim track branches right from this and goes south to enter Arroyo el Sáiz at 4.6 mi., which may be followed up to right to 8.6 mi. from M. 66.6. Here it comes to the old "pole line road" at M. 48.7 from La Ventana (see pp. 80 and 97).

The more traveled road continues to right, into the hills.

67.4	0.8	La Palmita. Occasionally inhabited Paipai Indian camp with spring. Five miles up the arroyo (said to be passable with 4-wheel drive, not visited by authors) is Agua Caliente, a larger Paipai rancheria.

The traffic encountered on these desert roads consists chiefly of dilapidated trucks of *leñeros*, or wood gatherers. These range over a large area of the desert in search of dried trunks and branches of ironwood. Large loads are hauled to Mexicali, where this heavy hard wood is esteemed for use in tortilla factories on account of its hot, smokeless flame (other woods such as mesquite, also an excellent fuel, are not gathered on such an extensive commercial scale). Some of the desert roads were originally opened by *leñeros*, and many a traveler has taken a promising looking fork or side road which soon rebranches and leads only to stump holes.

Mi. from Tijuana	Partial Mileage	
98.7	......	Past the Laguna Salada turnoff the highway to Mexicali leaves the north end of the Laguna Salada basin and goes through a low pass. To the left is the solitary peak of El Centinela (Mt. Signal), a barren mountain 2,560 ft. high just south of the border. Southeast is the bare, waterless Cucapás range.
		Beyond the hills the intensely cultivated area of the Mexicali Valley begins, in sharp contrast to the adjacent desert. Irrigation canals and fields of cotton are on all sides.
108.2	9.5	COLONIA PROGRESO. A collective farming colony, with store, gasoline pump, post office, etc.
110.7	2.5	COLONIA ZARAGOZA. Farming community.
112.8	2.1	A paved road right cuts across to the San Felipe highway (4.8 mi.), joining it at M. 7.1 (see page 77), a useful bypass for going to San Felipe or San Luis, Sonora, avoiding Mexicali traffic.
117.3	4.5	MEXICALI. Elevation: sea level. Population: 172,554 in 1960.

Climate: Generally pleasant in winter (average temperature, Nov.-Mar. 58.5° F.; coldest months, Dec. to Feb.); very hot and dry in summer (average temperature, Apr.-Oct. 82.0° F.; hottest months, June to Sep.). The extreme temperatures in the summer sometimes reach 120° F. during the day and drop to 60° at night. Rainfall is negligible, averaging 3.0 inches annually.

Communications: Land telegraph and telephone to Tijuana and Ensenada, connecting with lines in the United States; a telephone line connects Mexicali with San Luis, Sonora. Radio telegraph and telephone to Mexico City and other points in the interior. There are daily planes (carrying air mail and passengers) to Mexico City (see page 37). The airport is on the east side of town.

There are passenger bus lines from Mexicali to Tijuana via Tecate and between Mexicali and San Luis (Sonora), Guadalajara, and Mexico City. There is also bus service between Mexicali and San Felipe (see page 39).

One passenger-carrying railway operates out of Mexicali: F. C.

Sonora-Baja California has a daily train between Mexicali, Puerto Peñasco, Hermosillo, and Guadalajara.

A number of local bus lines serve the city of Mexicali.

Hotels: Most American tourists stay in Calexico, California, where there are several hotels and motels. However there are very good hotels in Mexicali, including the following: Del Norte (II-A), Av. Madero and Calle Melgar (at the border gate); Hilton Plaza (II-A), Av. Madero 366; Cucapah (II-A), Av. Madero 222; Corona (II-A), Av. Madero and Calle Martínez Zorrilla; Kino (II-B), Calle México 279; and Moreno (II-B), Av. Reforma 646. Motels include the following: Fortín de las Flores (II-A), Cristobal Colón 612; Cosmos (II-A), Calz. Justo Sierra 1493; and La Siesta (II-A), Calz. Justo Sierra 899.

Restaurants: Carmina, at Av. Reforma and Calle C, for continental cooking. Café Persia, Av. Reforma 949 features Arabian and international cooking. A good restaurant for Mexican food is the Bum Bum, Calle Irigoyen north of Av. Madero. The restaurant at the Sonora-Baja California railway station is clean and has good food. Chinese food is a specialty of Restaurant 19, Juárez 8. Restaurants are also located at the Del Norte hotel and the Hilton Plaza hotel.

Banks: Banco de Baja California; Banco Mercantil; Banco de Mexicali; Banco Mexicano de Occidente; Banco Nacional de México, and several others. A better rate for the dollar is offered at the banks than at the numerous exchange booths near the border. Both Mexican and United States currencies are accepted in Mexicali and Calexico.

Hospitals: There is a municipal hospital, as well as private clinics.

There is an American consulate in Mexicali. Tourist cards for travel to the interior can be obtained from Mexican officials at the border.

The Mexicali Chamber of Commerce *(Cámara de Comercio)* has a tourist information office on Calle Alfabetización south of Av. Reforma.

There are many stores and markets where supplies of all kinds can be purchased. As Baja California is a free zone, many American and other foreign goods are sold here free of duty, sometimes at prices considerably lower than in the United States. Since the completion of the Sonora-Baja California Railway merchandise of all kinds from central Mexico has been brought to Mexicali in increasing quantities. Fine silver and leather articles may be purchased at prices high for Mexico, but low when compared to those in the States.

Even more than Tijuana, Mexicali has changed within the last few years from a motley collection of shacks and grim-looking bars into an attractive, modern city, with many beautiful homes, paved streets, and handsome government buildings. What it has lost in frontier atmosphere it has gained in cleanliness, respectability, and civic pride. It is

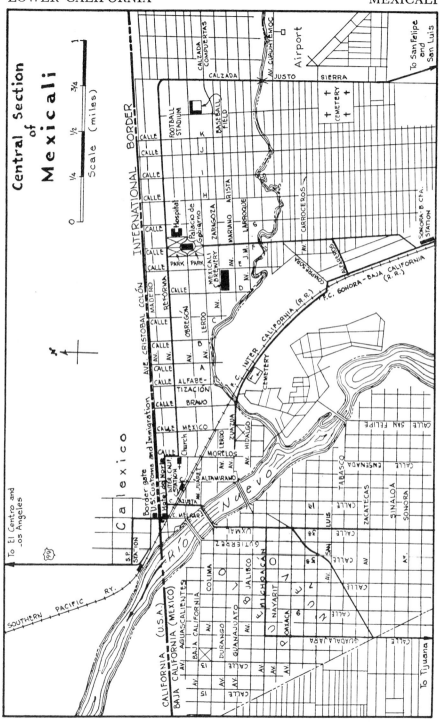

Central Section of **Mexicali**

Scale (miles)

the capital of the State of Baja California, the largest city in the peninsula, and the center of a rich agricultural district. Immediately adjacent across the border is the smaller town of Calexico, California, separated from Mexicali by a fence. The Valley of Mexicali, a continuation of the Imperial Valley, is a great flat basin partly below sea level. South of Mexicali the dark barren range known as Sierra de los Cucapás rises abruptly from the desert floor. The Río Nuevo, a shallow ravine carrying drainage water from the farming areas, runs through the center of town dividing it into the two sections of Mexicali proper (east) and Pueblo Nuevo (west).

The main business section of town begins at the border gate and extends along both sides of the railroad tracks. The new residential section is spread out to the east, with wide tree-lined avenues. In the center of the residential district, at the end of Avenida Obregón, is the Government Palace (Palacio de Gobierno), a handsome stone structure surrounded by parks. In front of the Palace is a statue of General Alvaro Obregón, onetime (1920-1928) President of Mexico, who lost an arm in the Revolution and was later assassinated. Two blocks southwest of the Palace is the Mexicali Brewery, which produces some of the finest beer in Mexico. Also worth a visit is the world's largest cotton gin (Compañía Industrial Jabonera del Pacífico), on the south edge of town.

The site of Mexicali, at first known as La Laguna del Álamo, was settled by ex-miners from El Álamo (above Ensenada) in 1898. The town began to flourish in 1902, when the Imperial Canal was finished and water from the Colorado River became available for irrigation in the valley. Within a few years Mexicali was a rip-roaring frontier town, and its growth has been phenomenal to the present time. There was a great flood in 1906, when the waters of the Colorado got out of control and inundated much of the valley. For several months in 1911, during the Revolution, Mexicali was occupied by an army of soldiers of fortune that had invaded Mexico from the United States. Stability was restored during the six-year tenure of Colonel Esteban Cantú, who ruled the Northern District practically independent of the central Mexican government from 1915 to 1920. It was during Cantú's term that the capital was moved from Ensenada to Mexicali. At this time practically all the land in the valley was owned by the Colorado River Land Company, an American concern. Long-staple cotton, introduced in 1912 has always been the principal crop. In recent years most of the cotton is trucked to Ensenada for shipment. Thousands of Chinese were brought to the valley as laborers, but their immigration was restricted in 1919. They were replaced by a steady stream of Mexican farmers from the interior.

In its early years Mexicali was a "wide open" town, specializing in the types of vice calculated to attract the American tourists and ranchers of the Imperial Valley. The government, in order to finance its many material improvements (including the first automobile road across the mountains to Tijuana), licensed gambling, prostitution, and opium refining. During the prohibition years thousands of Americans poured daily across the border and Mexicali earned a very wicked reputation. However, gambling was outlawed in 1935, and drug-peddling and prostitution have been strictly curtailed in recent years. About the only reminder of Mexicali's unsavory past is the relatively large number of bars and night clubs.

In 1936-37 the Colorado River Land Company was forced by the Mexican government to sell most of its properties to Mexican farmers and collective farming colonies, known as *ejidos*. Originally the irrigation water for the whole valley on both sides of the border was carried in the Imperial Canal, which dips down into Mexico. In 1934 construction began on the All-American Canal, running entirely on the United States side, which threatened to deprive the Valley of Mexicali of its water. An international water treaty solved this problem in 1945, guaranteeing to Mexico 1,500,000 acre feet of water a year. Now Mexico has asserted her sovereignty by building a new aqueduct entirely south of the border.

ROUTE 2

MEXICALI TO SAN FELIPE

AND BEYOND TO LAGUNA CHAPALA

An excellent paved highway (MEXICO 5), flat and with long straight stretches, to the fishing port of San Felipe on the upper Gulf of California. The first part traverses rich green farming country irrigated from the Colorado River, and the last part is barren desert.

Mi. from Mexicali	Partial Mileage	
0.0	0.0	MEXICALI (for description, see page 69), border gate. Follow signs to the east edge of town, then south.
6.4	6.4	Crossroads. The highway to San Felipe continues straight ahead (south) across the railroad tracks. To the left, paralleling the tracks on the north, is the paved highway to San Luis, Sonora (MEXICO 2).

	Mi. from M. 6.4	
(3.0)	3.0	PALACO (GONZÁLEZ ORTEGA). A bustling little community stretched along the highway and railroad. Many cotton gins are located in this area. There are gas stations here and in most other places named on the San Luis highway.
(0.7)	3.7	PASCUALITOS, to right of highway. Here the Sonora-Baja California Railway angles to the right away from the highway. The former Inter-California Railway (to Algodones) which paralleled the highway beyond here was torn up in 1960.

(2.3)   6.0   A paved road right loops south, then east to near the Colorado River, then returns to the San Luis highway. This passes EJIDO PUEBLA (0.5 mi. from junction) and EJIDO MICHOACÁN (8.7 mi.).

At 12.7 mi. is project headquarters of a government agency which has drilled (1961) some steam wells nearby in the mud volcano area east of CERRO PRIETO (see p. 77). It is planned to utilize the natural steam for generation of electricity.

The road continues past EJIDO HIDALGO (15.0 mi.); EJIDO NUEVO LEÓN (16.8 mi.); and EJIDO SALTILLO (20.6 mi.).

At 24.1 mi. a paved road crosses. To left is San Luis highway, 9.5 mi. To right it goes via VICTORIA (10.1 mi.) to the Carranza — K-57 highway (13.3 mi., see p. 78).

The San Luis highway (at M. 36.1) is rejoined after 40.7 mi.

Ejido originally referred to the communal grazing lands on the outskirts of a village. In Baja California ejidos are more often collective farming colonies sponsored by the government, where groups of immigrants from central Mexico are given land, loans for farming implements, etc. The ejido system has been extensively used to rehabilitate thousands of *braceros* (migrant farm workers) who have been refused entry to or deported from the United States. Most of the lands in this area formerly belonged to the Colorado River Land Company.

Mi. from Mexicali	Partial Mileage	Mi. from M. 6.4	
	(2.8)	8.8	SESVANIA. Small agricultural community.
	(4.4)	13.2	CUCAPAH. Small agricultural community.
	(0.9)	14.1	Paved road left which doubles back to Mexicali.
	(1.2)	15.3	PÓLVORA. Small agricultural community.
	(2.4)	17.7	HECHICERA. Small agricultural community.
	(3.1)	20.8	VOLCANO. Small agricultural community.
	(1.5)	22.3	Paved road right via EJIDO JIQUILPAN (3.4 mi.) to VICTORIA (19.6 mi.) and beyond (see p. 75).
	(0.5)	22.8	BATAQUES. Small agricultural community.
	(2.3)	25.1	SANTA ROSA. Fork in highway.

Left branch goes via TECOLOTE (2.2 mi. from junction), PAREDONES (fair-sized agricultural community, 6.7 mi), and CUERVOS (11.6 mi.), to PUENTE CALABAZAS (14.5 mi.) where it crosses a bridge over the *Canal Principal* and joins another road from the Mexicali-San Luis highway. It continues past PRESA MORELOS (23.8 mi., see below) to ALGODONES (24.8 mi. from Santa Rosa): Elev. 125 ft. Communications: telegraph and telephone to Mexicali and points in the U.S.   Bus to Mexicali.

Algodones is a rather bedraggled-looking border town which experienced a boom during the construction of Morelos Dam *(Presa Morelos)*, a large diversion dam across the Colorado River (see above), completed in 1952. Algodones is on the west bank of the Colorado immediately south of Andrade, California. Yuma, Arizona, is 8.5 mi. across the border via U.S. Route 80. The border gate (U.S. Customs) is open from 8 a.m. to 6 p.m. There are a number of stores and bars.

The first settlers of Algodones were cattlemen from Sonora who arrived soon after the international boundary was decided on, in the 1850's. In the early days Algodones was a station on the old stagecoach route from Yuma to San Diego.

Partial Mileage	Mi. from M. 6.4	
......	25.1	The San Luis highway is the right branch.
(6.8)	31.9	EJIDO HERMOSILLO. Cotton gin.
(4.2)	36.1	Road in from right, from Ejido Nuevo León, etc., (see p. 75). Here highway crosses the *Canal Principal*.
(0.3)	36.4	A paved road left follows the *Canal Principal* via PUENTE CALABAZAS (7.5 mi.) and PRESA MORELOS (16.8 mi.) to ALGODONES (17.8 mi. see above).
(1.9)	38.3	Crossing of Colorado River. A steel and concrete toll bridge ($5 pesos per car, 1961). The boundaries of three

states come together at this point: Baja California, Sonora, and Arizona. The road to San Luis (Sonora) continues beyond the river, just south of the international border.

(2.0) 40.3 SAN LUIS, Sonora. A fast-growing commercial and farming center. It is a port of entry, and there is a road to Yuma, Arizona (26 mi.). The Mexican highway continues across northern Sonora connecting with other roads to Puerto Peñasco, Hermosillo, and Mexico City. A paved road leads south out of San Luis to Riíto, Sonora (27.4 mi., see p. 78).

The main San Felipe highway crosses the tracks (at M. 6.4) and heads south through irrigated farming country.

7.1   0.7   Paved road right connects after 4.8 mi. with Tijuana-Mexicali highway at M. 112.8 (see p. 69).

9.0   1.9   Paved road right to Fraccionamiento Laguna Campestre (0.4 mi., a modern residential subdivision) and the Country Club (1.2 mi.).

17.3   8.3   Bridge across Canal de Cerro Prieto, a large irrigation canal. A prominent landmark seen to the southeast is CERRO PRIETO, a dark volcanic hill 750 ft. high, with two craters at the top.
A side road goes left at the bridge and runs along the north side of the canal, crosses the canal after 4.8 mi., and skirts the north edge of Cerro Prieto. At 5.9 mi., at a fork, the right branch leads to AGUA CALIENTE, 6.9 mi. from highway. Here are hot mineral springs popular locally for bathing, at the edge of a swampy area known as LAGUNA VOLCANO to the east of Cerro Prieto. In this area there are mud volcanoes, conical mounds formed by hot mud ejected with steam through craters.
The main highway continues south and approaches the barren range, Sierra de los Cucapás. It soon leaves the irrigated delta area to the left and begins to cross a sandy desert.

27.4   10.1   LA PUERTA. A farming community at the foot of the Cucapás mountains. Stores, gasoline stations, etc.

29.9   2.5   EL FARO, a store at left. A dirt road turns off to the left and crosses a number of sloughs in which there is reported to be good fishing.

30.6   0.7   PUERTO DE MAZATLÁN, restaurant. A road across the Cucapás starts here, angling to the right.
After 3 miles of going southerly this turns west up a broad

Mi. from Mexicali	Partial Mileage	

canyon to cross the Cucapás range on a low pass after 7.4 mi., and then descends through a valley. At 11.6 mi. a branch to right (one of several such) leads to an arroyo at the north side of the valley and down it past AGUA DE LAS PALMAS, a small palm grove (0.7 mi. right at 16.7 mi.), and on to the east edge of the Laguna Salada, 21.3 mi. from the highway. The left branch at 11.6 mi. continues down the arroyo through a little gorge (CAÑÓN DE DAVID) to emerge into the basin of the Laguna Salada 15.6 mi. from the highway. The road continues southerly along the edge of the Cucapás range, but four-wheel drive vehicles may make their way across sand onto the dry lake surface.

31.0   0.4   A paved side road branches left to the Colorado River and beyond:

Mi. from
M. 31.0

(4.5)	4.5	EJIDO DURANGO. Farming center, stores, etc.
(4.2)	8.7	Bridge across Estero Pescaderos, usually a good-sized river.
(1.4)	10.1	COLONIA V. CARRANZA. Farming center, stores, etc.
(1.3)	11.4	Crossroads at gas station. A dirt road branches left to PESCADEROS (4.9 mi.,) and other farming villages. Paved road keeps straight ahead.
(2.0)	13.4	Branch road left to VICTORIA (3.2 mi.) and beyond.
(3.4)	16.8	Colorado River crossing on the railroad bridge planked for automobiles and trucks. Toll $2 pesos per car (1961). See illustration p. 99.
(4.9)	21.7	COLONIA COAHUILA (Locally called KILÓMETRO 57 for its location on the railroad). A fair sized farming community. A road to right goes south to COLONIA ZACATECAS, 14 mi. The paved road turns left and crosses the line into Sonora.
(1.8)	23.5	Junction at a paved road. To left is San Luis, Sonora (24.5 mi., see p. 77). Right branch leads to
(2.9)	26.4	RIÍTO, Sonora; farming settlement. Railroad station. A dirt road continues 46.4 mi. farther to SANTA CLARA (EL GOLFO), a fishing village on the gulf shore. (See Preface page 9.)

The main road to San Felipe continues south through a cultivated area:

32.4   1.4   LA MARIANA. A scattered agricultural community.

37.6   5.2   Side road right through a pass (PUERTO DE AZUFRE, 2.4 mi.) over the Cucapás mountains to a fork, 4.3 mi.

The right branch goes 3.9 mi. to an abandoned sulfur mine. Left branch passes an abandoned field 8.4 mi. from the highway, and the Laguna Salada surface is most easily reached by taking a very dim track here to the left (south). In 1961 the Laguna

Salada could not be crossed this far south because of water in the flood channel.

The main road curves left and follows a narrow ledge between the barren Sierra El Mayor on the west and the Río Hardy (the principal delta channel of the Colorado) on the east.

41.6   4.0   EL MAYOR. Here and at Campo Río Hardy (40.8 mi.) are trailer camps, stores, etc. Launches can be rented for fishing in the river. El Mayor is the usual northern limit of tidewater from the Gulf.

The Indians seen in this area belong to the Cócopa (Cucapá) tribe, largest of the surviving native groups in Baja California. Once very numerous, the tribe is now reduced to about 250 individuals. Most of them have become "Mexicanized," but others live pretty much as their ancestors did when first seen by Spaniards 400 years ago. They have a primitive agriculture supplemented by game, fish, and wild plants. Their houses are well-ventilated brush shelters. Each year the tribe used to make a trip to the mountains (Sierra Juárez) to collect piñon nuts, and another to the Gulf to dig for clams, and even today some of them make these long annual treks across the desert.

47.0   5.4   Side road left to EJIDO MARÍTIMO.

The San Felipe highway leaves the mountains behind and continues south on top of a dike across an extensive mud flat separating the Colorado delta from the Laguna Salada basin.

55.4   8.4   A track left goes 5.8 mi. across the salt flats to VUELTA LA CURVINA, a sport fishing camp on a bend of the lower Colorado River. (See also Preface page 9.)

In 1962 tracks were reported from the camp to the site of LA BOMBA (ca. 11 mi.) a former settlement near the head of the Colorado River estuary. In the mid-1930s this was a port for medium draft sea-going vessels. Toward the middle of the last century the Colorado River was navigated by flat-bottomed steamboats to which cargoes were transferred from sea-going vessels. The coming of the railroad to Yuma in 1877 ended the romantic era of river steamboats.

Tracks, in varying locations, are seen going to the right of the highway across the salt flats. These are

Mi. from Mexicali	Partial Mileage	

used by *leñeros* (see page 68) to reach TRES POZOS, ca. 11 mi. (see page 80) and the desert basin to the south.

Ahead the highway passes through some sand dunes and skirts the edge of the low, barren Sierra Pinta following near the east base of these mountains. To the left is a vast expanse of tidal salt flats. Periodically the Gulf waters overflow this area (tides at this point sometimes exceed 30 feet).

72.7 17.3 ESTACIÓN LA VENTANA, gas station and restaurant. A dirt road right heads across the Sierra Pinta into the desert basin beyond, and four-wheel drive vehicles may cross the mountains to join the Ensenada-San Felipe road.

	Mi. from M. 72.7	
(18.2)	18.2	Road crosses Arroyo Grande, a wide sandy wash up which four-wheel drive vehicles can drive to left 22.3 mi. to ARROYO GRANDE, ranch, more easily reached via Arroyo Teráiso (see p. 101).
(4.3)	22.5	A junction. Right branch goes 13.5 mi. to TRES POZOS, waterhole near edge of the Laguna Salada, and ca. 11 mi. farther to the San Felipe highway.
		Left branch is passable with difficulty by four-wheel drive vehicles, leading across the mountains, via the old "pole line road" (see p. 97).
(12.0)	34.5	ARROYO JAQUEJEL crossing. Vehicles can drive to left up this rare desert stream for 1.5 mi. (See Preface page 9.)
(1.8)	36.3	Road enters ARROYO JAMAU, with very rough going for 1.3 mi. up the narrow boulder-strewn canyon.
(9.4)	45.7	A road to left ends after 0.8 mi. A trail continues a mile farther to JAMAU, cattle camp occupied in winter.
(1.7)	47.4	A road to right goes 1.3 mi. to GUATAMOTE, another winter cattle camp.
(1.3)	48.7	ARROYO EL SÁIZ crossing. The wash may be followed down to right 4.0 mi., after which the road climbs out and heads north for Laguna Salada. The Tijuana-Mexicali highway (M. 98.7) is 75.2 mi. from here (see page 68).
		East of here the old "pole line road" climbs a short, spectacularly steep grade.
(2.3)	51.0	PORTEZUELO DE JAMAU, summit, elev. 4,000 ft., on the peninsular divide. The descent on the west side is more gentle.

Mi. from Mexicali	Partial Mileage	Mi. from M. 72.7	
	(4.7)	55.7	ALAMITO, cattle camp, sometimes inhabited, water.
	(11.4)	67.1	Junction with the Ensenada-San Felipe road at M. 67.4 (see p. 97) near EL RODEO.

74.4	1.7	A little-traveled old track left follows the edge of the salt flats to the easternmost point of the Sierra Pinta, 1.4 mi. An outlying little hill has an opening through it which gives the name LA VENTANA ("window") to this entire area.
92.0	17.6	A dark volcanic butte to the left of the highway is called EL CHINERO. The story is that some years ago a party of Chinese immigrants bound for Mexicali disembarked at San Felipe and continued on foot to this place, where they all died of thirst.
95.3	3.3	Side road right is best route from this area to Ensenada. It branches after 15.0 mi. Right branch connects with the Ensenada-San Felipe road 28.4 mi. from highway, at the mouth of San Matías canyon (M. 101.0, see p. 101). Left branch at 15.0 mi. goes to Valle San Felipe and connects (25.9 mi. from highway) with the Ensenada-San Felipe road at M. 110.7, at the north end of the dry lake.
121.0	25.7	Side road left to PLAYA LAS ALMEJAS (Clam Beach), 1.3 mi., a fishing resort on the Gulf. This is one of several roads to the beach along this stretch of highway.
125.8	4.8	Dirt road to Ensenada goes right (see Route 4).
126.0	0.2	At entrance to San Felipe, a graded road to right is the main road to the south (see below).

126.3   0.3   SAN FELIPE. Estimated pop. in 1960: 1000. Climate: pleasant in winter and spring; very hot in summer. Rainfall practically nil.

A fishing settlement on the upper Gulf, 60 miles from the mouth of the Colorado River. The town itself is largely a ramshackle collection of fishermen's huts. The shallow anchorage is exposed to south and east winds, but somewhat protected from the prevailing winds on the north by a range of hills. San Felipe Point, at the north end of the bay, is 940 ft. high. To the south is a long steep sandy beach. Other good camping spots are north of the settlement. There are two shallow wells of brackish water, but bottled drinking water and good beer are available and recommended.

There are two modern hotels: Augie's Riviera (1-B, bar, restaurant) and El Cortez Motel (I-B, with a trailer park in connection). The Sands Trailer Court is just south of town. There are several other small hotels, but accommodations are limited and are apt to be filled during the best fishing months (most visitors come prepared to camp out). There are several restaurants, gasoline stations, and stores where some supplies may be purchased. South of the town is a landing field. Passage can occasionally be obtained on fishing vessels running down to Guaymas and other ports.

San Felipe has become popular with American fishermen since the completion of the paved highway from Mexicali. It is an important commercial fishing center; *totuava* (see page 44) and shrimp are caught and sent in trucks to Mexicali and the United States. Many varieties of game fish are found offshore, and surf fishing is also popular. Fishing launches can be rented and bait purchased. Spring is the best season for sport fishing.

The bay and water hole of San Felipe were used to a slight extent toward the end of the 18th century as a supply point for the northern Dominican missions. The place began to be developed as a port in 1858, when some shacks were built here, but there were no permanent inhabitants until the 1920's. Large-scale commercial fishing operations began in 1942.

South of San Felipe a dirt road continues along the Gulf of California and joins the main transpeninsular road (Route 5) at either Rancho Laguna Chapala or 18.0 mi. beyond.

Mi. from Mexicali	Partial Mileage	
126.3	0.0	SAN FELIPE. The old road heads south from center of town, joining the newer, graded road (see M. 126.0) after 2.5 mi.
129.5	3.2	A side road to the left leads to the Gulf

	Mi. from M. 129.5	
(3.4)	3.4	A junction. Keep left (right branch is older road to the south).
(7.6)	11.0	Road forks. Left leads almost to PUNTA ESTRELLA. Take right branch (south) among sand dunes parallel to Gulf, with several roads branching left to the beach.
(4.3)	15.3	A cross road. The left branch goes 0.2 mi. past PERSEBÚ (deserted ranch, water) and 1.0 mi. to a beach. Straight ahead also leads to a beach, 2.4 mi. Take right branch, angling away from the Gulf.
(5.7)	21.0	A road in from the right is the older "main" road which branched at 3.4 mi.
(2.1)	23.1	Junction with main road at M. 146.9 (see below).

Mi. from Mexicali	Partial Mileage	

The main road continues south over the sandy coastal plain.

146.9   17.4   A little-traveled road in from left rear is from Persebú (see above).

148.0   1.1   At the first signs of a sulfur mine at left, a branch left leads over a low hill and to the east to a beach called AGUA DE CHALE (4.8 mi.) named for a former nearby well. Surf fishing.

148.8   0.8   At the end of the sulfur mining area another road goes left around the hill to join the road to Agua de Chale.

The main road crosses some sandy washes and some spurs of hills which extend to the Gulf.

160.9   12.1   A side road goes 2.0 mi. to the Gulf shore.

167.5   6.6   Crossing of ARROYO MATOMÍ. A well is 0.2 mi. to right. This wash, here consisting of many branches, originates far back in the desert hills. Four-wheel drive vehicles may follow it for a considerable distance.

177.5   10.0   PUERTECITOS. A cove on the Gulf, developed as a fishing and camping resort. Gasoline, restaurant, boat launching.

The road follows close to the shore for several miles, a stretch of rocky cliffs, coves, and tidal pools. Then it goes a little inland.

188.7   11.2   Summit of a short grade. The dark volcanic hill to left, CERRO PRIETO, has a crater at its top. A few miles farther is a stretch of steep and narrow grades crossing ridges which come to the edge of the sea. Local truck drivers distinguish between three distinct grades: CUESTA LA LEONA, CUESTA LA VIRGEN (a little shrine at summit, M. 194.1), and CUESTA EL HUERFANITO.

197.2   8.5   A long straight stretch begins along the coastal plain. The little island close to shore here is EL HUERFANITO ("The Little Orphan"). (See Preface page 10.)

203.3   6.1   A road to right rear goes to ARROYO MIRAMAR (crossed by highway at M. 202.0). It is 1.9 mi. to where the arroyo emerges from the hills, and the road may be followed a mile farther up the canyon past signs of placer gold mining and caves formerly inhabited by miners. These placers were extensively worked in the early 1900's by Yaqui Indians from Sonora.

Mi. from Mexicali	Partial Mileage	
203.6	0.3	EL ALMACÉN. Stone ruins 0.2 mi. left (almost hidden from view by a rise) near the shore. This was a warehouse constructed in the heyday of gold mining at Miramar.
206.4	2.8	OKIE LANDING. A little cove. Boats may be rented for fishing among the adjacent islands. Camping space. The road crosses low ridges which come right down to the Gulf, before turning a little inland.
208.1	1.7	Crossing of ARROYO LOS ARQUITOS. At left near road is a "tinaja" which holds water for considerable periods after the infrequent rains. A spring (EL SAUCITO) is reported to be upstream ca. 4 mi.
208.8	0.7	A side road right 0.5 mi. to AGUA DEL MEZQUITITO, a small water hole. The road traverses a sandy coastal plain, then crosses low hills.
223.6	14.8	A branch road left to the shore of BAHÍA SAN LUIS GONZAGA (1.0 mi.).

A small fishing camp, where boats may usually be rented; good fishing; gasoline sometimes available; camping space. A beautiful little bay surrounded by extremely barren hills and plains. Until recent years it was only rarely visited except by fishermen arriving by sea, but the construction of the road down the Gulf has brought many tourists, and it is developing into a resort.

When explored by Jesuit Padre Fernando Consag in 1746, San Luis Gonzaga Bay was found uninhabited for lack of water, though frequently visited by Indians for fishing. In 1767 it became a supply point for the last Jesuit mission, Santa María, about 14 miles to the southwest (see pp. 120-21). Ruins of a stone structure, likely a storehouse, dating from the mission period may still be seen near the shore of the bay (see below). On the ARROYO ALFREDO (crossed by the main road at M. 223.3) there is a stone-faced well, Pozo de los Frailes, believed by "old-timers" to have been constructed in mission days (to reach it, take left branch 0.1 mi. toward the camp from junction of M. 223.6; well is 0.7 mi. further).

The main road passes through low hills and emerges onto a wide sandy coastal plain.

	Partial Mileage	
225.2	1.6	A sandy road branching left leads 0.9 mi. to the stone ruins on the shore of the bay (see above).
226.7	1.5	A road left leads to another tourist camp on Bahía San Luis Gonzaga (2.0 mi.), attractively located on a sandspit which separates this bay from the larger ENSENADA

Mi. from Mexicali	Partial Mileage	

DE SAN FRANCISQUITO. Landing field for light airplanes; usually gasoline; camping space.

232.1   5.4   Highway makes a sharp right turn (the cleared road straight ahead ends after 5.5 sandy miles). A road left leads to the Gulf shore:

Mi. from
M. 232.1

(4.0)   4.0   MOLINO DE LACY. A small hill with ruins of a former gold ore mill. A little-traveled road goes straight ahead, crosses hills, passes PIONEER MINE (0.2 mi. to left after 8.2 mi., not being worked in 1959), and rejoins the main road at M. 249.9, 14.3 mi. from Molino de Lacy.
Another branch turns left at Molino de Lacy and heads directly for the Gulf.

(2.8)   6.8   PUERTO DE SAN FRANCISQUITO, at the southern end of Ensenada de San Francisquito. A pleasant wide sandy beach. (See also Preface page 10.)

The main road, heading directly away from the Gulf, goes to the edge of the plain, and then crosses low hills, roughly following the Arroyo de San Francisquito.

247.7   15.6   LAS ARRASTRAS (DE ARRIOLA). A wide clearing. At right in gully is a well of good water. The place was named for the old ore mills here.

248.0   0.3   Road forks. Either branch may be taken to join the Ensenada-Santa Rosalía road. The right branch goes to Chapala:

Mi. from
M. 248.0

(3.5)   3.5   A road left goes 3.2 mi. to rejoin the road to Calamajué at M. 252.5.

(11.4)   14.9   RANCHO LAGUNA CHAPALA, at M. 273.9 on the main Ensenada-Santa Rosalía road (see p. 122).

The left branch at M. 248.0 goes via Calamajué.

249.9   1.9   A cross road. From left is the road from Molino de Lacy and Pioneer Mine (see above).

252.5   2.6   A road in from right connects with the Chapala road after 3.2 mi. (see above).

254.2   1.7   A little traveled road left leads to the Gulf.

Mi. from
M. 254.2

(1.0)   1.0   KING RICHARD (LA JOSEFINA), an abandoned gold mine discovered and worked in the early 1900's by an Englishman, Dick Daggett.

Mi. from Mexicali	Partial Mileage	Mi. from M. 254.2	
	(4.5)	5.5	The valley of Arroyo Calamajué is reached and followed to the Gulf.
	(10.5)	16.0	PUERTO DE CALAMAJUÉ. A little cove (not very sheltered) on the Gulf shore, with a sand beach, used occasionally by fishermen. A well is 0.9 mi. up from the beach (0.2 mi. past ruined shacks). Behind the beach is an area sometimes used as a landing place for light planes.

The main road enters and crosses the broad valley of Calamajué.

263.0   8.8   MOLINO DE CALAMAJUÉ, abandoned gold ore mill near edge of a low bluff overlooking Arroyo Calamajué.

The ruins of the old mission of CALAMAJUÉ, barely traceable, are on a gravelly terrace across the arroyo. The site of Calamajué was discovered by the Jesuit Padre Consag in 1753. The place was a visiting station of San Borja mission (see pp. 124-25) until 1766, when Padres Arnés and Díez founded a separate mission here. They were unable to grow crops because of the bad water, so after seven months they moved the mission north to Santa María (see pp. 120-21).

At the mill the road descends into the arroyo and goes up the creek bottom. The water, which runs all year around, is heavily mineralized near the mill, but two miles upstream may be drunk without ill effect. Deer and mountain sheep are found in the desert ranges east of here.

Partial Mileage

270.3   7.3   The road climbs out the head of the canyon and crosses a wide valley.

278.8   8.5   Junction with main Ensenada-Santa Rosalía road at M. 291.9 (Route 5, see p. 123).

ROUTE 3

TIJUANA TO ENSENADA

A road, UNDER CONSTRUCTION but passable in 1961, leads along the beach from the international line to Rosarito. If reported plans to establish a border gate on the coast are carried out, this will be an excellent means of by-passing the city of Tijuana for travelers heading further south. At present this is reached by driving west through the city: (See also Preface page 10.)

Mi. from Tijuana	Partial Mileage	
0.0	0.0	TIJUANA (for description see page 57). Drive west on Calle Segunda (2nd St.) which becomes a paved highway.
5.1	5.1	PLAYAS DE TIJUANA, a subdivision under construction. Paved road goes right 0.4 mi. to Plaza Monumental bull ring (see page 59) near the beach and alongside the international fence. The new road (unpaved) turns south and follows close to the coast.
10.9	5.8	A fishing camp at right, one of several in this district of SAN ANTONIO DE LOS BUENOS.
18.5	7.6	Road joins the highway into ROSARITO on the north outskirts of the settlement (see below).

The present highway (MEXICO 1) is paved and a beautiful drive, mostly along the coast, with spectacular views of the Pacific. There are many fine beaches and camping spots close to the road, with several motels comparable to those north of the border.

Mi. from Tijuana	Partial Mileage	
0.0	0.0	TIJUANA, junction of Boulevard Agua Caliente and Boulevard Cuauhtémoc. The road goes up a canyon with many small ranches.
5.6	5.6	Branch road right to ranches of SAN ANTONIO DE LOS BUENOS district and the coast. The highway goes over a low pass and approaches the sea.
11.5	5.9	An alternate highway angling right goes past the Rosarito Beach area.

Mi. from Tijuana	Partial Mileage	Mi. from M. 11.5	
	(1.3)	1.3	A road in from the right connects with the beach highway (see above).

(1.5)   2.8   ROSARITO. Communications: Telephone to Tijuana and Ensenada. A beach resort (good swimming). Stores, gas stations, hotels, motels, trailer camps. The Rosarito Beach Hotel (1-A) has three bars, a dining room, swimming pool, and tennis court. De Anza Motel (1-B) has a dining room and bar. Rene's Motel (1-B, on the main highway) has a bar, restaurant, and trailer park. There is a powerful radio station, XERB. Landing strip, 2,000 ft. long.

The small valley of Rosarito was chosen in 1788 as the boundary between Upper and Lower California. However, when the peace treaty was signed after the Mexican War the boundary was moved up to Tijuana. The 1788 line ran from Rosarito across to the mouth of the Colorado River.

	Partial Mileage	Mi. from M. 11.5	
14.5	(0.4)	3.2	Rosarito road rejoins main highway, which follows a line of cliffs immediately above the sea.

22.6   8.1   DON PANCHO. Restaurant and bar. Camping area.

24.9   2.3   PUERTO NUEVO. Fishing camp; bar, restaurant.

28.0   3.1   DESCANSO. An agricultural community spread out along both sides of Arroyo Descanso. At the mouth of the arroyo is a fresh-water pond and a pebble beach. Store, gas station, motel. Wheat and barley are the chief dry-farm crops.

A side road just north of the arroyo goes left (0.4 mi.) to a new brick church being built on the exact location of Descanso mission, founded by the Dominican Padre Ahumada about 1814. A second church was completed about 1830, but the mission was abandoned soon afterwards. Apparently Descanso was intended as a new site for the mission of San Miguel (see below).

A poor dirt road left starts across from the motel and goes up onto the plateau. There are many branching roads, and in 1950 it was possible to go from LA ZORRA (14.7 mi. from highway) over a grade to SAN JOSÉ DE LA ZORRA, an Indian rancheria, 18.4 mi. From here a fair road (1958) leads to AGUA ESCONDIDA (more Indian ranches 23.6 mi. from highway), and after 28.9 mi. comes to the main road at EJIDO PORVENIR, 0.3 mi. north of the main intersection (see p. 62).

	Partial Mileage		
30.1	2.1		HALF WAY HOUSE (Medio Camino). Bar and gas station. Camping area. Several miles farther the highway leaves the coast and winds down into a broad valley:

37.1   7.0   LA MISIÓN. A small settlement occupying the site of the old mission of San Miguel, 1¼ miles from the sea in a broad valley lined with flat-topped cliffs. At the mouth of the arroyo is a large fresh-water pond, or *estero*, and a fine bathing beach.

Before the Spaniards arrived there was an important Indian
rancheria here called Jakwatljap (hot water, because of some
hot springs in the valley). The original mission of San Miguel
de la Frontera was founded by the Dominican Padre Sales in
1787 about 7 miles inland, but was moved to its present site
in 1788. It became one of the more prosperous missions, with
many horses, mules and cattle. The ruins near the road (behind a schoolhouse) on the south edge of the arroyo, consist
of low walls and mounds of adobe. Most of the Indians died
in epidemics, but there are still a few families living in isolated ranches nearby.

Just beyond the bridge, a side road runs down the left side of the
arroyo to the sea and south. There are several tourist camps along here,
including RANCHO PUNTA PIEDRA (1.9 mi.) and SALINA BEACH (3.3
mi.). This road continues past JATAY (ranch, 6.5 mi.), and ends 12.3
mi. from highway.

Leaving La Misión, the road to Ensenada climbs up the
cliffside and comes out on a bare, flat-topped mesa.

Mi. from Tijuana	Partial Mileage	
47.2	10.1	Side road right to SALSIPUEDES (3.9 mi.), a ranch on the beach where there are some tourist cabins for rent.
49.1	1.9	A well graded side road left goes 7.4 mi. to join the Tecate-Ensenada highway at M. 57.2 (see p. 62). At 4.8 mi. on this road a dirt road branching to left heads to Ejido Porvenir, 6.5 mi. beyond (see p. 62).
		The main road leaves the mesa and drops down into a narrow canyon leading to the sea.
56.3	7.2	Driveway right to "San Miguel Village," a resort with trailer park, restaurant, camping space, and boats for rent. (See Preface page 10.)
57.6	1.3	Paved highway to left to Tecate, 65.4 mi: MEXICO 3 (see pp. 61-63).
58.1	0.5	EL SAUZAL. A fishing port and village built around the largest fish cannery on the west coast of Mexico (Pesquera del Pacífico). It is owned by General Abelardo Rodríguez, former president of Mexico, whose palatial residence is off the road to the left north of town. The fish are packed in olive oil from orchards nearby, and are sold throughout Mexico.

A kelp plant was established at El Sauzal in 1918 for the
purpose of making explosives. Two years later it was leased
to an American company to be operated as a fertilizer plant,
and in 1927 it was converted to a fish cannery.

The highway south of El Sauzal follows the coast past several motels and then cuts inland, then back to the coast.

Mi. from Tijuana	Partial Mileage	
64.1	6.0	**ENSENADA.** Sea level. Population: 42,770 in 1960.

Climate: Cold and raw in winter (average temperature, Nov.-Apr., 57.9° F.; coldest months, Dec. to Mar.); very pleasant in summer (average temperature, May-Oct., 65.6° F.; warmest months, July and Aug.). Average annual rainfall: 10.7 in., nearly all from Nov. to Mar. There is usually some fog early in the morning, particularly in summer.

Communications: Land telegraph and telephone to Tijuana, connecting with lines in the United States. Government telephone south to El Rosario. Radio telegraph and telephone to points in the interior. In March 1962 there was no major air line service to Ensenada. The airport is at El Ciprés, 5 miles south of town on the main highway.

There are passenger bus lines between Ensenada and Tijuana, and from Ensenada south to El Rosario (see page 39).

Freighters with limited passenger accommodations occasionally call at Ensenada bound for La Paz and other west coast ports.

Hotels: Most of the hotels and motels are on Calle Primera (First St.) along the water front. These are all strictly American style and are generally clean and comfortable. The palatial Riviera Pacífico (i-a), a former gambling casino, is in a class by itself for grounds and atmosphere. Others are the Bahía (i-a), Casa del Sol (i-b), Villa Marina (i-b), Misión Santa Isabel (i-b), Santa María (i-b), and Cortez Motel (i-b). There are many others equally as good. Away from the sea, on Ruiz and 14th is Hotel Montemar (i-b). Along the shore out of town to the west are Quintas Papagayo (i-a) and El Morro Cabañas (i-b). There are several trailer courts. (See also Preface page 10.)

Ranchers from the country, when visiting Ensenada, stay at Hotel Virginia, 3rd and Miramar (iii); or Hotel El Polo Notre, 3rd and Gastélum (iii).

There are numerous restaurants, including the Velasco (Ruiz between 2nd and 3rd), Café Colonial (2nd between Ruiz and Obregón), El Rey Sol (1st, at Casa del Sol Motel), and Calmarisco (3rd between Ruiz and Gastélum). The Bahía Motel has a dinner floor show.

Banks: Banco Nacional de México; Banco de Baja California; Banco Mercantil; Banco Mexicano de Occidente.

Hospitals: There is a small municipal hospital.

The third largest city in Baja California, Ensenada is beautifully located on the northeast side of Todos Santos Bay, surrounded by low, barren hills. To the south is a perfect half-moon beach of hard sand ten miles long. The southwest end of the bay is limited by the moun-

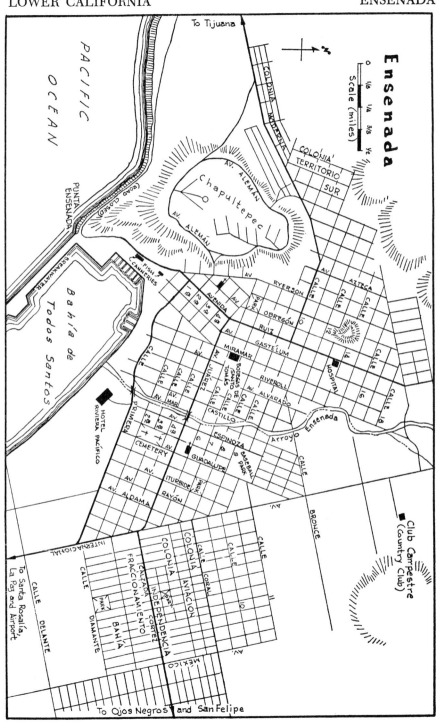

tainous peninsula of Punta Banda, off which are the rocky Todos Santos Islands. The harbor is protected from prevailing winds by a line of cliffs and a breakwater on the west.

Within the last fifteen years Ensenada has changed radically from a sleepy little Mexican port to a modern city of California-style residences, motels, and intense commercial activity. It is a favorite summer resort for weekend tourists and sport fishermen from Southern California. A number of Americans have retired here, attracted by the climate, scenery, and relatively low cost of living.

The main street, Avenida Ruiz, is lined with stores, banks, curio shops, bars, and two modern movie theaters. A westward continuation leads to a large fish cannery, the principal industry of Ensenada. At Miramar and 6th Streets is the winery of Bodegas de Santo Tomás, worth a visit. Parallel to the shore is First Street, lined with hotels. On a hill above the town is the residential section of Chapultepec.

Numerous sport fishing boats are available in Ensenada. During the summer months many varieties of game fish are caught, including an occasional marlin and swordfish.

There is a Yacht Club (Club de Yates de Ensenada), and an electric bridge crane is available for launching boats from trailers.

Ensenada, or rather Todos Santos Bay, was discovered by Rodríguez Cabrillo on his exploration of the California coast in 1542. At that time there was an Indian rancheria on the shore. During the mission era the port was occasionally visited by whalers and fur traders, but it was not chosen for a mission site because of the lack of surface water for irrigation. In 1804 the surrounding region was granted to a sailor, José Manuel Ruiz, who developed it into a prosperous cattle ranch. When gold was discovered at Real del Castillo in 1870, the town of Ensenada sprang up as a supply base for the mines. The seat of government of the northern frontier area was moved in 1882 from Real del Castillo to Ensenada, and when the peninsula was divided into two federal districts in 1887 Ensenada continued as capital of the north. In its early days Ensenada was a boom town, the headquarters of an American land company organized in 1884 which later sold out to an English syndicate. This company obtained a huge land grant from the Mexican government extending through most of the peninsula. American and English colonists arrived and attempted to raise wheat by dry farming, without much success. Many of the old wooden buildings in the town date from this period. During the Mexican Revolution in 1915 the company's grant was cancelled, the capital was moved to Mexicali, and Ensenada became a forgotten little fishing village. In recent years, particularly since 1940, the town has grown considerably and prospers from tourist trade, fish canneries, and new agricultural developments.

ROUTE 4

ENSENADA TO SAN FELIPE

A rough dirt road (except for a few miles out of Ensenada) which climbs through the mountains over a low pass and crosses the desert to the Gulf of California.

Mi. from Ensenada	Partial Mileage	
0.0	0.0	ENSENADA (for description, see page 90), corner of Avenida Ruiz and Avenida Juárez. The road leaves town as a continuation of Avenida Juárez, passes a cemetery, and gradually climbs into the mountains. In 1961 a new highway was under construction for about 10 miles out of Ensenada, following the same general route as the old road. Several side roads turn off to ranches. (See also Preface page 10.)
10.1	10.1	EL TRIUNFO, ranch off road to left. This region is called EL TULE.
12.2	2.1	A ranch house at left is the largest of an area known as PIEDRAS GORDAS, with several ranches and rocky little vineyards.
14.0	1.8	Branch road left to RANCHO NELSON.
17.5	3.5	Private side road right to AGUA CALIENTE DE RAMÍREZ (7.9 mi.), a hot spring.
17.6	0.1	LAS CRUCES (MINA DE LA FELICIDAD), houses at left belonging to former gold mine.
18.1	0.5	RANCHO LULESAL (formerly RANCHO ESPANTADO), right.
18.6	0.5	RANCHO EL BARRIL, right, in a setting of live oaks. The road continues up past several more ranches. Then it goes over a high point (elev. 2,900 ft.) and comes out in the broad valley of Real del Castillo, or Ojos Negros (once known as San Rafael), an extensive plain between the coast ranges on the west and Sierra Juárez on the east.
22.2	3.6	Branch road left to REAL DEL CASTILLO (4.4 mi.); Elev. 2,000 ft. An almost deserted town of ruined adobe houses,

picturesquely located in a broad valley enclosed by barren mountains. Gold was discovered here in 1870 and for a few years there was a thriving settlement of several hundred miners. From 1871 to 1882 Real del Castillo was the seat of government for the whole northern Fronteras area (from the border to Santa Gertrudis) and the residence of the deputy governor. Then the mining boom subsided, the capital was moved to Ensenada, and Real became a sleepy little village of cattle owners. Beyond Real del Castillo a side road continues 4.0 mi. to AGUA CALIENTE DE MARCONI, a hot spring.

A poor road (not traveled by authors) heads north from Real del Castillo, going via VALLE SECO and EL BURRO to join the Tecate-Ensenada highway at M. 39.8 (see p. 62).

Mi. from Ensenada	Partial Mileage	
22.8	0.6	The main road curves to a southeasterly direction. A side road straight ahead (left) leads to ranches and farms. One of the largest of these is LA LAGUNA, 4.7 mi.
25.9	3.1	OJOS NEGROS (store). Elev. 2,350 ft. Limited supplies (gasoline usually available). This place was once the headquarters of Circle Bar Ranch, a 1,500,000-acre property owned by Americans until it was broken up in the 1930's. Some old wooden buildings date from that era. The road continues past scattered ranches.
26.6	0.7	A road branches left which crosses the valley to the Sierra Juárez, with connections to the Tijuana-Mexicali highway.

Mi. from M. 26.6		
(1.1)	1.1	Another center of OJOS NEGROS. Store, school, post office.
(1.2)	2.3	EL BRILLANTE, ranch.
(5.9)	8.2	Road forks. The left branch goes along the west edge of the mountains to connect with the Tijuana-Mexicali highway east of Tecate, at M. 47.4 (see p. 63), 53.5 mi. from here. Keep to right for Sierra Juárez.
(1.3)	9.5	A road left to the Indian village of LA HUERTA (1.2 mi., see p. 64), then continuing 0.9 mi. to connect with the road just mentioned.
(0.1)	9.6	A road right goes 4.2 mi. to join the Ensenada-San Felipe road at M. 37.6 (see p. 96).
(0.1)	9.7	ENCINO SOLO, ranch, left. Beyond here the road begins to climb a rocky canyon.
(2.2)	11.9	Another road right goes to join that branching at 9.6 mi. (above) and after 4.5 mi. comes to M. 37.6 on the Ensenada-San Felipe road.

Mi. from Ensenada	Partial Mileage	Mi. from M. 26.6

The main road climbs to a rolling plateau and enters the first scattered growth of pine trees.

(8.0)   19.9   A right branch leads across the Sierra Juárez, and is an alternate route to Santa Catarina. It goes through pine forests and meadows, past LAS CUEVITAS (cattle ranch, 9.1 mi.) and BAJÍO LARGO DEL SUR (cattle ranch, 11.5 mi.). At 14.5 mi. the road to Santa Catarina branches right past LAS FILIPINAS (uninhabited in 1961, 15.0 mi.), past a branch left to SANTA ISABEL at 17.8 mi., and a branch left to CERRO PRIETO (ranch) at 18.9 mi., to drop to a lower elevation, and heads southerly past RANCHO VIEJO (ranch, 25.6 mi., not to be confused with the ranch of the same name a few miles south of here), and LA CIÉNEGA (ranch, 27.8 mi.) to SANTA CATARINA, 33.5 mi. from the junction.

At 14.5 mi. from the junction the left branch (straight ahead) goes northerly past SANTA ISABEL (ranch, 3.1 mi., uninhabited in 1961) to end at SANTA ISABEL VIEJO (cattle ranch, 6.0 mi.) near the head of Arroyo Santa Isabel (see p. 68).

Mi. from M. 26.6

(1.5)   21.4   EL RAYO. Ranch to right in meadow, elev. 5,090 ft. The road continues through stands of ponderosa pines.

(0.8)   22.2   A road in from right is another branch of that which took off at M. 19.9 above.

(2.0)   24.2   ASERRADERO SIERRA JUÁREZ. Sawmill and settlement. Store.

(3.4)   27.6   A road right goes to EL CALABOZO, 5.3 mi., a ranch near the eastern edge of the Sierra Juárez plateau.

(0.5)   28.1   LAGUNA HANSON (see page 66). The road continues in a northerly direction along the top of Sierra Juárez, to connect with the Tijuana-Mexicali highway at M. 61.3 (see page 65 for description).

The main road keeps straight ahead at M. 26.6.

27.7   1.1   Side road right, an alternate route to EL ÁLAMO (see p. 96).

Mi. from M. 27.7

(1.1)   1.1   Road forks. Right branch goes 8.2 mi. to AGUA CALIENTE DE SAN ANTONIO, a hot spring on Arroyo San Carlos.

(4.1)   5.2   EL MEZCAL, ranch, on Arroyo San Carlos.

(5.4)   10.6   ESCONDIDO, small cattle ranch.

(7.0)   17.6   SANTA CLARA, ranch in a valley. A little used road right (not traveled by authors) goes west down to Ejido Uruapan to join the main coast highway at M. 23.2 south of Ensenada (see p. 104). The road followed here turns left up the valley.

Mi. from Ensenada	Partial Mileage	Mi. from M. 27.7	
	(3.8)	21.4	Another older SANTA CLARA ranch, not inhabited in 1960.
	(2.9)	24.3	A side road branches right and passes EL PORVENIR, ranch (1.5 mi.), coming back in at M. 26.4. The valley narrows.
	(4.4)	28.7	Take right branch for El Álamo. (Straight ahead, left, goes via CERRO COLORADO, ranch [1.7 mi.] to join the main Ensenada-San Felipe road at M. 47.8 after 2.2 mi.)
	(11.9)	40.6	EL ÁLAMO (see below).

The main road, beyond M. 27.7, widens for a straight stretch of several miles.

29.0	1.3	EL RECREO, cattle ranch at right
35.9	6.9	SANGRE DE CRISTO (0.3 mi. off road to left). Ranch, not visible from road. Elev. 2,760 ft.
37.6	1.7	Side road left which branches after 1.1 mi. Left branch goes 3.1 mi. further to join Ojos Negros-Laguna Hanson road at M. 9.6, and the right goes 3.4 mi. to join it at M. 11.9. The main road bears right and climbs up a narrow cultivated valley.
41.8	4.2	SAN SALVADOR. Valley and group of ranches. The road continues climbing to a divide (elev. 4,000 ft.), then begins a gradual descent.
47.8	6.0	The main road to San Felipe swings to the left. A less traveled road straight ahead goes to CERRO COLORADO (0.5 mi., ranch), and may be used as an alternate route to El Álamo (turn left after 2.2 mi.).
50.0	2.2	PINO SOLO. A lone ponderosa pine long used as a landmark, but in 1961 it had died. The road forks. The left branch is an alternate route to Santa Catarina (13.9 mi.) via AGUA BLANCA ranch (6.5 mi.). Both branches cross a broad plateau (average elev. ca. 3,500 ft.) where the characteristic vegetation is juniper. Keep to right.
51.3	1.3	The main road to San Felipe turns left.

Branch road right to EL ÁLAMO. After 4.1 mi. this in turn forks, one branch going around each side of CERRO EL PIÑÓN (hill, elev. 5,100 ft.). By the west branch El Álamo is 11.3 mi. from M. 51.3, and by the east branch it is 13.0 mi. EL ÁLAMO, elev. 3,500 ft., once a gold mining center of about 5,000 inhabitants, is now a nearly deserted ghost town. It is at the southwest corner of the plateau, with barren hills on all but the east side.

Mi. from Ensenada	Partial Mileage	

There is a store where gasoline and limited supplies may be obtained.

A gold rush began near here in the Santa Clara placers in 1889. There are many ruins of old houses as well as of the stamp mills which were operated successfully for some years. Mining and cattle raising are now conducted on a reduced scale.

54.3	3.0	AGUA FLORES. Small goat ranch. The road now crosses a dry lake area known as LLANO COLORADO.
59.7	5.4	A junction, at south end of Llano Colorado, with a road in from the left, from El Álamo (8.1 mi., see above).
60.8	1.1	Road fork.

The left branch goes to SAN MIGUEL (5.0 mi.; go right after 4.7 mi.) and SANTA CATARINA (6.9 mi.; go left after 4.7 mi.), both settlements of Paipai Indians. In 1960 San Miguel was practically deserted, and the Paipais were living in and around Santa Catarina. Santa Catalina (as it was originally called), at an elevation of 3,600 ft., is the site of a Dominican frontier mission founded in 1797. Only low mounds of adobe remain of the extensive buildings, arranged as a fortress on a low hill on the west side of the arroyo. Just below the mission ruins are the remains of a stone-and-adobe dam once used to irrigate crops in the valley below. There is a stream of water forming a series of little cascades and pools above the dam.

The missionaries had a good deal of trouble with the unruly mountain Indians in the vicinity of Santa Catalina, and with the warlike tribes from the Colorado delta who used to come each year to the Sierra to gather piñon nuts. The mission was attacked several times, and finally destroyed by a major uprising in 1840.

Keep to right for San Felipe.

64.1	3.3	RANCHO VIEJO. Cattle ranch. A side road goes left to San Miguel (see above).
67.4	3.3	A little-traveled side road turns left and ascends a canyon to PORTEZUELO DE JAMAU (16.1 mi., elev. 4,000 ft.), a high pass on the peninsular divide. This road was built during World War II to follow a telephone line (since abandoned) from Ensenada to San Felipe. East of the pass the road (four-wheel-drive recommended) drops precipitously to the desert floor. It is described on pages 80-81.

EL RODEO, ranch, is to right here.

69.2	1.8	At right is a scattered group of houses, a struggling agricultural colony called EL RODEO (the name of this area is Valle El Rodeo). The road heads up a narrowing valley.

Mi. from Ensenada	Partial Mileage	
73.7	4.5	CAÑADA ANCHA, ranch, right. The road continues across a low divide, then drops down a short steep grade into VALLE TRINIDAD, a large arid valley 2,400 ft. above sea level, which runs roughly east and west.
80.6	6.9	At base of grade there is a branch road right, an alternate route to west end of the valley (see below). Main road turns left.
81.5	0.9	COLONIA LÁZARO CÁRDENAS (VALLE TRINIDAD), center of an agricultural colony, or collective farm, which is in possession of the eastern or upper end of Valle Trinidad. Stores, gasoline station.
		A road heads back to the west end of the valley and to the coast highway.

Mi. from
M. 81.5

(3.8)	3.8	EJIDO VALLE TRINIDAD, at lower end of the valley, a scattered community consisting largely of Paipai Indians. A dead end road continues 0.2 mi. to a hot spring. Turn left at houses.
		The road climbs out of the valley to begin a long descent.
(10.1)	13.9	EL ENCINO, spring and shack (uninhabited in 1961) in oak grove in canyon. After a few miles more the road goes down several steep switchback grades, normally used only for going down.
(11.5)	25.4	Floor of LA CALENTURA valley is reached.
(11.5)	36.9	Junction with Ensenada-Santa Rosalía highway at Llano Colorado turnoff, M. 60.8 (see p. 106).

The road to San Felipe heads easterly up Valle Trinidad.

92.4	10.9	Side road right via Arroyo León to Tepí.
		The ARROYO LEÓN area is the home of several families of Indians, survivors of the Kiliwa tribe. Three of their rancherias were accessible by this road in 1960: CUATRO (branch left 4.8 mi. from junction, then go 2.5 mi.), LA PARRA (branch right 10.1 mi. from junction, then go 0.8 mi.), and RANCHO NUEVO (down to right of road in ARROYO EL PLEITO at 11.5 mi.). From TEPÍ (cattle ranch, with grain fields and orchard, 19.2 mi. from junction) a trail leads 4½ mi. south to CERROS CUATES on ARROYO SAN RAFAEL.
93.0	0.6	SAN MATÍAS PASS. Elev. 3,200 ft. A flat pass separating the Pacific and Gulf drainage slopes, at the east end of Valle Trinidad. It is the lowest point in the peninsular

RAILROAD BRIDGE ACROSS THE COLORADO RIVER

LA CORONA MEADOW IN THE SIERRA SAN PEDRO MÁRTIR
See text pages 108-109.

Mi. from Ensenada	Partial Mileage	

divide for 200 mi. north and 100 mi. south. Beyond San Matías Pass there is a descent to the desert floor on the east. Plenty of gasoline and extra water should be carried.

94.9	1.9	A road right to SAN MATÍAS, cattle ranch (3.2 mi.) and nearby springs of same name.

101.0   6.1   At mouth of San Matías Canyon, on edge of Valle de San Felipe. Here the best and most traveled road branches left, cuts across the valley to the east, going 28.4 mi. to join the Mexicali-San Felipe highway at M. 95.3.

At 0.2 mi. on this left branch, a side road angles left. This goes up ARROYO TERAIZO for 6.4 mi., then climbs out the north bank, and after 13.7 miles reaches ARROYO GRANDE ranch (see p. 80).

The right branch at M. 101.0, followed here, starts down the sandy wash.

108.6   7.6   CAÑÓN DE LA ESPERANZA (a dim road here approaches its mouth, ca. 5 miles). The first of several canyons on the right, dropping down abruptly 6,000 ft. from the top of Sierra San Pedro Mártir. This east face of the mountains is almost a sheer drop of 5,000-8,000 ft. Several of the arroyos have water running down toward their mouths, but it sinks into the sand upon reaching the desert floor.

The road continues southeasterly across the extremely barren VALLE DE SAN FELIPE, a broad basin with no outlet.

110.7   2.1   (Near north end of dry lake). Side road left connecting after 10.9 mi. with the road going directly from M. 101.0 (above), and after 25.9 mi. joining the Mexicali-San Felipe highway at M. 95.3.

Road traverses the dry lake bed (impassable after heavy rain). Above, to the southwest, looms EL PICACHO DEL DIABLO (Devil's Peak), 10,100 ft. high, the tallest mountain in Baja California.

117.7   7.0   A branch road angles right to SANTA CLARA, 2.5 mi.

120.2   2.5   A road in from right from SANTA CLARA, cattle ranch among mesquites near edge of dry lake (1.4 mi.).

This side road continues to base of Sierra San Pedro Mártir. At 4.7 mi. from Santa Clara the left branch (straight ahead)

Mi. from Ensenada	Partial Mileage	
		goes to the mouth of Cañón el Diablito (5.7 mi. from ranch). The poor right branch goes 1.3 mi. to approach the mouth of Cañón el Diablo. Both canyons have water near their mouths. The latter is used by hikers to climb the Sierra San Pedro Mártir.
123.3	3.1	Branch road right continues down the valley.

	Mi. from M. 123.3	
(1.2)	1.2	Rancho Fonseca. Here a road goes west 3.4 mi. to the mouth of Cañón la Providencia. Trail to water, ca. 1 mi.
(13.9)	15.1	Road right goes 0.7 mi. to end in Cañón el Cajón. A trail up this canyon leads to the plateau at top of Sierra San Pedro Mártir.
(5.9)	21.0	Algodón, seasonally occupied cattle camp.
(11.0)	32.0	Arroyo Agua Caliente. Passable road ends (1957) here 0.8 mi. up canyon from its mouth. A hot spring is a short distance further up.

Main road swings left and climbs out of the Valle de San Felipe over Sierra San Felipe through a low pass (Paso de Buena Vista, elev. 2,000 ft.) at M. 131.0, emerging on the barren desert which borders the Gulf of California.

149.6	26.3	SAN FELIPE. For description see page 81.

ROUTE 5

ENSENADA TO SANTA ROSALÍA

The first section of the "Trans-Peninsular Highway," a real desert road which in some places follows the *camino real* built by the missionaries. The pavement extends from Ensenada 72 miles to Arroyo Seco, and the completed grading to San Quintín, another 51 miles. Beginning a few miles beyond here the road is an unimproved track through the desert, recommended only to the adventurous.

Mi. from Ensenada	Partial Mileage	
0.0	0.0	ENSENADA, corner of Avenida Ruiz and Avenida Juárez. Leave town on Avenida Juárez and Avenida Internacional. The road turns south parallel to the coast.
5.6	5.6	EL CIPRÉS, off road to right. Ensenada airport (long enough for heavy aircraft, hangars, etc.) and Army post.
6.7	1.1	Side road right to EL ESTERO (1.6 mi.), a motel and trailer park (electricity, showers) at the mouth of a long tidal estuary. There are boats for rent, and surf fishing is also popular. Fine sand beach.
8.7	2.0	Side road left up a canyon to AGUA CALIENTE DE SAN CARLOS (11.8 mi.). Hot springs; cabins for rent.
9.9	1.2	Immigration station. Tourist cards are checked here.
10.5	0.6	MANEADERO. Center of the Maneadero Valley, a large community farming area. Corn, beans, alfalfa, and chile are the usual crops. Gas stations, stores, packing plant.

A paved branch road to the right leads southwest to the little peninsula of Punta Banda. This passes La Grulla Gun Club (turn right 4.0 mi. from junction), and reaches the shore of Todos Santos Bay at a tourist area known as PUNTA BANDA (beginning at 7.4 mi.) which consists of several campgrounds with trailer space, some with boat ramp, small cabins, etc. There are boats for rent. At 8.2 mi. a side road left climbs to the top of the ridge and one branch of this continues to ARBOLITOS (1.4 mi. from the pavement) on the other side of the peninsula. The paved road continues toward Punta Banda, climbing to the ridge of the peninsula. In the summer of 1961 the pavement ended 12.1 mi.

Mi. from Ensenada	Partial Mileage	
		from Maneadero, but construction was continuing down toward a cove on the sea side of the peninsula. (See Preface p. 10.)
		The main highway goes inland up a valley.
23.2	12.7	A side road goes left to Ejido Uruapan (agricultural colony in the valley) and continues past Santo Domingo (5.1 mi. from highway). A little used road (not traveled by authors) continues to Santa Clara (see p. 95).
		The highway goes through a low mountain pass, then winds down into the broad valley of Santo Tomás.
27.1	3.9	Side road right down Santo Tomás valley:

Mi. from M. 27.1		
(1.9)	1.9	Ejido Ajusco. Farming community.
(1.6)	3.5	Off the road to right are some adobe mounds, the ruins of the old mission church of Santo Tomás (see below).
(0.5)	4.0	Poor alternate route left back to Santo Tomás (4.2 mi.).
(12.7)	16.7	La Bocana. Ranch on a little cove at the mouth of Arroyo Santo Tomás. The road continues north along the coast to Puerto de Santo Tomás (2.8 mi.), a fishing camp (cabins for tourists).

29.1   2.0   SANTO TOMÁS. Elev. 550 ft. 1950 pop. 294. Communications: Telephone to Ensenada. An old agricultural settlement and former mission, situated in a broad valley walled in by steep mountains 15 mi. from the sea. Santo Tomás is famous all over Mexico for its wine (actually the wine is made in Ensenada, and only some of the grapes come from Santo Tomás). Most of the valley bottom is laid out in orderly vineyards with an intricate system of irrigation ditches.

There are several stores where supplies, refreshments, and gasoline are sold. "El Palomar" has grocery and curio store, trailer park, restaurant, and motel (1-B).

The original site of Santo Tomás de Aquino mission, founded by the Dominican Padre Loriente in 1791, was 3½ mi. down the arroyo, where the adobe ruins of a chapel are still traceable (see above). Three years later the mission was moved up to the site of the present village. The second church has disappeared, but there are some ruins which may be one of the mission outbuildings. Originally the area had about 1,000 Indians, and supported 1,200 head of cattle and 2,600 sheep. Grapevines were cultivated by the Dominicans to produce altar wine, and the mission had a brief period of prosperity before epidemics wiped out the Indians. In 1849 the last missionary left, and Santo Tomás became a tiny farming village.

A road south from Santo Tomás crosses the hills via EL CHOCOLATE (ranch, 3.5 mi.) to a junction 5.1 mi. from Santo Tomás. Right branch goes via SAN JOSÉ (grain farm, 9.7 mi.) to the coast and ends at PUNTA SAN JOSÉ (abandoned fishing camp, 21.2 mi. from Santo Tomás). Left branch goes via EL REFUGIO (10.0 m.i), joins the above mentioned road at 20.7 mi., 5.2 mi. before Punta San José. A branch road goes down the coast to end just past a region called SAN JUAN.

The main road from Santo Tomás climbs up the south side of the valley to a pass at 1,400 ft., and then follows along the edge of a broad flat area planted to grain, Llano de San Jacinto.

Mi. from Ensenada	Partial Mileage	
40.0	10.9	Side road left to SAN JACINTO (3.3 mi.) and other ranches. The main road continues down a canyon.
46.1	6.1	(Km 181) Branch road right to a junction at 0.5 mi.

The left branch is the best road to the coast. It joins the road down from San Vicente (9.1 mi. from highway) and reaches the sea at EJIDO ERÉNDIRA (11.4 mi., agricultural colony). Road continues up the coast past PUERTO SAN ISIDRO (12.9 mi. from highway, fishing camp), and Punta Cabras to end near Punta Calaveras (21.2 mi.). Another road goes down the coast from Eréndira to San Antonio del Mar (see p. 107).

The right branch goes through grain fields, SANTA CRUZ (4.1 mi. from highway), past a junction (6.3 mi., right branch to Punta San José), to join the coast road (see above) near Punta Cabras (12.1 mi.).

The paved road turns left out of the canyon:

53.2	7.1	SAN VICENTE. Elev. 300 ft. 1950 pop. 450. An agricultural center of growing importance on the broad sandy arroyo of San Vicente, surrounded by barren hills. Most of the settlement is on the south side of the arroyo on an extensive mesa. There are several stores, restaurants, gas stations, etc. The old mission of San Vicente Ferrer, consisting of extensive adobe ruins, is on the north edge of the arroyo a short distance downstream from the road crossing.

San Vicente, founded by the Dominicans in 1780, was the administrative center of the northern Frontera mission district. The principal garrison of troops for the area was stationed here until 1849, although the mission itself was abandoned about 1833. Afterward the valley was inhabited by only a few families until the 1940's, since which time several agricultural colonies have sprung up in the vicinity.

A side road right goes down the cultivated canyon, joins the road from M. 46.1 after 7.1 mi., to continue to the sea at Ejido Eréndira (10.8 mi., see above). (See Preface p. 10.)

The main road from San Vicente climbs through low hills to a pass, then descends to a broad plain known as Llano Colorado.

Mi. from Ensenada	Partial Mileage	
60.8	7.6	Side road left past LLANO COLORADO (grain, poultry, hog farm, 1.8 mi.) to a junction at 2.0 mi.

Left branch goes via Los COCHES (ranch 5.9 mi. from highway), BUENOS AIRES (12.6 mi.), and Los ALAMOS (18.0 mi.) to AGUA CALIENTE (20.5 mi.) hot springs on the Arroyo San Vicente. Right branch goes through LA CALENTURA valley (ranches extending for 5.7 mi., beginning 3.9 mi. from the highway). A road continues through the mountains to VALLE TRINIDAD, joining the Ensenada-San Felipe road at Colonia Lázaro Cárdenas (M. 81.5, see page 98), 36.9 mi. from highway. Because of some steep grades this road is little used, and normally on the down trip (westward) only.

63.0	2.2	Side road right to RINCÓN DE GUADALUPE (3.0 mi., ranch), SAN ANTONIO DE LA MESA (4.9 mi., ranch), and back to San Vicente.

The main paved road crosses Arroyo Salado and climbs over a pass to Arroyo Seco:

69.5	6.5	Branch road left, an unpaved alternate route to San Telmo Valley.

Mi. from M. 69.5

(3.8)	3.8	SAN RAFAEL DE EN MEDIO, grain farm.
(0.2)	4.0	A branch road left goes up Arroyo San Rafael for 12.5 mi., a pretty canyon with running water in places.
(0.5)	4.5	A road left to another SAN RAFAEL ranch.
(8.3)	12.8	A road in from left, from Los CONEJOS.
(4.0)	16.8	In San Telmo Valley, join valley road 7.0 mi. from highway (see p. 107).

The main paved highway follows down the right bank of Arroyo Seco. (See Preface page 11.)

71.9	2.4	End of pavement and beginning of a rough gravel surface. Across the valley to left is the ranch house of ARROYO SECO (0.3 mi.), uninhabited in 1961.
75.8	3.9	RANCHO GRANDE. Gasoline, meals, rooms. Side road right.

Mi. from M. 75.8

(5.0)	5.0	A road left crosses Mesa de Colnett to sea at PUNTA COLNETT fishing camp (10.5 mi.) and follows the coast to the main highway near Camalú (see p. 109).
(0.7)	5.7	A junction. Right branch passes the former JOHNSON

Mi. from Ensenada	Partial Mileage	Mi. from M. 75.8	

RANCH (0.1 mi.) and continues up the coast to Ejido Eréndira (see p. 105), 16.5 mi. from junction. Most traffic turns left.

(2.0)   7.7   SAN ANTONIO DEL MAR. Beach, popular for camping, surf fishing, and clam digging.

The main highway crosses Arroyo Seco:

76.3   0.5   COLONIA COLNETT (EJIDO MÉXICO). A small farming center; store, school.

77.7   1.4   Side road right to PUNTA COLNETT fishing camp (ca. 7.5 mi.). The main highway continues south across a broad coastal plain recently being cleared and irrigated for cultivation.

83.5   5.8   Side road left to San Telmo and Sierra San Pedro Mártir:

Mi. from M. 83.5

(1.9)   1.9   SAN TELMO DE ABAJO, ranch, across arroyo to right (alternate route back to the highway, see below).

The road follows the arroyo through a narrow canyon and comes to a small meadow:

(4.0)   5.9   SAN TELMO DE ARRIBA, village. Store, gasoline sometimes available. Here are the barely visible ruins of an adobe chapel built by the Dominicans in 1800. Fr. Junípero Serra camped here for two days in 1769 and was impressed by the agricultural possibilities. The site was developed in 1798 by the Dominicans as a farm and visiting station of Santo Domingo mission (see p. 109).

Road crosses a low ridge and emerges into the Valle de San Telmo.

(1.1)   7.0   A road left goes across valley and via San Rafael back to M. 69.5 on the highway (see p. 106).

(4.6)   11.6   HACIENDA SINALOA. Ranch. The valley floor at this point is extensively cultivated.

(1.4)   13.0   A side road left goes to LAS FLORES (ranch, 1.1 mi.) on north side of valley. The north side road may be followed (taking left branch at 3.5 and 3.7 mi.) into the foothills to BUENA VISTA (ranch, 16.1 mi. from junction), EL COYOTE (ranch, 20.3 mi.), and junction at 20.7 mi. with road right from San José. This point is usually reached from the San José road; see below for continuation of this road into the San Pedro Mártir mountains.

(3.2)   16.2   Road fork. For San José go to left. The right branch crosses rolling hills and gullies past VALLADARES (ranch and old mine on side road 23.2 mi. from fork) to SANTA CRUZ (ranch off road to right, 28.7 mi. from fork) and EL POTRERO (32.2 mi., cattle ranch).

Mi. from Ensenada	Partial Mileage	Mi. from M. 83.5	
(4.1)		20.3	Branch road right to Las Cabras, ranch.

(10.3) 30.6 A road left leads to the north end of the San Pedro Mártir. After 4.7 mi. (just past El Coyote, ranch) this joins the road in from left from Buena Vista (see above), and continues past Cerro de Costilla (ranch, 7.2 mi. from fork). This was the proposed site of a lumber mill, and the road beyond here was built about 1950 to haul lumber from the mountains (but never used for that purpose). It passes Los Encinos (uninhabited ranch at 12.3 mi.), and at 16.3 mi. is on a ridge with the deep Arroyo San Rafael down to left (trout fishing). Beginning at 18.5 mi. the road follows for 1.5 mi. the easy grade of the canal built by Harry Johnson about 1896 to transport water from Arroyo San Rafael to the Socorro mine (see below). Then a very steep grade leads up to the ponderosa pine forest in the northern Sierra San Pedro Mártir, elev. 7,000 ft., in the area known as Corral de Sam, the road ending 23.5 mi. from fork. Lumbering operations were never carried out here, and the road was not maintained; however it was passable in 1960.

	Mi. from M. 83.5	
(1.7)	32.3	San José (Meling Ranch). Cattle ranch. Elev. 2,200 ft.

Nearby is an airstrip long enough for light planes. A lodge is operated at the ranch with comfortable accommodations for 10 or 12 visitors. Horses and guides are available for pack trips into the highest mountains of Baja California, Sierra San Pedro Mártir. The best time for such a trip is May to October, because of winter snow storms. One popular "circle tour" (not taken by authors) takes a week. The trail leaves San José and climbs to the first pine and oak forests about 15 mi. above the ranch. The next point reached is La Grulla, about 35 mi. from San José, a beautiful meadow surrounded by pine forests at an elevation of 6,700 ft. The valley has several small ponds. There is good hunting for deer and there are trout in the streams. (Some years ago an American named Utt carried the trout, then found only in one river, to all the other streams in the vicinity, making it an angler's paradise.) About 5 hours beyond La Grulla is La Encantada, elev. 7,000 ft., a similar but larger expanse of grassy meadow through which runs a mountain stream of clear, cold water. On all sides are great jagged hills covered with huge granite boulders and tall pine trees. Leaving La Encantada the trail climbs to another camp at an elevation of over 9,000 ft., through thick forests of conifers. Here a good view may be had (in clear weather) of El Picacho del Diablo (Devil's Peak), 10,100 ft. high, the tallest mountain in Baja California. From this place the trail begins to descend abruptly through birch forests to a series of little meadows (Vallecitos, elev. 7,600 ft.), and continues to another pretty mountain valley called La Corona (see illustration p. 100). A watershed is crossed, and the trail drops steeply to Arroyo San José and back to the ranch (see Map 3).

The old Dominican mission ruins of San Pedro Mártir (elev. 5,100 ft., uninhabited) can be reached in about seven hours on horseback from La Grulla (a closer approach by automobile can be made via Santa Cruz; see p. 107). The mission was founded in 1794 in a small mountain valley surrounded by granite hills. There are extensive adobe ruins. Water for irrigation came from springs above the ruins and was carried to the fields below in stone ditches which may still be seen on either side of the canyon. The mission, abandoned about 1806, had few Indians and was used chiefly for cattle raising. (This has not been visited by authors).

From San José a logging road was built in 1950 to the edge of the pine forest in the San Pedro Mártir, but it was never used to haul timber. This passes SOCORRO (10.0 mi.), site of a placer mine opened in the late 1890's with water brought in a 20 mile ditch from Arroyo San Rafael (see above). Beyond here the road is bad and passable with great difficulty to its end at a small meadow, CORONA DE ABAJO, elev. 6,300 ft., in the pines, 16.3 mi. from San José. LA CORONA meadow (see above) is reached by trail, ca. 2 mi. beyond.

The main highway from M. 83.5 continues southeast along the coastal plain:

Mi. from Ensenada	Partial Mileage	
84.8	1.3	VILLA HIDALGO (also called San Telmo de Abajo). Small agricultural settlement on Arroyo San Telmo. A road right goes 6.0 mi. to the beach at the mouth of the arroyo. A road left joins the road to San Telmo.
89.8	5.0	RANCHO IBARRA, cultivated area.
91.2	1.4	RANCHO LAS MARGARITAS. The highway crosses some low hills.
95.3	4.1	VALLE DE CAMALÚ. Settlement, store. Side road right to the beach and up the coast.
102.6	7.3	Branch road left to SANTO DOMINGO (5.1 mi., elev. 200 ft.) and alternate route to HAMILTON RANCH, 3.3 mi.; a better road to Hamilton Ranch is that beyond Colonia Guerrero (see below).

Santo Domingo is a small farming community picturesquely situated in a narrow canyon walled in by barren hills, the site of a mission founded by the Dominicans in 1775. The original church, of which only a few traces of adobe remain, was near Hamilton Ranch, but within a few years the mission was moved up the canyon to this place. The adobe walls are still erect, three feet thick with stone foundations. Above the mission is the old cemetery and a stone dam built by the missionaries. Epidemic disease carried off the Indians, and the mission was abandoned in 1839.

A road continues up the river beyond Santo Domingo 4.5 mi. to the cattle ranch of SAN MIGUEL.

103.8	1.2	COLONIA GUERRERO. 1950 pop. 710. Communications: Telephone line to Ensenada.

An agricultural colony on Arroyo Santo Domingo, 4 mi. from the sea. Most of the houses are about a mile east of the main road. There are several stores and gas stations, a restaurant, and a motel (III). This is the center of an important agricultural development; several thousand acres are irrigated from wells.

From Colonia Guerrero junction a side road goes left through the center of the community. Another road turns right to the beach at SAN RAMÓN (4.3 mi.).

104.9   1.1   Side road left to HAMILTON RANCH (2.9 mi., a guest ranch patronized by Americans; good hunting in vicinity; airstrip for medium planes).

The main highway leaves Colonia Guerrero and heads south in a perfectly straight line across the broad coastal plain of San Quintín (Valle de San Quintín) much of which has been irrigated and brought under cultivation within recent years. Crops include tomatoes, peas, potatoes, and grain. There are numerous ranches along the highway and side roads to others. Those listed here are surrounded by small settlements.

113.8   8.9   A road left heads past a ranch and into the mountains to Cañón de Nueva York and the ranch of NUEVA YORK (uninhabited in 1954) 20.0 mi. from highway. Two roads continue for short distances beyond.

116.0   2.2   SANTA GERTRUDIS, ranch.

116.9   0.9   SAN LUIS, ranch.

119.6   2.7   Side road right to BAHÍA SAN QUINTÍN.

A large lagoon-like bay with good shelter for boats of shallow draft. Landing field long enough for light planes. West of the bay are five conspicuous hills of volcanic origin (a sixth is offshore on the small island of SAN MARTÍN). The salt lagoons just north of the bay were exploited during mission times, and the harbor was frequented in the early 1800's by American ships indulging in contraband trade. About 1885 an American (later English) land company chose San Quintín as the center of an ambitious colonization project. A pier and flour mill were built and a railroad constructed 20 mi. north toward San Diego, but soon afterward the whole scheme collapsed (because rain was insufficient for dry farming) and San Quintín became a ghost town.

EL MOLINO, fishing village, is 4.5 mi. from highway. Store, motel. Roads run in both directions around the bay from here, one of these going via the salt lagoons at the north to the beach on the open sea. South of El Molino 2.0 mi. pilings of the ruined pier may still be seen at the site of the village, of which nothing remains. The old cemetery, with the forlorn graves of English colonists, is on the shore of the bay 2.6 mi. south of the old pier.

121.4   1.8   A road branching left was until 1956 the main road. It keeps closer to the edge of the hills. (See Preface p. 11.)

Mi. from Ensenada	Partial Mileage	Mi. from M. 121.4	
	(3.8)	3.8	SAN SIMÓN. An agricultural colony.
	(1.7)	5.5	SANTA MARÍA. Small farming community.
	(5.0)	10.5	Road branches. To right the old main road continues to Arroyo Socorro and after 7.0 mi. rejoins the main highway at M. 135.1. The left branch leads toward the mountains and climbs several steep grades through barren foothills.
	(13.4)	23.9	EL CIPRÉS, ranch.
	(8.9)	32.8	Side road left to AGUA ESCONDIDA (3.5 mi.), ranch.
	(8.1)	40.9	EL SALTO, cattle ranch, off road to left.
	(10.0)	50.9	ROSARITO. Elev. 2,500 ft. A cattle ranch. Road follows up the arroyo.
	(6.8)	57.7	RANCHO NUEVO. Ranch. An old mule trail continues up the arroyo and crosses the mountains to the San Felipe desert, but it should not be attempted without a guide. There is good hunting for deer and small game. The motor road turns north away from the main arroyo.
	(1.7)	59.4	EL PALMARITO. Deserted grove of fan palms. From here the road climbs to a plateau.
	(6.1)	65.5	LA SUERTE. Elev. 3,700 ft. End of the road, a cattle ranch on the southern slope of Sierra San Pedro Mártir.

The main highway continues across the coastal plain.

122.9	1.5	A side road right to shore of San Quintín Bay. The old cemetery (see above) is 0.4 mi. left after 1.2 mi. The old wharf pilings are 3.3 mi. and El Molino is 5.3 mi. from highway. The highway, here in bad condition, continues through farming country.
126.6	3.7	Entrance right to SANTA MARÍA SKY RANCH. Motel (I-B), camping space, access to beach reserved for guests; meals. Landing strip for light planes. Bass fishing in a fresh water pond. Road left to village of Santa María (1.5 mi., see above).
129.5	2.9	Side road right to "PAVILLION BEACH," 1.6 mi. Highway continues across the coastal plain and over a sandy hill to another coastal plain.
135.1	5.6	Road right 0.6 mi. to EL SOCORRO, agricultural ranch on the coast. The highway continues south along a coastal plain parallel to the beach. Several side roads go to the sea with good swimming and camping spots.
146.5	11.4	EL CONSUELO, restaurant. A branch road right con-

tinues along the shore to an old fishing camp (2.6 mi.). The main road turns inland up a canyon, climbing to a broad flat-topped mesa.

153.6   7.1   Side road right to the airfield of El Rosario on the top of the plateau (1.0 mi.), long enough for heavy planes. The main road left drops off the edge of the mesa and descends a steep, narrow canyon.

156.0   2.4   EL ROSARIO. Elev. 100 ft. 1950 pop. 372. Climate: Similar to that of Ensenada, but considerably dryer. Communications: Government telephone to Ensenada (Rosario is the end of the line). Weekly bus from Ensenada. Mail service extends to El Rosario, but there is no such service between here and San Ignacio.

A small agricultural village and mission site attractively located between tall cliffs in the broad Arroyo del Rosario, a permanent stream, three miles from the Pacific. It is divided into two settlements: ROSARIO DE ARRIBA (through which the main road passes), on the north side of the arroyo); and ROSARIO DE ABAJO (reached by a side road), 1.6 mi. downstream on the left bank. A continuation of this road down the valley branches 2.9 mi. from Rosario de Arriba. The right branch may be followed across the arroyo to a fresh water *estero* (pond) and beach (La Bocana) 5.5 mi. from Rosario de Arriba; the left branch leaves the valley and goes to PUNTA BAJA, 11.5 mi. from Rosario de Arriba, at the north entrance to Rosario Bay, where there is a fishing camp. The best way to reach the beach from Rosario de Arriba is to take the road which follows the right side of the valley (4.6 mi.).

Both settlements consist of a scattering of adobe houses surrounded by cultivated fields and orchards, with groves of fan palms. The principal crops are chile peppers and beans. In both upper and lower towns are stores where supplies and gasoline may be purchased at somewhat higher prices than in Ensenada. Because of the increasing distance from the source of supply prices in general tend to rise as one goes south until San Ignacio is reached, where there is a sharp drop. In Rosario de Arriba there are gasoline pumps, restaurants, and tourist cabins.

In pre-Spanish times Rosario was the site of an Indian rancheria called Viñadaco. The place was chosen for the first mission founded by the Dominicans in 1774. Large numbers of Indians died in epidemics from 1777 to 1782, but Rosario continued to be an important mission until it was abandoned about 1832. Later it was chosen as the seat of military government for the northern area, and was gradually repopulated by mestizos from the mainland. The remains of the original mission buildings near Rosario de Arriba may still be seen. In 1802 the mission was moved to Rosario de Abajo, where there are also adobe ruins. The old bells have been moved to a new church.

A side trip may be made from El Rosario down the coast to Puerto San Carlos, a sometimes-inhabited fishing camp. This road leaves from the south side of the arroyo, between the two settlements of Upper and Lower Rosario:

Mi. from Ensenada	Partial Mileage	Mi. from El Rosario	
(0.0)	0.0		The road begins 0.7 mi. below Rosario de Arriba, following up the left (south) edge of the arroyo.
(1.3)	1.3		The road turns right up Cañada de San Fernando, crosses a pass 1,400 ft. high, and drops down another canyon.
(18.1)	19.4		VALLE DE SAN VICENTE, a wide flat valley, scene of recent attempts at agriculture. In 1955 this was the last inhabited place on the road.
			A side road right to the mouth of Arroyo San Vicente (5.0 mi.). The main road crosses the dry arroyo and continues south.
(8.0)	27.4		Arroyo de San Fernando, dry crossing.
(10.7)	38.1		Side road right to CAJILOA (2.5 mi.), an abandoned fishing camp on the coast. There is a tiny well of poor brackish water on the road 1 mi. inland.
(7.6)	45.7		PUERTO SAN CARLOS. A seasonally occupied fishing camp on a bay offering fair protection from the prevailing winds. There is no fresh water. San Carlos was once used as a supply point for the mines in the interior.

Leaving El Rosario de Arriba, the main road now continues up the north bank of the valley, with several small farms off to the right, and after 4.5 mi. turns to cross to the south side, where it joins the road formerly used. (See also Preface page 11.)

162.1   6.1   Fork in road. Across the valley on the north side is a conspicuous cliff called EL CASTILLO because of its resemblance to a gigantic castle.

A side road goes left to continue up the valley to LA VÍBORA, uninhabited ranch, 7.9 mi. from fork. At 7.4 mi. a road (reported impassable in 1961) branches right via SAUZALITO (abandoned copper mine, 22.7 mi.) and eventually rejoins the main road at M. 186.0, near Arenoso (see below), 26.5 mi. from fork.

At 0.1 mi. beyond the fork the main road turns to the right away from Arroyo del Rosario and climbs a tributary canyon. Ahead the typical vegetation of the Baja California desert begins to be encountered. Here is the giant *cardón* cactus which resembles the *saguaro* of Arizona. Farther south these form dense forests; individual plants sometimes reach a height of 60 feet. The edible fruits ripen in July and August. Here also for the first time the curious *cirio* plant is noticed. It has a tall tapering trunk covered with short spiny branches, a cluster of yellow flowers at the top. Forests of these weird-looking trees are encountered from here to the 28th parallel, and are found nowhere else in the world, except for a very limited area in Sonora.

Mi. from Ensenada	Partial Mileage	
175.6	13.5	EL AGUAJITO, ranch off road 0.1 mi. to left. Coffee and sodas sold. The road climbs out of the canyon and starts up the steep Aguajito Grade.
177.6	2.0	LA TURQUESA. A turquoise mine worked intermittently on a small scale. The road continues to climb until it reaches the top of the long Aguajito grade at an elevation of 1,700 ft., 1.8 mi. from La Turquesa.
183.3	5.7	A less traveled road left goes via Sauzalito (abandoned copper mine, 2.5 mi.), rejoining main road after 6.3 mi.
186.0	2.7	Another road in from left from Sauzalito (see above).
187.5	1.5	EL ARENOSO. Elev. 2,000 ft. Cattle ranch with an irrigated garden. Restaurant.
190.2	2.7	Side road left into the southern foothills of the San Pedro Mártir mountains:

Mi. from M. 190.2		
(6.1)	6.1	EL CARTABÓN. Cattle ranch.
(10.4)	16.5	SAN JUAN DE DIOS (abandoned). An old ranch once used as a cattle *estancia* and visiting station of San Fernando mission. It is an attractive spot with a few palm trees and a trickle of water in the arroyo. Fr. Junípero Serra, on his long overland trek to found the missions of Upper California in 1769, arrived here in such agony from a sore on his leg that he could go no further. One of the muleteers in the expedition relieved Serra's pain with a poultice which he used to cure his mules.
(2.5)	19.0	EL METATE. Cattle ranch at the end of the road. Water from a spring is used to irrigate a small garden. Just south of here is the peak of San Juan de Dios, 4,300 ft. high, while to the north looms another barren mountain, El Matomí, 4,500 ft. (see illustration p. 117).

The main road continues across rough but fairly level country:

Mi. from Ensenada	Partial Mileage	
197.0	6.8	Road forks. The left branch is shorter.
197.8	0.8	EL PROGRESO. Meals, refreshments, and sometimes gasoline.

A road to the right goes down the arroyo to SAN FERNANDO (1.8 mi.). Elev. 1,700 ft. A fertile valley surrounded by barren hills. Two families live here and raise a few crops. This is the site of the only mission in Baja California founded by the Franciscans. The place, known to the Indians as Guiricatá, or Velicatá, was discovered by the Jesuit Padre Link in 1766. The Jesuits were expelled before they could establish a mission here, but this was done in 1769 by the Franciscan president Fr. Junípero Serra, on his way to Upper California. The Franciscans and their successors the Dominicans developed San Fernando into a large and important mission which at one time had about 1,500 Indians. The population was practically wiped out by epidemics in 1777-80, and the mission seems to have been abandoned in 1818. Many of the fields have been washed away, but part of the old irrigation ditch is still in use. Some adobe walls mark the site of the mission church.

201.7	3.9	Branch road right joining (8.5 mi.) the Santa Catarina road (see below).
204.4	2.7	PÉNJAMO. Ranch with an irrigated garden. The road begins to cross the LLANO (Plain) DE BUENOS AIRES.
207.2	2.8	EL ÁGUILA. Cattle ranch with good water from three wells. There is a small garden. From here the road follows the bed of a dry arroyo, with several dusty places and alternate tracks.
214.0	6.8	Just before crossing the arroyo by San Agustín (see page 119) there is a branch road right to Santa Catarina, and a little-used road follows down the Pacific coast to near San Andrés. (NOTE: This road can be used as an alternate through route to the south. There is no gasoline available.)

Mi. from M. 214.0		
(8.7)	8.7	A road in from right is the alternate route in from M. 201.7 on the main road (see above). The road ahead goes down the Arroyo de Santa Catarina.
(4.3)	13.0	LA RAMONA. Cattle ranch (uninhabited in 1960).
(2.4)	15.4	EL COLOSAL. Cattle ranch, windmill well (uninhabited in 1960).
(5.4)	20.8	SANTA CATARINA. Cattle ranch with several out-buildings. There is a good supply of water used to irrigate a

Mi. from Ensenada	Partial Mileage	Mi. from M. 214.0	

garden and orchard. The road leaves the Arroyo de Santa Catarina.

(2.3)   23.1   The road forks. The right branch, little used and badly washed out in places, goes to Santa Catarina Landing. This passes (12.2 mi. from fork) an area where ammonites (fossilized cephalopod mollusks) have been found in quantities, and returns to Arroyo Santa Catarina (12.7 mi.) here a wide valley. At 15.7 mi. is an abandoned wildcat well where an unsuccessful attempt was made to find oil in 1924. The hole is 2,025 ft. deep. There is a small spring of bad water here. PUERTO DE SANTA CATARINA (Santa Catarina Landing), a seasonally occupied fishing camp on the beach at the arroyo mouth, is 17.0 mi. from the fork. It is an unprotected roadstead with a small stone jetty, once used for shipping onyx blocks from the quarry at El Mármol (see p. 119).

The left branch goes through valleys and hills, with signs of mining activity, and then approaches the coast.

(22.2)   45.3   A road branches right to LA LOBERA, 4.0 mi., an abandoned fishing camp on the mesa of Punta Canoas.

(2.6)   47.9   An airstrip in a broad flat valley. Just beyond, a side road goes right 0.6 mi. to a seasonally occupied fishing camp known as PUNTA CANOAS, in the shelter of the point. The road crosses the valley and heads away from the ocean.

(1.3)   49.2   A junction. A road continues up the valley to SANTA MARÍA (a mine ca. 16 mo.) and EL CHILENO (ranch ca. 23 mi.), places not visited by authors. The through road turns right and parallels the coast.

(10.3)   59.5   LOS MORROS, a seasonally occupied fishing camp. Road continues over barren coastal hills and crosses the mouths of dry arroyos.

(16.9)   76.4   Mouth of ARROYO SAN JOSÉ, a narrow canyon. A seasonally occupied fishing camp is across the estuary to the south. The road turns and heads up the canyon.

(1.8)   78.2   A junction. The road straight ahead up the arroyo goes via CERRO BLANCO to join the main Ensenada-Santa Rosalía road at M. 232.5 (see p. 120) after 48.2 mi. The coastal road branches right, crosses hills, returns to the coast, and follows fairly close to the sea, passing several good beaches. Clams are plentiful on the beaches and abalones are easily found among the rocks.

After 26.1 mi. the road leaves the coast and goes 5.7 mi. up a flat barren valley.

(31.8)   110.0   LAS PALOMAS, site of an unsuccessful agricultural colony (Colonia Nicolás Bravo) abandoned in 1960. Water,

TYPICAL VEGETATION OF THE NORTHERN DESERT REGION

BARREN PEAK OF EL MATOMÍ
In the rugged, little-known region north of San Juan de Dios. See text page 114.

A PALM CANYON ALONG THE TRAIL TO SANTA MARIA MISSION

Mi. from   Partial   Mi. from
Ensenada   Mileage   M. 214.0

quail and doves. A branch road up the valley goes via LAS CODORNICES to join the main Ensenada-Santa Rosalía road at M. 286.1 (see p. 123) after 29.4 mi. The coastal road branches right and goes over low hills.

(5.2) 115.2   In a valley, a road leads 5.1 mi. right to a muddy salt flat, EL SALINITO, beyond which is a pebbly beach.

(6.9) 122.1   A road branches right to join that from M. 123.5.

(1.4) 123.5   A road in from right rear leads 2.6 mi. to the beach. Four-wheel drive vehicles may run the beach to 3.4 mi., where the road climbs up on the low headland of PUNTA MARÍA. At 4.7 mi. from the junction it again enters the the beach, which may be followed ca. 4 mi. further to near PUNTA CONO.

The through road follows close to the coast.

(5.5) 129.0   EL CARDÓN, remains of former fishing camp. Dry well.

(10.0) 139.0   A road right to the beach at BOCA DE MARRÓN, 1.5 mi., a beautiful crescent beach at the mouth of a small valley. The road leaves the coast to head up this valley.

(7.7) 146.7   A road right to BOCANA DE SAN ANDRÉS, fishing camp, 7.8 mi.

(4.7) 151.4   Junction with the "coastal route," 14.2 mi. from Punta Prieta (see p. 126).

214.2   0.2   SAN AGUSTÍN. Elev. 1,900 ft. Cattle ranch. A deep well furnishes some excellent water. There is a restaurant, with kerosene refrigerator (cold beer). This ranch was started about 1905 to provide water and supplies for El Mármol.

The road straight ahead (left) goes to EL MÁRMOL (10.1 mi. from San Agustín, elev. 2,300 ft.) an onyx mine owned by the Southwest Onyx and Marble Company. The quarry was opened shortly after 1900 by an American company which brought a number of Yaqui Indians from Sonora as miners. Blocks of high grade onyx were originally hauled to Puerto de Santa Catarina (see page 116), where they were lightered out to ships; more recently they were hauled by truck to San Diego. Operations ceased here about 1958, and in 1961 the only inhabitants were caretakers. The settlement at the edge of a barren plain has a bleak appearance. It is perhaps the only place in the world that has a school house made of onyx (unpolished blocks). There is an airfield long enough for medium planes.

No road exists from El Mármol to the Gulf. A little-traveled jeep trail which formerly led to a prospect may still be followed northeast from El Mármol. After 1.1 mi. a foot trail to the right leads over the divide to EL VOLCÁN (ca. 2 mi. from the road), a soda spring on the arroyo of the same name. At 2.6 mi. from El Mármol, on the peninsular divide, the Gulf may be seen, and a short distance beyond the road is impassable.

A poor road from El Mármol goes 10.3 mi. to rejoin the main road at M. 226.5.

Leaving San Agustín the main road branches right .

Mi. from Ensenada	Partial Mileage	
216.2	2.0	TRES ENRIQUES, ranch. Gasoline, refreshments.
216.5	0.3	Side road left to SAN SIMÓN, ranch (0.5 mi.). This branch continues to join the road to El Mármol. (See also Preface page 11.)
224.1	7.6	AGUA DULCE. Adobe ruins of an abandoned ranch. Just beyond here is a dim track running off to the left ¼ mi. to the water hole of Agua Dulce, a natural reservoir in the rocks filled from a tiny spring.
226.5	2.4	The road from El Mármol (10.3 mi., see above) comes in from the left. From here the road traverses a sandy rolling desert, winding among huge granite boulders. There are many giant *cardón* cactus, *cirios,* and weird looking elephant trees *(copalquín).*
228.3	1.8	LA VIRGEN, a little shrine in a large rock. A resident sells coffee, sodas, and sometimes gasoline.
232.5	4.2	Side road right leads to the Pacific coast.

	Mi. from M. 232.5	
(21.7)	21.7	CERRO BLANCO, abandoned onyx mine, with a soda water spring.
(5.2)	26.9	TODOS SANTOS, small ranch.
(12.5)	39.4	SAN JOSÉ, ranch on side road right, 0.6 mi. After a short down grade the road enters the narrow valley of Arroyo San José which it descends.
(8.8)	48.2	Junction with Pacific coast road at M. 78.2 (see page 116). The mouth of the arroyo is 1.8 mi. straight ahead.

The main road leaves the rocky plain mentioned above and crosses the Arroyo de Cataviñacito, a small canyon which usually has pools of fresh water, with clusters of tall, graceful blue palms. Then the road goes over a low divide to Arroyo Cataviñá, a similar arroyo with palms and much vegetation. (See Preface page 11.)

238.7	6.2	SAN LUIS. Cattle ranch with small garden plots irrigated from the arroyo. Good drinking water from a well. (See Preface page 11.)
239.7	1.0	SANTA INÉS. Cattle ranch with several houses and two windmill wells. Gasoline sometimes available.

From here in 1961 a road was under construction to the ruins of SANTA MARÍA, the uninhabited site of the last mission founded by the

Jesuits in Baja California. This continues up the arroyo and crosses the peninsular divide (10.0 mi.), ending 12.1 mi. from Santa Inés, about 2 mi. from the ruins. The trail from here to the mission is difficult to discern (see illustration p. 118). The roofless adobe walls of a chapel and outbuildings are in a small valley, elev. ca. 1,000 ft., on a terrace near the edge of the arroyo. There are two small springs, one above the ruins in an extensive palm grove, and the other below the ruins. The surroundings are barren hills.

The mission of Santa María de los Angeles was moved in 1767 to this spot, known to the Indians as Cabujacaamang, when the first site at Calamajué (see p. 86) proved unfit for a mission. The founder, Padre Arnés, was here less than a year before he and all the rest of the Jesuits were expelled from California by royal decree. The chapel was built by the Franciscans in 1768, but in the following year the place was abandoned in preference to the more fertile site of San Fernando (see p. 115). Santa María continued to be a visiting station for some years, and had a small vineyard and a few fig trees, but these have disappeared.

The "lost mission" of Santa Isabel

During their seventy years (1697-1767) in Baja California the Jesuits ruled the peninsula practically as an independent theocracy. No Spanish or other settlers were allowed to come in, and even visitors were excluded. All that was known of California in the outside world was what the Jesuits themselves chose to divulge in occasional reports. Even the governor of California and soldiers under his command were selected by the Jesuit father superior and were subordinate to the missionaries. Because of this "closed door" policy a legend arose that the Jesuits had accumulated a great treasure of gold, silver and pearls. According to one version of the story, shortly after the mission of Santa María was founded a confidential message from the Jesuit general in Rome arrived at Loreto, informing the missionaries that they were about to be expelled from New Spain by order of the king. They were instructed to submit peacefully, *but to leave no trace of their wealth.* Accordingly a vast amount of treasure was collected from all the missions and transported by burro train to a deep gorge in the mountains some place beyond Santa María, where the Jesuits founded one more mission known as Santa Isabel. When the order for their expulsion arrived, they closed off the entrance to the gorge by means of a land-slide and retired obediently to Loreto, where they were imprisoned and exiled to Europe.

Unfortunately very little of this legend is confirmed by history. It is true that pearls, gold and silver all existed in Baja California, but the

Jesuits were far too busy producing food for themselves and their Indians to devote much time to fortune collecting. The evidence indicates that the missionaries had a hard struggle just to keep going. They were constantly on the verge of economic collapse, and had to rely on alms in order to support the missions. However, the legend of the "lost mission" persists to the present day, and many expeditions have trudged over the barren hillsides looking for it. According to one theory it should be in a steep canyon on the east side of Sierra San Pedro Mártir. Others say it is farther south, in the region around Laguna Chapala or in one of the barren uninhabited mountain ranges near the Gulf.

The main road continues across a rough, rocky desert with numerous cross washes. (See also Preface page 11.)

Mi. from Ensenada	Partial Mileage	
246.7	7.0	SAN IGNACITO. A small ranch, sometimes inhabited.
249.9	3.2	JARAGUAY. Cattle ranch in an arroyo with several fan palms. There is a small outbuilding where travelers may bathe, quite a luxury in this area. The road climbs a steep rocky grade to an elevation of 3,300 ft. and drops down to Laguna Seca, a dry lake bed.
259.6	9.7	EL PEDREGOSO. A cattle ranch with windmill well. The name refers to the nearby hill composed of enormous granite boulders. From here the road crosses monotonous country until it begins to approach the dry basin of Laguna Chapala. There is a maze of ruts running through deep, fine dust, very uncomfortable driving. It is best to keep toward the left and head for Laguna Chapala ranch, marked by a grove of trees.
273.9	14.3	RANCHO LAGUNA CHAPALA. A cattle ranch on a windswept plain. Good water. Meals and sometimes gasoline are available. A side road left comes in from the Gulf route, from Mexicali and San Luis Gonzaga Bay (see p. 85). The main road continues across flat barren ground.
274.8	0.9	LAGUNA CHAPALA. A large dry lake which normally has a hard earth surface suitable for landing heavy aircraft. The road goes across the middle of the lake, and for the first time in many rocky miles a car may be "opened up" for the distance of 1.6 mi. After a rain (extremely rare in this area) the surface becomes a sea of mud and it is necessary to detour around the east side of the lake.

Mi. from Ensenada	Partial Mileage	
		The road continues to the edge of the flat country and climbs out of the lake basin.
280.3	5.5	EL PORTEZUELO. A low pass (elev. 2,300 ft.) across the peninsular divide.
286.1	5.8	Side road right leads to the Pacific coast. This is a fair road to LAS CODORNICES (10.0 mi., cattle ranch); then a poor road climbs to a rough rocky mesa before dropping down to LAS PALOMAS (29.4 mi.), at M. 110.0 on the Pacific coast road (see p. 116).
		The main road continues across the LLANOS DE SANTA ANA, a rough valley, and back into the Pacific drainage slope.
288.7	2.6	CERRITO BLANCO, small ranch, left.
291.9	3.2	Road in from left is the Gulf route from Mexicali via San Felipe, San Luis Gonzaga Bay, and Calamajué. Mexicali is 278.8 mi. distant. (See Route 2, pp. 75-86).

297.9   6.0   Branch road left to Los Angeles Bay and alternate route south by way of the old mission of San Borja. This is a more interesting route than the main road, but is 33.4 mi. longer.

Mi. from M. 297.9	Partial Mileage	
8.3	(8.3)	DESENGAÑO. Abandoned mine. A trail 0.3 mi. beyond goes left to the TINAJA DE YUBAY, ca. 5 mi., a historical waterhole on the old mission trail.
9.3	(1.0)	A branch road right to Punta Prieta, 15.6 mi.
13.5	(4.2)	A side road right from Punta Prieta, 14.0 mi. (see p. 126). Barren country except for many white-trunked elephant trees (copalquines).
25.1	(11.6)	AGUA AMARGA. Remains of an old stamp mill. There is a spring of mineralized water in a gully off the road to left.
27.7	(2.6)	On the left is a large flat dry lake, suitable for landing heavy planes.
30.8	(3.1)	A road right goes to San Borja and beyond (see below, page 124).
31.7	(0.9)	Another branch, in from right, of the road to San Borja. The Los Angeles Bay road follows a valley, then descends a narrow canyon.
43.0	(11.3)	Side road left to LA GRINGA (5.9 mi.), on Los Angeles Bay, a region of little coves, sand spits, and salt flats.
46.1	(3.1)	BAHÍA DE LOS ANGELES (Los Angeles Bay). Climate: Pleasant in winter and spring; very hot in summer; rainfall practically nil. A beautiful

harbor with shelter and anchorage for vessels of any size, directly across from Angel de la Guarda Island. The entrance to the bay is protected by a barrage of small islands, and there are three deep entrance channels. On the shore is a small fishing village with about 20 shacks, including a store. Gasoline is usually available. Drinking water comes from a spring above the village. There is a landing strip long enough for light planes. Some cabins with shower baths have been fitted up by Antero Díaz, who also serves excellent meals for tourists. Fishing boats (skiffs with outboards) can be rented.

Fish of many kinds are caught in the quiet waters of the bay. The chief occupation of the inhabitants is the harpooning of giant sea turtles *(caguamas)*, which are shipped by truck to Ensenada. The fishing season is from about April to September. Los Angeles Bay is a good starting place for hunting trips (deer) in the nearby mountains.

The Jesuit Padre Consag visited and named Bahía de los Angeles in 1746 on his exploration trip of the upper Gulf and reported that there was a large rancheria of Indians on the shore who lived mostly on shellfish. When the mission of San Borja was founded (1762) the bay became an important supply point and visiting station, but not long afterward the Indians were moved inland to the mission. In the 1890's and later the port was used as a shipping point for the nearby mines of San Juan (see below). The present settlement dates from about 1930.

The road continues south along the bay shore, past a little hill with traces of the onetime SANTA MARTA ore mill (1.3 mi. from settlement). After 5.1 mi. a branch goes inland to the abandoned ore mill of LAS FLORES (10.3 mi. from settlement). Beginning in 1889, silver ore to the value of $2,000,000 from the mine of San Juan was processed here by an American company, which went out of business during the Mexican Revolution. Another branch continues across tidal flats around the edge of the bay for a distance of 10.5 mi. from the settlement.

The San Borja mission route turns south from the Los Angeles Bay road, 30.8 mi. from main road (15.3 mi. from bay):

Mi. from M. 297.9	Partial Mileage	
31.4	(0.6)	Junction left with the short cut back to the Los Angeles Bay road. (See also Preface page 11.)
33.5	(2.1)	A road branches right to AGUA DE HIGUERA, a spring of bad green water, 0.5 mi. Keep left. (See Preface page 11.)
41.1	(7.6)	A summit, elev. 2,000 ft., after following up to the head of ARROYO EL PRINCIPIO. The road now descends across low ridges and arroyos. (See also Preface page 12.)

52.7 (11.6) SAN BORJA. Elev. ca. 1,600 ft. A ruined mission, once the cultural center of an area comprising some 3,600 sq. mi., today a tiny ranching community centering around a massive stone church. The mission buildings are in a broad valley dominated by barren mountains covered with forests of *cirio* and giant cactus. Near the church is a cluster of adobe shacks with a palm grove, orchard, and garden irrigated from several tiny hot springs. The water has a sulfur taste which disappears if it is left standing. There is a landing strip suitable for light planes.

San Francisco de Borja was an important link in the chain of missions which the Jesuits planned to extend around the Gulf of California, connecting with the mission settlements of Sonora. Several years were spent hunting for a location with enough water to raise crops and support cattle. This water hole and camping spot, known to the Indians as ADAC, was investigated by order of the Jesuit Padre Jorge Retz in 1758, and the following year Retz arrived and began work on the irrigation ditches and the first adobe chapel. His successor, Padre Link, formally inaugurated the mission in 1762. There were originally some 3,000 Indians in the area, but epidemics reduced their number to 400 by the end of the century, and in 1810 only 175 remained. The mission was finally abandoned in 1818.

The first Jesuit chapel was replaced by another adobe church built by the Franciscan Fray Lasuén, the ruins of which can still be seen. The stone church, a handsome Moorish building with carved portals, was finished by the Dominicans in 1801, except for the tower which was never completed. It has a vaulted roof supported by massive keyed arches. The mission buildings form a rectangle with the church on one side, adobe ruins opposite, and several other apartments in between once used as missionaries' quarters, store rooms, etc. The walls have been somewhat undermined by treasure-seekers looking for gold and pearls the missionaries are supposed to have hidden (a most improbable legend). There are two bells, one dating from 1759. Off to one side are two stone reservoirs, also built by the Dominicans, with old irrigation ditches. At one time there was more cultivated land than at present, much of it now washed away by floods. See illustration page 127.

A little-used road climbs to the southeast of the mission, past the landing strip, to a junction at 1.5 mi. To the left up Arroyo San Juan, the road ends at SAN GREGORIO, 8.6 mi. from San Borja. The ranch house is in a picturesque setting reached by trail ca. 0.3 mi. from end of road (see illustration p. 127). The right branch goes down the arroyo via SANTA ANA (8.1 mi., see below) and at 13.7 mi. from San Borja joins the San Borja-Rosarito road at M. 60.8.

Leaving San Borja, the road follows down the arroyo:

Mi. from M. 297.9	Partial Mileage	
58.6	(5.9)	SAN IGNACITO. Cattle ranch with a small garden, one of the old visiting stations of San Borja mission. Parts of the irrigation ditch built by the missionaries are still in use. The road continues down the arroyo, very rough and stony.
60.8	(2.2)	Road left to SANTA ANA (ranch, 5.6 mi.), another former visiting station of San Borja mission. Ruins of the chapel and irrigation ditch may still be seen. The road continues to SAN GREGORIO, 19.3 mi. from junction (see above).
72.1	(11.3)	Fork in road. The poor left branch is a short cut going 3.3 mi. to join the main road 3.2 mi. below Rosarito. Right branch is best.
74.8	(2.7)	ROSARITO. Junction with main road at M. 339.3.

The main transpeninsular road continues in a southerly direction from the Los Angeles Bay turn-off at M. 297.9, across a broad rolling plain with a thick growth of desert plants.

Mi. from Ensenada	Partial Mileage	
315.6	17.7	PUNTA PRIETA. Elev. ca. 850 ft. A small and bleak-appearing settlement of cattle ranchers. There are two stores with limited supplies. Meals and gasoline can be purchased. The water,

from wells, has a disagreeable salty taste. There is a good landing strip, long enough for heavy planes.

A side road leaves Punta Prieta in a northeasterly direction, branching after 8.6 mi. Left branch joins the Los Angeles Bay road near Desengaño, 15.6 mi. from Punta Prieta. Take right branch for Los Angeles Bay; it joins the Los Angeles Bay road at M. 13.5, after 14.0 mi. from Punta Prieta (see p. 123).

A few miles south of Punta Prieta the road branches, and the right fork leads to a route which keeps well to the west of the main road. There are several alternates to this road and connections between it and the main road. Sections of the "coastal route" described here are receiving (1961) increasing traffic, largely because of the salt works at Guerrero Negro. Described here is the most westerly of the possible combinations between Punta Prieta and Los Mártires.

Mi. from Pta. Prieta	Partial Mileage	
7.3	7.3	The main road (see p. 133) branches left here and an alternate turnoff goes left 0.3 mi. beyond. Go straight ahead for coastal route. (See also Preface page 12.)
8.4	1.1	A side road branches left and passes BACHANDRES (0.8 mi.), a farm, coming back in at M. 10.6.
10.2	1.8	SAN ANDRÉS. An old cattle ranch, uninhabited in 1961.
10.6	0.4	Another road in from left, from BACHANDRES (1.7 mi.). Beyond here the road descends a narrow canyon with salt water pools.
13.1	2.5	EL TOROTE. Goat ranch.
14.2	1.1	A side road right leads to the coast and north via Las Palomas and Santa Catarina to the main road near San Agustín at M. 214.0 (see pp. 115-19).
20.3	6.1	Branch road right to seasonally occupied fishing camp of SANTA ROSALILLITA, 1.4 mi.
21.9	1.6	The road comes out on the beach, which is followed for thirteen miles.
31.3	9.4	EL MUERTITO. A solitary grave on the right side of the road. Seasonally occupied fishing camp.
34.5	3.2	The road leaves the beach and heads inland past ALTAMIRA, seasonally occupied fishing camp.
38.2	3.7	A road in from left, from Rosarito, 7.2 mi. (see page 133). Now road heads down the canyon of SAN JAVIER.
42.8	4.6	A more direct road branches left to go over a low hill. Right branch is followed here.
43.1	0.3	A road right goes 1.0 mi. (take right branch after 0.6 mi., at old graves) to EL TOMATAL, fishing camp.
43.9	0.8	Road in from right from El Tomatal, 0.9 mi. The beach is now seen to the right.
45.1	1.2	A cross road. To right is MILLER'S LANDING on the beach (0.3 mi.), a long-abandoned loading point for onyx from El Marmo-

THE MOUNTAIN RANCH OF SAN GREGORIO
Near the San Borja Mission. See text page 125.

STONE MISSION CHURCH OF SAN BORJA
See text page 124.

FISHING VILLAGE AND CANNERY AT TURTLE BAY
See text page 131.

MAIN ROAD THROUGH THE VIZCAÍNO DESERT NEAR EL ARCO
Bordered by cholla, pitahaya agria, and datilillo. See text pages 134-35, 137.

Mí. from Pta. Prieta	Partial Mileage	
		lito. The road to left leads inland to main road at M. 353.0, 4.6 mi. from here.
45.3	0.2	The road which branched left at M. 42.8 rejoins from left, having come 1.9 mi. over the low hills.
46.5	1.2	Road branches just after leaving the beach and crossing a sand dune. (This place is called LOMA AMARILLA after a nearby hill). The left branch goes 4.1 mi. to join main road at M. 358.6.
		The right branch, followed here, continues parallel to the coast behind some sand dunes, toward the large coastal lagoons.
56.0	9.5	A poor road left goes via JESÚS MARÍA (3.7 mi.) to EL JUNCO (10.1 mi.), ranches. (See p. 134).
57.8	1.8	A better road to Jesús María, etc.
61.7	3.9	A junction near a salt marsh. Road right goes 0.8 mi. to a former fishermen's camp on the shore of shallow LAGUNA MANUELA. This place was once called Santo Domingo Landing. Supplies were landed here for the Calmallí mines in the early 1900's.
		Road continues left across salt flats. Follow main traveled ruts, bearing right after 0.4 mi.
67.4	5.7	A road in from left rear just after climbing to a higher sandy plain is from El Junco (9.3 mi.) and M. 371.9 on main road (14.5 mi. from here). This branch was in frequent use in 1961.
67.7	0.3	A less-traveled road branching left goes 19.3 mi. to join the main road at La Vuelta, M. 386.7.
		The right branch continues over a sandy plain of the Vizcaíno Desert with the coast out of sight beyond large sand dunes.
78.6	10.9	LA ESPINA (LA ESPINITA), a solitary group of shacks serving as a saloon for salt works employees. Roads leave here in several directions. (Straight ahead leads to Las Bombas, 5.5 mi. see below). The most direct route to Guerrero Negro is probably one angling a little to the right (not traveled by authors). Another road to the right leads to the shore of LAGUNA GUERRERO NEGRO (BLACK WARRIOR LAGOON), then turns south.
88.6	10.0	GUERRERO NEGRO. Estimated pop. in 1960: 900. A company town belonging to Exportadora de Sal, S.A., subsidiary of an American corporation with a concession for harvesting salt used for industrial purposes. The vast salt beds of SALINA VIZCAÍNO are dyked off into large "pans"; sea water is pumped in and allowed to evaporate; the salt is then trucked to the port facilities for loading onto ships. Some five miles of highway leads from the salt beds to the town (offices, shops, housing) and some six miles beyond on a causeway across Guerrero Negro Lagoon to the port facilities (PUERTO VENUSTIANO CARRANZA) on an island near the mouth of the lagoon. Operations here commenced approximately in 1958.
		There is a public restaurant, a few stores, and a government radio telegraph station.

Mi. from Pta. Prieta	Partial Mileage	

A road to the north shore of SCAMMON's LAGOON (LAGUNA OJO DE LIEBRE) goes via the company's highway (obtain permission and instructions at the office) past the salt pans, and continues across salt beds and sand dunes (ca. 18 mi., not traveled by authors).

There are many roads in this area of the Vizcaíno Desert, most of them very little traveled and some impassably sandy. Those described below were being traveled in 1961.

A wide, hard-surfaced road leaves Guerrero Negro in an easterly direction.

| 93.9 | 5.3 | The "coastal route" followed here branches to the right. This is a bulldozed road constructed by Petróleos Mexicanos ("Pemex"), the government oil monopoly, about 1959 when exploring for oil in this area. |

The road straight ahead leads to El Arco.

Mi. from
M. 93.9

(1.0)	1.0	LAS BOMBAS, a group of shacks. Store, gasoline. The hard road ends here, and a sandy desert road begins.
(3.3)	4.3	EL SOLITO, ruined shack of former ranch.
(10.0)	14.3	EL MATOMÍ, a well at site of former ranch.
(0.2)	14.5	A cross road. Right branch leads via LA BANDERITA (cattle ranch, 4.2 mi.) and SANTA MARÍA (cattle ranch, 8.7 mi., uninhabited in 1961) to cross the "Pemex road" after 12.5 mi. from junction (at M. 111.5, see below).
(1.2)	15.7	Road in from right rear, also from La Banderita (4.6 mi.) etc.
(24.3)	40.0	EL ARCO, on main road, M. 410.3 (see p. 135).

From M. 93.9 the "Pemex road" leads off to the south across a sandy plain:

| 111.5 | 17.6 | A cross road is the old road from El Arco to Ojo de Liebre. El Arco is to left via Santa María and La Banderita (see above). |

Straight ahead the "Pemex road" was being little traveled in 1961, most of the traffic turning right on the older road, followed here.

| 117.8 | 6.3 | OJO DE LIEBRE (Jackrabbit Spring), historic water hole (almost dry in 1961), uninhabited, with a stunted cottonwood tree. |
| 118.5 | 0.7 | EL HUISACHE, ranch. A road branches west here and goes to cross a large salt bed (SALINA OJO DE LIEBRE) toward the easterly edge of SCAMMON'S LAGOON (known as LAGUNA OJO DE LIEBRE, named for the nearby water hole). After 4.8 mi. it comes to a ruined causeway, treacherous to drive on or alongside, which leads a mile or two out to the lagoon. Here are remains of a narrow-gauge railway. These salt deposits have been exploited at intervals since about 1860. |

Mi. from Pta. Prieta	Partial Mileage	
122.8	4.3	A road branches right to Bahía Tortugas. In 1961 this was reported to be the easiest way to get started to that bay. (The first 4.8 miles have not been traveled by authors.) The road has some very sandy stretches and is recommended only for four-wheel drive vehicles.

	Mi. from M. 122.8	
(4.8)	4.8	A road from left is that by which authors reached this point from Las Lagunas in 1955. The road traverses a region of alternate salt flats and sand dunes.
(34.2)	39.0	The road leaves the flat country and climbs westward into the barren Sierra Pintada, with a view of Scammon's Lagoon to the north.
(2.2)	41.2	A road branching left (not traveled by authors) was reported in 1961 to join the coastal road between San Andrés and Asunción.
(9.8)	51.0	Here for 3½ mi. the road traverses a very treacherous sand dune known as LOS VOLADORES. In 1955 this was the usual route westbound, as it is downhill, but on the return trip traffic was taking a detour south about 17 mi. long which comes in at this point.
(8.6)	59.6	Junction left with detour mentioned above.
(8.9)	68.5	Branch road left to SAN JOSÉ DE CASTRO (0.9 mi.), a nice oasis and ranch with a good spring of sulfur water, the only water for many miles. This road continues as an alternate route back to San Ignacio via Punta Abreojos, see pp. 139-40.
(0.3)	68.8	Another road, left, to San José and, immediately beyond, a side road right to MALARRIMO (26 mi., not traveled by authors), a long beach stretching west from the mouth of Scammon's Lagoon (see page 198). Fishermen cross the coastal dunes and run the beach at low tide ca. 10 mi. east to the mouth of Scammon's Lagoon. The Bahía Tortugas road climbs over low passes and down to the southwest coast.
(29.1)	97.9	The coast is reached, and the road continues up it and around the bay.

(16.2) 114.1 BAHÍA TORTUGAS (Turtle Bay; shown on most maps as Puerto San Bartolomé). 1950 pop. 315. A snug harbor, protected from all winds and deep enough for the largest ships. On the shore there is a fishing village with a pier and an abalone cannery. Its chief disadvantage as a port is the fact that there is no fresh water in the vicinity; drinking water is made by distilling sea water. There is a landing field and a radio station. The bay is visited during the spring and early summer by numerous fishing boats from Ensenada and elsewhere. *Caguamas*, the great sea turtles from which the place gets its name, are no longer plentiful, but there is good sport fishing from May to September. A fishing camp with rustic accommodations has been established for sport fishermen, and its management flies the guests in from Ensenada.

Supplies and gasoline may be purchased from the cannery store.

Rodríguez Cabrillo visited this bay in 1542 and called it Puerto San Pedro Víncula. It was renamed San Bartolomé by the explorer Sebastián Vizcaíno in 1602. Early in the last century it was much visited by American whaling ships. In the 1900's a colony of Japanese abalone fishermen was founded here; a cannery was built and the product shipped to Japan. This enterprise was abandoned about 1920, and the settlement was repopulated with Mexican fishermen in the 1940's. See illustration page 128.

The main traveled "coastal route" continues straight ahead at the Turtle Bay turnoff (M. 122.8):

Mi. from Pta. Prieta	Partial Mileage	
123.8	1.0	The "Pemex road" is crossed, having come 11.9 mi. from where it was left at M. 111.5. Going right on this road takes one to its end at the abandoned Pemex camp, 9.2 mi. From the camp site, little-traveled, confusing roads radiate out in all directions. One of these is said to lead to Bahía Tortugas. Cross the Pemex road.
124.6	0.8	LA CANTINA. Cattle ranch with windmill well and garden. A branch road left crosses sandy plains past several ranches (uninhabited in 1955) and joins the main road after 29.6 mi. at M. 429.7 (see p. 137).
136.8	12.2	A side road to right rear, formerly leading to Bahía Tortugas, was reported in 1961 to be no longer passable.
139.0	2.2	LAS LAGUNAS, cattle ranch. A branch right goes by way of a dry lake used as an airstrip (3.4 mi.) to the abandoned Pemex camp mentioned above (8.1 mi.).
141.8	2.8	Side road left to SAN FRANCISQUITO, cattle ranch with windmill well, 1.7 mi. From here a road goes left across sandy plains in an area of many confusing tracks to RANCHO DE WILSON (9.0 mi.) and continues to the main road at M. 439.7, 15.9 mi. from San Francisquito (see p. 137).
145.3	3.5	Side road in from left from San Francisquito, 2.7 mi.
158.5	13.2	SAN ESTEBAN, cattle ranch on a short alternate to right of direct road.
161.9	3.4	A less traveled road branches left toward a ranch. The right branch is that used by truckers. It joins the road in from Los Mártires and continues via San Angel (see page 138; the connecting stretch not traveled by authors). Left branch is followed here.
162.0	0.1	GUADALUPE, ranch, uninhabited in 1961.
170.8	8.8	LOS MÁRTIRES, at M. 461.8 on the main road (see p. 138). The "coastal route" just described has come 24.6 mi. farther than the main road to reach this point.

The main road below Punta Prieta (M. 315.6) follows down the valley, starting out on the road described above (see p. 126). There are many branches, through deep dust. It is usually best to keep right.

◉

Mi. from Ensenada	Partial Mileage	
322.6	7.0	A road left to LA BACHATA, 0.7 mi., a group of ranches.
322.9	0.3	Main road angles to left. (Straight ahead is the coastal route described above. At 0.3 mi. further another branch angles left to main road). (See Preface p. 12.)
330.8	7.9	AGUA DE REFUGIO. Small cattle ranch on ARROYO SANTO DOMINGUITO.
339.3	8.5	ROSARITO. Collection of ranches in a valley. A side road left up the arroyo to San Borja mission (22.1 mi.), Bahía de los Angeles, etc. (see pp. 123-25). Another side road goes right, starting down the valley, and cuts over to join the "coastal route" at M. 38.2 from Punta Prieta, near Altamira (see page 126) after 7.2 mi. Two miles from Rosarito this side road traverses a marsh which occasionally becomes impassable. Inquire in Rosarito before taking this branch. (See Preface p. 12.)
342.5	3.2	Side road from left, connecting (after 3.3 mi.) with the road to San Borja.
345.6	3.1	Side road left up a canyon to EL CARDONAL (3.8 mi. from fork), SAN MIGUEL (10.9 mi.), and SAN REGIS (13.0 mi.), ranches. The last two places were visiting stations of San Borja mission; both have irrigation works built by the missionaries, and San Regis has an old ruined adobe chapel and cemetery.
346.7	1.1	Branch road left to EL MARMOLITO (2.9 mi.), an occasionally worked onyx quarry on ARROYO SALINITO. Beyond here 0.8 mi. the main road runs along a little stream of mineralized water (AGUA AMARGA).
350.9	4.2	Side road in from left from El Marmolito, 3.7 mi. Main road goes down valley of ARROYO SALINITO.
353.0	2.1	A junction where the arroyo emerges from the hills. The less traveled right branch goes to the sea at Miller's Landing, 4.9 mi. (see page 126). Take left branch across arroyo and onto the coastal plain.
358.6	5.6	Junction with road in from right, a connection with the "coastal route." The junction at M. 46.5 from Punta Prieta is 4.1 mi. from here (see page 129). Road continues along the coastal plain, then crosses low hills into a wide valley, with a high black mesa ahead.
371.6	13.0	SAN JERÓNIMO, ranch, at left, located 0.3 mi. beyond crossing of ARROYO PARAÍSO, here a narrow wash (see below).

Mi. from   Partial
Ensenada   Mileage
371.9   0.3   Roads right and left.

In 1961 the right branch was being frequently used by truckers going to Guerrero Negro. It heads west toward the wide coastal plain.

Partial   Mi. from
Mileage   M. 371.9
(5.2)   5.2   EL JUNCO, cattle ranch.

(1.2)   6.4   A junction (go left). The road straight ahead (to right) leads to JESÚS MARÍA, ranch (5.3 mi.) and joins the "coastal route" at M. 56.0, 9.0 mi. from junction, or at M. 57.8.

(5.8)   12.2 Take left branch at fork.

(2.3)   14.5 Junction with the "coastal route" in from right, where the latter climbs out of the mud flats at M. 67.4.

The left branch goes 1.5 mi. to SAN JUAN (cattle ranch), and a ranch road continues up the valley. At 5.8 mi. from San Juan a branch goes right 0.2 mi. to end across the wash from BOCA DE PARAÍSO, where Arroyo Paraíso emerges from the mountains. In the high altitudes where this water-course begins it is a deep winding canyon, a formidable obstacle to travelers on the old trails of the region.

Partial
Mileage
374.9   3.0   MEZQUITAL. Cattle ranch with a well of good water. A side road goes to San Juan, 3.4 mi. (see above). Main road goes left of the black mesa to emerge on the coastal plain.

376.7   1.8   Side road left to RANCHO GRANDE and RANCHO ALEGRE (2.5 mi.), and EL RETIRO (3.9 mi. from junction).

376.9   0.2   RIO GRANDE, new ranch house being built in 1961.

378.8   1.9   Another road left to Rancho Grande and Rancho Alegre (1.8 mi.).

386.7   7.9   Road angles left to head more easterly. This region is called LA VUELTA. A road in from right is from M. 67.7 on "coastal route," 19.3 mi. A branch of this cuts across to Guerrero Negro.

388.1   1.4   A road left to MIRAMAR, cattle ranch, 7.3 mi., in the foothills.

397.9   9.8   Road forks in the broad ARROYO SAN LUIS. The main road via El Arco continues straight ahead. An alternate route via Calmallí, 4.5 mi. longer, branches left.

Mi. from
M. 397.9
(7.1)   7.1   EL CAÑÓN DE CALMALLÍ. Ranch.

(1.6)   8.7   A side road left goes north. After 4.0 mi. on this road a

Mi. from Ensenada	Partial Mileage	Mi. from M. 397.9	

left branch goes to LA ESPERANZA (ranch, 10.3 mi.) and continues to SANTA CRUZ (ranch, 14.1 mi. from junction); right branch goes to LAS PALOMAS, old ranch (7.5 mi. from junction), from which a trail leads ca. 3 mi. right to the waterhole of CALMALLÍ VIEJO, mentioned by early explorers.

(0.6)   9.3   CALMALLÍ. Elev. 1,200 ft. A nearly deserted mining town consisting of several adobe buildings and a few wooden shacks and ruined stamp mills.

Water, which is fairly good, comes from three wells. There is a landing strip long enough for large planes.

Gold was discovered here in 1882, causing a brief but profitable rush. By mid-1883 there were about 300 miners with 20 stamp mills in operation, and a reported $250,000 in gold was recovered before the placers began to play out. The hillside behind the town is littered with old mine workings.

(5.2)   14.5   POZO ALEMÁN. Another nearly abandoned mining camp. Store. Branch road left to El Barril (see below).

(2.4)   16.9   EL ARCO (see description below).

The main road keeps to the right at the intersection in Arroyo San Luis (M. 397.9), and after a few miles winds through low hills.

410.3   12.4   EL ARCO. Elev. 950. Estimated 1960 pop. 150. A small community at the site of a former gold mine, about two miles north of the boundary between the State of Baja California and the Southern Territory. It consists of two groups of adobe and wooden shacks on opposite banks of the arroyo, with extensive mine workings below. El Arco is a supply point for the surrounding area. There are two stores, one of which has a kerosene-operated refrigerator. Gasoline is sold. There is a well of poor water. A field next to the town serves for small aircraft, and two miles south of town there is another one long enough for heavy planes.

The gold mines of El Arco, which at one time employed over 1,000 workers, began to be developed by an American company in the 1920's, but operations ceased after a prolonged strike of the miners.

Several side trips may be made from El Arco. The road to Santa Cruz has been described above. Other roads go to El Barril and San Francisquito on the Gulf, to Santa Gertrudis mission, and to Guerrero Negro salt works on the Pacific.

Mi. from Ensenada	Partial Mileage	Mi. from El Arco	

(2.4)   2.4   POZO ALEMÁN (see above). Turn right at center of town and bear left beyond last houses.

Mi. from Ensenada	Partial Mileage	Mi. from El Arco	
	(7.8)	10.2	Branch road left to LA UNIÓN (5.0 mi.), ranch. The road continues ahead up a long valley, then winds through low hills.
	(14.0)	24.2	LAS LAGUNITAS, abandoned ranch 0.5 mi. off road to left.
	(5.5)	29.7	Summit of steep grade (CUESTA LA LEY) on the peninsular divide, elev. 2,100 ft. There is a fine view of the Gulf of California at its narrowest point. The largest of the string of islands is San Lorenzo; beyond are the peaks of Tiburón Island and the Sonora mainland.
	(8.4)	38.1	Road forks. Take right branch for El Barril. The left branch goes 11.8 mi. to BAHÍA SAN FRANCISQUITO, a snug little harbor, not inhabited in 1959. After 6.1 mi. on this branch a road comes from the right, from near El Barril.
	(8.6)	46.7	A road left cuts across to the San Francisquito road, 6.7 mi.
	(1.0)	47.7	EL BARRIL. A ranch on the Gulf shore inhabited by a large family. Gardens and a small orchard irrigated from wells. The water is good.

The road to the old mission of Santa Gertrudis leaves El Arco in an easterly direction.

Partial Mileage	Mi. from El Arco	
(2.4)	2.4	Faint road straight ahead; keep to left.
(2.7)	5.1	Junction with a road from Pozo Alemán on left; turn right.
(7.3)	12.4	MIRAFLORES. Cattle ranch. The road follows up a canyon.
(4.5)	16.9	GUADALUPE. Cattle ranch.
(5.3)	22.2	SANTA TERESA, off road to left: ranch with a little garden among date palms.
(1.0)	23.2	SANTA GERTRUDIS. Elev. ca. 1,800 ft. A small ranching

settlement in a narrow arroyo, the site of an old mission which in its heyday administered to more than 3,000 Indians in a vast territory stretching from the Gulf to the Pacific.

The Jesuit Padre Consag discovered the site of Santa Gertrudis about 1740, but it was not until 1752 that a mission was established here by a German Jesuit, Padre Jorge Retz. It was the center of the frontier region and base for further exploration until San Borja was founded ten years later. The Jesuits made great efforts to develop Santa Gertrudis as a self-sufficient community, but were never completely successful because of the scarcity of water. Some tiny springs were diverted into a long irrigation ditch (which is still partly used) cut into the cliffside and leading to the cultivated area below the mission. The Indian population, decimated by disease, dwindled to 300 in 1785. Less than a hundred remained when the mission was abandoned in 1822.

When the Dominicans arrived they began work on the small stone church, which was finished in 1796. It is a graceful touch of civilization in a lonely spot, on a narrow ledge between the cliffside and the arroyo. Behind the chapel are several rooms intended for missionaries' quarters, and off to one side is a low bell tower. There are several ruined stone outbuildings, also built by the Dominicans, as well as a masonry reservoir. Much of the land once cultivated has been washed away, but there are still a few date palms, grapevines, and olive trees.

The road to Guerrero Negro leaves El Arco in a southwesterly direction from the buildings on the right bank of the arroyo, or from the main road 0.5 mi. north of town (going past the cemetery). See page 130 for road description. Guerrero Negro is 45.3 mi. from El Arco.

The main transpeninsular highway leaves El Arco in a southeasterly direction and crosses the 28th parallel, dividing line between the northern (Estado de Baja California) and southern (Territorio Sur de Baja California) halves of the peninsula. The road runs in long, straight sections along the eastern edge of Desierto de Sebastián Vizcaíno, or Llano del Berrendo (Antelope Plain), a flat desert with a dense and varied cover of thorny shrubs, cacti and tree yuccas.

Mi. from Ensenada	Partial Mileage	
429.7	19.4	Side road right crosses the sandy plains past several ranches (uninhabited in 1955) and confusing branches to join the "coastal route" at M. 124.6 (La Cantina) after 29.6 mi. (see p. 132).
436.7	7.0	Crossing of ARROYO CUEVA COLORADA (LA CUEVA). A trail is said to go from here into the mountains, to the tiny oasis and ruins of SAN PABLO (not visited by authors), once a visiting station of Santa Gertrudis mission.
439.7	3.0	Side road right to farm locally referred to as RANCHO DE WILSON (6.9 mi.), started about 1959 with American capital. Many acres of former desert are irrigated with an ample supply of good well water.
		A road continues beyond the clearing, into an area of many sandy roads. In 1961 San Francisquito, on the "coastal route" (see page 132) could be reached, 15.9 mi. from the main road, by taking the left branch 9.1 mi. from the main road.
440.7	1.0	EL TABLÓN, cattle ranch 0.3 mi. off road to left, with a good well and a large reservoir. Ahead is a sandy stretch, which, when in bad condition is avoided by detouring via El Tablón and rejoining main road 2.7 mi. beyond here. (Also see Preface page 12.)
446.7	6.0	EL CARACOL. Well at site of former ranch. Beyond here the road crosses sandy plains for some twenty miles.

Mi. from Ensenada	Partial Mileage	
450.9	4.2	Los ANGELES. Ranch. Meals sold.
456.3	5.4	EL PORVENIR. Cattle ranch, usually uninhabited.
461.8	5.5	Los MÁRTIRES. Cattle ranch, small garden. The main road to San Ignacio goes straight ahead.

In from the right rear is the "coastal route" (see page 132) which comes via Guerrero Negro from Punta Prieta (170.8 mi.).

A road branching directly to the right goes to join the road coming directly from Guadalupe (see page 132). In 1961 this route was being used by truckers going to La Paz via the Pacific Coast, avoiding San Ignacio and Santa Rosalía. The following was logged in 1952 and 1955:

	Mi. from Mártires	
(2.5)	2.5	Road joins another in from right, directly from Guadalupe (see p. 132) on the "coastal route."
(8.9)	11.4	Road in from right, from Punta Abreojos and Turtle Bay (see pp. 139-40).
(0.7)	12.1	SAN ÁNGEL, attractive oasis with some date palms and ranch (uninhabited) 0.1 mi. off road to left.
(5.2)	17.3	SAN JUAN, ranch. In 1961 the truckers were reported to be taking a branch to the right (not traveled by authors) to El Álamo (see page 141), ca. 18 mi., leading to the Pacific coast route.
(6.2)	23.5	SAN SABÁS. Abandoned ranch on lower Arroyo San Ignacio. This was once an important visiting station of San Ignacio mission. General direction of road is up the arroyo.
(8.8)	32.3	SAN IGNACIO, plaza (see below).

Below Los Martires the main road (straight ahead) continues across the plains and then begins to climb across rocky foothills.

484.4	22.6	SAN LINO. A suburb of San Ignacio. Straight ahead is the main highway to Santa Rosalía. Turn right, across the river, to

485.7   1.3   SAN IGNACIO. Elev. 500 ft. Estimated pop. in 1960: 900. Climate: cool in winter (average temperature Nov.-Apr., 63.7° F.; coldest months, Dec.-Feb.); pleasant in summer (average temperature May-Oct., 77.0° F.; warmest months, July-Sep.). Average annual rainfall: 4.8 inches. Communications: Telegraph line to Santa Rosalía. See frontispiece illustration.

The first glimpse of San Ignacio after plodding through hundreds of miles of barren desert is one of the really spectacular sights in Baja California. Bleak sunbaked cactus-covered hills suddenly give way to the welcome shade of a huge grove of date palms. Several springs in the arroyo irrigate a fertile valley for a number of miles before the water sinks into the ground. Figs, oranges, grapes, and many other fruits are grown, but the main crop is dates. They are harvested with a minimum of effort, dried, and shipped out through Santa Rosalía.

The town itself, on a slight elevation on the edge of the arroyo, is a group of thatch-roofed adobe houses clustered around a little plaza. Dominating everything is the massive stone church, finished by the Dominican Padre Gómez in 1786. It is entirely of cut lava rock with walls four feet thick and an arched ceiling. Behind the church are the remains of an old irrigation ditch used to water the mission garden. Several other mission buildings along the west side of the plaza, originally used as storehouses, a school for the Indian children, missionaries' quarters, etc., are now occupied by government offices.

There are a number of stores where gasoline and supplies may be purchased. Travelers who wish to spend the night are accommodated at the house of Señora Leree (III). Meals can be obtained at several other private houses. In 1961 Pilar Cota had limited space for tourists to spend the night (III) and served meals. Auto servicing and repairing (and expert blacksmith work) are done at Frank Fischer's shop.

Originally the site of San Ignacio was occupied by an Indian rancheria known as Cadacaaman. The place was visited by the Jesuit Padre Píccolo in 1716, and a mission was established here in 1728. During the next 25 years San Ignacio was the northernmost mission and a base for exploration of the wild frontier region beyond. At one time there were about 5,000 Indians in the area, but disease reduced their number to 120 by the end of the 18th century. Later San Ignacio was gradually repopulated with settlers from across the Gulf. In the early years the missionaries' fields were periodically swept down the arroyo by disastrous floods, which still occur from time to time. The first crops produced were wheat and corn; later grapes and figs became more important. The original date palms were probably introduced by the Jesuits about 1765.

On the mesa above the town is a landing strip long enough for large aircraft, but aviation gas is not usually available.

San Ignacio is the starting place for several side trips. Bahía Tortugas (Turtle Bay) may be reached by driving to Los Mártires and branching off on the "coastal route" (see pp. 131-32). An alternate route via Punta Abreojos leaves San Ignacio in a southwesterly direction down the left bank of the arroyo, past cultivated fields and groves of date palms, following the road described above (see p. 138) via San Sabás (8.8 mi.), San Juan (15.0 mi.), and San Angel.

Mi. from S. Ignacio	Partial Mileage	
20.2	(20.2)	SAN ÁNGEL (off road to right, see p. 138).
20.9	(0.7)	(Exact location subject to variation). Take a less traveled left fork. (Right branch goes to Los Mártires or Guadalupe, see page 138). The Abreojos road runs down the arroyo, crosses a salt flat, then shifting sand dunes (called EL RÁBICH), and continues across rolling sandy terrain. To the west are the barren SANTA CLARA mountains, amazingly steep rugged buttes which seem to rise vertically from the flat desert floor. A legend identifies this area as the site of the "lost mission" of Santa Clara, where a fabulous treasure is supposed to lie buried. The early Jesuit records mention a proposed mission of Santa María Magdalena, to be founded near the Pacific coast west of San Ignacio, but apparently the Indians of this region were instead moved in to San Ignacio. Some of the old maps show a mission in this general direction called San Juan Bautista. If the Jesuits actually founded a mission here it was a well-guarded secret.
59.3	(38.4)	Here the road approaches the shore of Estero del Coyote, a salt water lagoon running inland from Bahía Ballenas. It then comes out near a fine sand beach and passes several seasonally occupied fishing camps.
69.5	(10.2)	PUNTA ABREOJOS. Lighthouse and fishing camp, on a low sandy point. There is a sandy beach and good anchorage for small boats just east of the point. Fresh water must be brought in from elsewhere. Store, gasoline sometimes available. The road goes northwest up the coast, following the shore of a long lagoon.
81.6	(12.1)	LA BOCANA. Stone monument on a hill, near the mouth of the lagoon; usually uninhabited.
111.0	(29.4)	SAN HIPÓLITO. Seasonally occupied fishing camp; no water.
115.6	(4.6)	PUNTA PRIETA. Another fishing camp sometimes inhabited.
135.6	(20.0)	Side road left to PUNTA ASUNCIÓN (1.6 mi.). Fishing camp, store. Here the road turns inland and begins climbing into the bare, waterless Sierra Pintada.
137.7	(2.1)	Landing strip at right.
146.9	(9.2)	SAN ANDRÉS. Ranch and mining camp, sometimes inhabited. There are several wells of fresh water, slightly alkaline but perfectly drinkable. The best water is that found in the deeper holes. Gold was discovered in this area about 1893 causing a mining boom which lasted some ten years. Several thousand prospectors, mostly Yaqui Indians, extracted an estimated $75,000 in gold before 1920. It is reported that there are still rich placers in the vicinity, but the scarcity of water and the extreme isolation make profitable mining very difficult.
172.2	(25.3)	SAN JOSÉ DE CASTRO. Ranch and garden, good spring of water.
173.1	(0.9)	Junction with northerly route to Bahía Tortugas via El Huisache or Las Lagunas (see pp. 130-31).
218.4	(45.3)	BAHÍA TORTUGAS (see p. 131).

A road goes from San Ignacio to La Purísima and the south parallel to the Pacific coast. While not traveled as much as the main road via the Gulf shore and Santa Rosalía, this route was receiving increased traffic in 1961 because it is ca. 50 mi. shorter and there are no substantial grades. Two alternate routes are possible for a part of the way, but both become impassable in wet weather.

Mi. from S. Ignacio	Partial Mileage	
0.0	0.0	SAN IGNACIO. Road leaves in a southerly direction (from the south side of the plaza, past the cemetery).
5.7	(5.7)	Side road left to SAN LUIS (7.7 mi.), ranch.
6.1	(0.4)	BATEQUE DE SANTA BRÍGIDA. Ranch. (Uninhabited in 1961).
8.8	(2.7)	SAN JOAQUÍN. A small farming community, once a *pueblo de visita* of San Ignacio mission. The road follows down the arroyo.
9.7	(0.9)	EL SAUZAL. Collection of ranches.
13.2	(3.5)	SAN ZACARÍAS. An old ranching community in an oasis of palm trees and small gardens. Here the road climbs out of the canyon and continues across flat country.
16.2	(3.0)	EL ÁLAMO. Ranch. In 1961 a road in from right from San Juan (ca. 18 mi., see page 138, not traveled by authors) was being used by truckers who used the Pacific coast route and avoided San Ignacio. They could go north either via Los Mártires on the main road or via Guadalupe to Guerrero Negro on the "coastal route" (see pp. 129-32).
23.5	(7.3)	Fork in road. The right branch via the Laguna San Ignacio and the *salitrales* (tidal flats) is that usually taken by the truckers. Although 16.6 miles longer than the left branch it permits higher speeds (but becomes impassable after rains or extreme tides).

	Mi. from M. 23.5	
	(15.5)	15.5	LA LAGUNA, turtle fishing camp on the shore of LAGUNA SAN IGNACIO (see illustration p. 145).
	(0.9)	16.4	EL ALMACÉN, another turtle fishing camp. The road enters a long area of tidal salt flats interspersed with sand dunes, past ESTERO EL DELGADITO (seen at a distance) and ESTERO EL DÁTIL. This long, narrow lagoon is followed along mangrove-lined shores in places.
	(40.2)	56.6	In 1961 a turtle camp was here on the shore of Estero el Dátil.
	(7.5)	64.1	Road enters mouth of ARROYO SAN JUAN.
	(1.6)	65.7	A left branch heads up the valley to the other road. Keep right on road which climbs out onto a coastal mesa.
	(7.0)	72.7	Junction with the other road at M. 80.0.

The left branch, described immediately below, is bad in places and less frequently used. It should be attempted only by high clearance vehicles with plenty of extra gasoline and water. Local inquiry should be made on other recent travel this way.

Mi. from S. Ignacio	Partial Mileage	
30.7	(7.2)	LA RINCONADA. Ranch off road to left. A few miles beyond here a trail (reported in 1961 to be passable in motor vehicles) goes to PATROCINIO (ca. 15 mi., not visited by authors), a collection of ranches with a good spring of water by means of which a little grain and sugar cane are grown.
41.8	(11.1)	SALINA CUARENTA. A salt bed from which salt is occasionally mined on a small scale. The road crosses flats for several miles, then turns up a canyon.
55.8	(14.0)	CUARENTA. Abandoned ranch off road at left. The road continues through a valley (VALLE LA TORTUGA) with deep ruts and loose dust.
69.6	(13.8)	Side road left to SAN JOSÉ DE GRACIA (4.7 mi.). A small agricultural settlement in a narrow valley, isolated and picturesque. There is an abundant supply of good water, used to irrigate about 100 acres of corn, beans, sugar cane, and fruit trees. San José was developed as a ranch and visiting station of Guadalupe mission by the Jesuits, who built a dam, the ruins of which can still be seen.
		The road follows coastal mesas and dips down to cross rough canyons.
75.2	(5.6)	ARROYO DE SAN JUAN crossing.
80.0	(4.8)	The road which branched at M. 23.5 and has come by way of the tidal flats joins from right.
85.1	(5.1)	SAN RAYMUNDO (LA BALLENA). Ranch in Arroyo San Raymundo. Water.
91.7	(6.6)	CADEJÉ. A tiny settlement which owes its existence to a spring of good water. There are a few date palms and subsistence crops are grown. Airstrip.
94.7	(3.0)	EL CARRIZAL. Ranch and water hole.
98.5	(3.8)	Road forks. Left branch goes directly to SAN JUANICO waterhole, 2.2 mi., good water among some date palms near the beach. Clams and lobsters are plentiful. After 2.3 mi. this rejoins the other branch.
		The right branch is followed here.
101.4	(2.9)	SAN JUANICO, fishing camp and cannery in the lee of Punta Pequeña.
103.1	(1.7)	The direct road joins from left, near beach.
110.5	(7.4)	ARROYO DEL MEZQUITAL.
121.0	(10.5)	Branch road right to LA BOCANA (9.1 mi.), a sand beach at the mouth of Estero San Gregorio. Just ahead road crosses ARROYO SAN GREGORIO.
131.1	(10.1)	Junction with main road; right to La Paz, left to La Purísima.
135.3	(4.2)	LA PURÍSIMA (see p. 160).

The main transpeninsular highway leaves San Ignacio (plaza) and returns to the road junction mentioned above at San Lino, on the right bank of the arroyo (if the town of San Ignacio is not entered, subtract 2.6 mi. from total mileage):

Mi. from Ensenada	Partial Mileage	
487.0	1.3	SAN LINO. Turn right, up the arroyo.
494.9	7.9	Side road right to SAN REGIS (2.3 mi.), cattle ranch.
498.9	4.0	LA ESPERANZA. Abandoned ranch. The road crosses a level valley, then winds through the foothills of the great volcano Las Tres Vírgenes (6,550 ft. high) which rises spectacularly on the north, quite close to the road. Probably the most recent active volcano in the peninsula, Las Vírgenes was the source of some of the great lava flows which cover the surrounding country.
509.1	10.2	EL MEZQUITAL. House where refreshments are sold.
511.7	2.6	Divide (elev. 1,600 ft.) between the waters of the Pacific and those of the Gulf. The road begins a steep (0.9 mi. long) descent, Cuesta de las Vírgenes, with many hairpin curves.
514.4	2.7	A road left to LAS VÍRGENES (0.3 mi), cattle ranch. It continues northerly through the ranch over a pass east of of the Tres Vírgenes volcano (10.6 mi. from highway) and down a narrow gorge (CAÑÓN DE AZUFRE), over rough country past LA PALMA (ranch, 20.5 mi.) to SAN CARLOS (28.9 mi.), an old ranch a few miles from the Gulf. All traffic on this road is four-wheel drive.
523.1	8.7	Another series of spectacular curves, Cuesta del Infiernillo (Cuesta Lúcifer). The road drops 1,000 ft. to the desert floor.
525.0	1.9	A side road right up a canyon to LÚCIFER, mining village (0.6 mi.) and on to a manganese mine (1.0 mi.).
529.8	4.8	The road arrives at the Gulf shore, which is followed south. A branch road left goes to Santa María Beach (also known as Biarritz).
534.6	4.8	SANTA ROSALÍA. Sea level. Pop., 5,361 in 1960.

Climate: Pleasant in winter (average temperature, Oct.-May, 71° F.; coldest months, Dec.-Feb.); oppressively hot in summer (average temperature, June-Sep., 87° F.; hottest months, July and Aug.). Average annual rainfall: 4.9 in. See illustration page 145.

Communications: Radio-telegraph service. Land telegraph to San Ignacio, Comondú, and Loreto. Air mail and passenger service.

Hotels: The old company hotel (Hotel Francés) (III) is on the Mesa Norte; it has a good restaurant. Hotel Central (III) is in the center of town near the church.

Bank: Banco Nacional de México (agency).

Recently in a period of decline because of a curtailment in mining activity, Santa Rosalía (locally known as "Cachanilla") was once a prosperous city of over 10,000 inhabitants. It is still the most important commercial center in central Baja California. The town is divided into three sections: "Mesa Norte" (or Mesa Francesa), a plateau on the left side of the arroyo overlooking the port, where the offices and houses of the mining officials are located; "Mesa Sur," a similar elevation on the right bank occupied by Government officials, garrison, etc.; and "La Playa," in the floor of the arroyo, where most of the workers live in company-built houses arranged in depressingly uniform rows. Public buildings include the market, customhouse, church (a galvanized iron structure brought in sections from Europe), municipal palace, a hospital, and a secondary school.

Santa Rosalía came into existence in the 1870's, when copper-bearing ore was discovered in the vicinity. In 1884-85 the holdings of a number of independent miners were bought up by the Boleo Mining Company, a French corporation associated with the Rothschild interests. For a time the company was very prosperous and controlled more than 2,000 square miles of the surrounding country. Yaqui Indians were brought across from Sonora to work in the mines. There was no fresh water in the vicinity, so the company laid a pipeline from the oasis of Santa Águeda, 10 mi. inland (see below). An artificial port was built, as well as a narrow-gauge railway connecting with the mines. The ore was processed in a smelter and then shipped out for refining, at first to Europe and later to Tacoma, Washington. Company ranches were developed in the interior to provide the new city with meat and vegetables, sold in company stores.

During the 1920's the quality of easily mined copper-bearing ore deteriorated to such an extent that the Boleo directors began to consider disposing of their properties, but they could not find a buyer. Production fell off, due not only to the scarcity of good ore but also to the low price of copper on the world market, difficulties with the labor unions, and other reasons. In 1953 the company ceased operations, but two years later a Mexican company resumed operations. Meanwhile a separate corporation (Compañía Minera Lúcifer) had been organized to exploit the manganese deposits in the vicinity. These companies are operating on a much smaller scale than the Boleo in its heyday.

Santa Rosalía, surrounded by barren hills and simmering much of the year in an oppressive heat rarely mitigated by breezes from the Gulf, is not a very picturesque town and has little of interest to the

MINING TOWN OF SANTA ROSALÍA
Looking northwest from the Mesa Sur. See text pages 143-144.

TURTLE CAMP ON LAGUNA SAN IGNACIO
Turtle meat being dried in the sun. See text page 141.

PACK BURROS ON THE ROAD ALONG CONCEPCIÓN BAY
A frequent sight in the peninsula's southern portion. See text page 152.

SHELF ROAD ALONG THE CLIFF ON CONCEPCIÓN BAY
Typical of several miles of the road in this area. See text page 152.

tourist. It does, however, offer a welcome touch of "civilization" to the traveler who arrives by land after the long trip down from Ensenada or up from La Paz.

The principal store is that of Alfonso Nuño Benson. The Pemex gas station is on the main street three blocks up from the plaza, and there are several small garages where limited repairs and spare parts are available.

The airport is 1.5 mi. south of town, on the Mesa Sur, although commercial aircraft use a better field at San Lucas (see page 149). There are boats which run across the Gulf from Santa Rosalía, and it is occasionally possible to ship an automobile to Guaymas, but there is no regular ferry service.

There is a fairly good road inland to the source of Santa Rosalía's water, the old agricultural settlement of Santa Águeda:

Mi. from Sta. Rosalía	Partial Mileage	
0.0	0.0	SANTA ROSALÍA, plaza. Follow the main street up the arroyo out of town past the abandoned Providencia mines. The road leaves the arroyo and climbs to a mesa.
5.4	5.4	Side road enters from left (this is an alternate route from Santa Rosalía via the airport, 7.1 mi. from the plaza). The road climbs down into Arroyo Santa Águeda.
7.3	1.9	EL RANCHITO. An attractive ranch with a small garden and date palms.
8.4	1.1	EL JAPÓN. Ranch.
9.1	0.7	SANTA ÁGUEDA. Site of the Indian ranchería of Guajandeví, and an important visiting station of Mulegé mission in the 1720's. Santa Águeda was a subsistence farming village long before Santa Rosalía came into existence, in fact the "boleo" copper formation was first discovered by a rancher from Santa Águeda, Rosas Villavicencio, in 1868. With the development of the mines it became important as the source of Santa Rosalía's fresh water and much of its food. The water is pumped from a spring above the settlement. It is a pretty little town, with many fruit trees and date and fan palms. The road continues up the arroyo.
13.7	4.6	EL BULE. Ranch with garden.
17.8	4.1	SAN JAVIER. Cattle ranch.
21.2	3.4	EL TAJO. Small cattle ranch.
24.9	3.7	Road junction; keep left. A branch to right goes 3.3 mi. to LA CANDELARIA, cattle ranch at edge of mountains.
25.1	0.2	SANTA ROSA. Cattle ranch with garden and fruit trees.
26.9	1.8	EL RINCÓN. Small ranch at edge of mountains.

ROUTE 6

SANTA ROSALÍA TO LA PAZ

The rugged condition of this route is compensated for by the scenery, as it passes through some of the prettiest towns in the peninsula and runs for many miles along the shore of beautiful Concepción Bay. The last half into La Paz has been graded and partially paved.

Mi. from Sta. Rosalía	Partial Mileage	
0.0	0.0	SANTA ROSALÍA (for description, see page 143). From the plaza a road may be followed along the sea, or a street at a higher level may be taken through the residential district of the Mesa Sur. They soon unite.
1.0	1.0	Junction with road right to airport (0.5 mi.) and alternate route to Santa Águeda (9.8 mi., see page 147).
3.8	2.8	Junction with San Luciano road, to right. The main road goes inland and returns to the sea at
10.1	6.3	BELLAVISTA. A group of ranches on the shallow lagoon of San Lucas. This is a good place to gather oysters from the rocks and mangrove roots at low tide.
11.3	1.2	SAN LUCAS. A fishing and truck farming settlement on the Gulf shore opposite San Marcos Island. The beach, lined with date palms, is fairly good for bathing. There is a landing strip used by large planes.
		The most direct road takes right branch beyond San Lucas, though a more picturesque alternate is the left branch along the beach.
16.0	4.7	SAN BRUNO. A road left here leads to center. A village of fishermen and subsistence farmers. The beach is backed with sand dunes and has excellent bathing. This side road continues, and rejoins the main road at M. 29.0:

	Mi. from M. 16.0	
(0.8)	0.8	SAN BRUNO, school.
(7.3)	8.1	SAN MARCOS. A prosperous dairy ranch and garden near the mouth of Arroyo Magdalena. There is a fresh water lagoon and side road extending to the Gulf (1.1 mi.),

Mi. from Sta. Rosalía	Partial Mileage	Mi. from M. 16.0	

where there is a fine camping spot and a white sand beach. This place, known to the Indians as CAHELCA (big pond), was an important rancheria and visiting station of Mulegé mission in the early 18th century. The road goes inland.

(2.4)   10.5   MEZQUITAL. Palm grove and ruined cattle trough, the site of a short-lived American colonization project in the 1860's. Poor and little-used road with loose sand (1953).

(4.9)   15.4   LA VÍBORA. Cattle ranch.

(2.1)   17.5   Junction with main road at M. 29.0.

16.9   0.9   Road junction, main highway straight ahead. The Magdalena road branches off to the right.

Mi. from junction

(6.3)   6.3   BOCA DE MAGDALENA. Scattered ranches. Crossroads; left to main road (4.3 mi.), straight ahead (0.8) mi.) to ruined MAGDALENA chapel and irrigation works built by the Dominicans in 1774. Turn to right up Arroyo Magdalena:

(4.7)   11.0   SAN JOSÉ DE MAGDALENA. Subsistence farming community, store. The road, rough and rocky, climbs into the mountains, closely following the arroyo.

(5.3)   16.3   Branch road left to SAN ISIDRO.

(9.1)   25.4   LAS MARIOLAS. Goat ranch.

(2.4)   27.8   LAS CRUCES. Cattle ranch.

(1.3)   29.1   Branch road left to SAN JERÓNIMO (2.8 mi., collection of ranches). Keep to right.

(2.5)   31.6   SAN SEBASTIÁN. Elev. 2,400 ft. Cattle ranch, date palms, orchard. From here an interesting excursion can be made on muleback across the mountains to the old mission settlement of GUADALUPE (3-4 hrs., elev. 2,900 ft.). In the arroyo above San Sebastián is the only known stand of *güérivo* trees in this part of the peninsula. This forest was discovered by the Jesuit Padre Juan de Ugarte in 1719. He and his Indians spent four months cutting lumber, which was then hauled down to the beach and made into a stout ship, "El Triunfo de la Cruz," used by Ugarte to explore the upper Gulf. The mission of NUESTRA SEÑORA DE GUADALUPE was founded in 1720 and abandoned in 1795. The stone foundations of the church, built about 1750, can still be seen.

Partial Mileage

22.0   5.1   A cross road; to right goes to Boca de Magdalena (4.3 mi.) etc. (see above).

24.1   2.1   EL POZO DE LA BRECHA. Cattle ranch

Mi. from   Partial
Sta. Rosalía Mileage

29.0   4.9   Junction with La Víbora road, to left (see p. 150, and see also Preface page 12.)

36.3   7.3   Rancho de Chávez, to right. One of several farms established in what was formerly a *cardón* forest.

41.7   5.4   Mulegé. Elev. 25 ft. Estimated 1960 pop. 950. Climate: slightly cooler and dryer than that of Santa Rosalía. Communications: Telegraph to Santa Rosalía and Loreto; mail three times a week to Santa Rosalía and Comondú; airfield for medium planes, with aviation gas tank.

Mulegé is an attractive oasis settlement two miles from the Gulf, on the Arroyo de Santa Rosalía. Dense groves of date palms make a welcome contrast to the surrounding barren country and give the impression of a tropical paradise such as one might expect to find in the South Seas. There is a pervasive atmosphere of ease and tranquility, perhaps due in part to the high occurrence of malaria among the inhabitants (the anopheles mosquito has been destroyed, so this is no longer a danger to the visitor).

The town itself is on a slight elevation on the left bank of the arroyo, a neat compact group of low adobe houses centering on a tiny plaza. Below on all sides are small plots of irrigated land among the date palms, where many kinds of semi-tropical fruits and vegetables are grown. Above the town is a large whitewashed federal prison. The inmates are allowed considerable freedom and may work for wages anywhere in the town. Prisoners rarely want to escape from Mulegé. Across the river, about a half mile up the arroyo, is the mission church of Santa Rosalía de Mulegé, built in 1766 by the Jesuit Padre Escalante and since repaired and remodeled several times. Below the mission is a stone dam and a small lake, the source of Mulegé's irrigation water.

The Jesuits founded the mission of Mulegé in 1705, on the site of an Indian rancheria called Caamanc-ca-galejá. The settlement was ruined by a flood in 1770, but was later restored. The original Indian population of the area, about 2,000, dwindled to less than a hundred in 1782. Mestizo settlers from across the Gulf began to arrive in the 1830's and formed the nucleus of the present population. Mulegé was occupied by American troops for one day, in 1847.

Roads run out to the Gulf along both sides of the estuary, which usually has water enough for small boats to go up to the town. At the mouth of the river on the north side is a tall hill, El Sombrerito, with a lighthouse on top. There are several good bathing beaches.

Hotels: Club Aereo (Loma Linda, I-A), beautifully situated on a terrace on the north side overlooking the mouth of the estuary.

Hacienda de Mulegé (1-B), in the village. Both are patronized by American fishermen who arrive by plane. In 1961 Mulegé Beach Lodge was in operation on the beach with several thatched cabins.

Gasoline is usually available at a store two blocks east of the plaza. Mulegé is a good place to buy *teguas*, shoes made of buckskin.

A side road goes up the arroyo past the mission to EL POTRERO (20.5 mi. from Mulegé), a goat ranch at an elevation of 900 ft. From here old mission trails go across the mountains to Cadejé and La Purísima.

Leaving Mulegé, the main road follows the south bank of the river to its mouth, and then keeps slightly inland and parallel to the coast.

Mi. from Sta. Rosalía	Partial Mileage	
56.0	14.3	A white sand beach (good bathing) on the shore of Bahía Concepción, a broad deep bay 25 mi. long. For the next few miles the road is a narrow track cut into the cliff above the bay, with occasional detours around salt flats (see illustrations p. 146).
57.5	1.5	SANTISPAC. A little cove on the bay, with beaches and mangroves.
60.6	3.1	(At end of a narrow shelf road). To right of the road, near the mouth of a short arroyo, are some petroglyphs on large rocks. Here begins an area of beaches with perfectly clear water, ideal bathing, and camping sites.
62.1	1.5	EL COYOTE. A goat ranch and fishing camp with a good beach and shade trees. Wells of brackish water. The road climbs a steep switchback and loses sight of the bay.
69.3	7.2	EL FRIJOL. Goat ranch, occasionally inhabited. The road returns to the bay.
71.5	2.2	EL REQUESÓN. A small island connected with the mainland at low tide, making a sandy isthmus which is an ideal camping spot. There are several other beaches along the bay south of here, but none as nice as this.
72.3	0.8	ARMENTA. Ranch and fishing camp.
79.0	6.7	CADEJÉ. Site of sometimes occupied goat and cattle ranch. (See also Preface page 12.)
82.6	3.6	A branch road left crosses the tidal flats on the south shore of Bahía Concepción to SANTA ROSALILLITA (5.2 mi., cattle ranch) and junction with the main road at M. 88.1 (6.8 mi.). This branch is impassable after rains. The right branch loses sight of the bay.

Mi. from Sta. Rosalía	Partial Mileage	
87.4	4.8	LA TRAVESÍA, goat ranch.
88.1	0.7	Junction with road to Santa Rosalillita, left, 1.6 mi. (see above). Beyond here the road crosses a low ridge with a dense growth of giant *cardón* cactus.
95.7	7.6	AÑO NUEVO. Ranch.
96.5	0.8	EL ROSARITO. Cattle and goat ranch, with a well of good water. A branch road left connects with the Canipolé-Loreto road (see below), 5.6 mi.
100.0	3.5	CANIPOLÉ. Cattle ranch. Good water and meals, and

often gasoline, are obtainable.

From here there is a branch road left to Loreto and beyond:

Mi. from Canipolé	Partial Mileage	
4.4	(4.4)	Road enters from EL ROSARITO, left (see above).
5.0	(0.6)	BOMBEDOR. Cattle ranch.
8.7	(3.7)	LA LUZ. Ranch.
12.1	(3.4)	SANTA ROSA. Cattle ranch. Between here and Arroyo de San Pedro the road crosses the Llano de San Juan, a dry lake bed covered most of the year with soft, fine dust, turning into a quagmire after a rain.
18.0	(5.9)	ARROYO DE SAN PEDRO. Cattle ranch.
20.1	(2.1)	SAN JUAN BAUTISTA LONDÓ. A small farming and cattle-raising community on Arroyo San Bruno. There is a ruined stone chapel built by the Jesuits about 1705, when San Juan was an important visiting station of Loreto mission. The place was discovered by Father Kino and Admiral Atondo in 1683, used by them as a cattle ranch, and rediscovered by Father Salvatierra in 1699. To the southwest looms the mountain mass of La Giganta, 5,800 ft. high, so named from its shape of a reclining giantess. There is a mule trail across the mountains from San Juan to Comondú, using a pass north of La Giganta.
21.1	(1.0)	LA ENVIDIA. Cattle ranch. Branch road right to another ranch, EL DESCANSO.
23.2	(2.1)	RENTOY. Cattle ranch.
23.6	(0.4)	Alternate branch road left to BUENA VISTA (see below).
27.0	(3.4)	Branch road left to BUENA VISTA (4.9 mi.), where there is a road to the white sand beach (excellent bathing). Another branch is passable as far as EL CABALLO (1.8 mi. from Buena Vista). One mi. further, by trail, are the ruins of SAN BRUNO on a hill overlooking the sea. This was the site of one of the Spaniards' unsuccessful attempts to colonize Baja California. In 1683 the famed Jesuit Padre Eusebio Francisco Kino and Admiral Atondo, with 200 colonists, landed here and chose San Bruno as their capital. The remains of the triangular fort, chapel,

Mi. from   Partial
Canipolé   Mileage

houses, etc., can still be seen. After 19 months of precarious existence the colony was abandoned in 1685.

40.0   (13.0)   LORETO. Elev., sea level. Estimated pop. in 1960: 1600. Climate: cool and windy in winter (average temperature Nov.-Apr., 69° F.; coldest months, Jan.-Feb.); warm in summer (average temperature May-Oct., 86° F.; warmest months, June-Oct.). Average annual rainfall: 5.0 in. Communications: Radio telegraph; land telegraph to Comondú and Santa Rosalía; air mail service. The landing strip, just north of town, is long enough for heavy planes.

The capital of California for 132 years, then almost abandoned for a century, Loreto is now a rather progressive little community with more life than any other town in the central section. It is built around the mouth of Arroyo de las Parras, which occasionally brings flood waters down from the mountains. The peninsular range is quite close to the Gulf, and forms an impressive backdrop of jagged peaks.

Fronting on the Loreto plaza is the municipal palace (mayor's office, post office), while behind the palace is the church of Nuestra Señora de Loreto. This consists of a central nave with choir loft, and separate wings for the baptistry, sacristy, and a chapel. The oldest bells in the tower date from 1743. What was originally the mission quadrangle is now a government school. The church was completed in 1752. Much damaged by earthquakes, notably in 1877 when the tower collapsed, it has been extensively remodeled and practically rebuilt in recent years.

Loreto was the first permanent Spanish settlement in California, selected by the Jesuit Padre Juan María Salvatierra for the site of his capital in 1697. During the next 70 years the Jesuits, using Loreto as a center of operations, explored most of the peninsula and founded 19 more missions. From Loreto the Jesuits were expelled in 1768, and in the following year the Franciscans left from here on their land expedition which led to the settling of Upper California. During all this period Loreto was the center of Government and residence of the Father Superior of the missions. Between the church and the Gulf shore was the garrison (presidio) and soldiers' suburb, and beyond this on the beach were the shipyards and sailors' houses. The town was practically wiped out in a hurricane in 1829, after which the capital was moved to La Paz and Loreto dwindled into oblivion. Its recent revival is due to the transfer of municipal offices from Comondú, and a growth in the tourist industry.

Along the sea front is a cement walk (malecón) much frequented by the inhabitants on warm evenings. On Sunday nights there is usually an informal dance in the plaza.

Hotels: A mile south of the plaza is the Flying Sportsman Lodge (I-B), operated by Americans, with swimming pool, bar, and food flown in from the United States.

The guest house of Doña Blanca de Garayzar, across the street from the church, has clean accommodations, bath, and excellent food (III). (See Preface p. 13.)

There are several stores and a gasoline pump. Small clinic with resident doctor.

South of Loreto a little-traveled road runs along the Gulf shore to LIGÜÍ:

Mi. from   Partial
Loreto   Mileage
3.6   (3.6)   Branch road right to PRIMER AGUA (4.3 mi.), a prosperous farm originally developed by the missionaries as a garden to supply Loreto.

Mi. from Loreto	Partial Mileage	
5.4	(1.8)	Bonó. Nearby is an old stone reservoir, probably built by the Jesuits. A branch road right goes to Zacatal (1.5 mi.), an experiment in irrigating from wells.
7.7	(2.3)	Nopoló. Site of occasionally occupied goat ranch. At left (other side of salt flat) at Punta Nopoló, is an excellent beach for swimming. The road climbs a very steep grade and returns to the beach at
10.9	(3.2)	Notrí. Goat ranch. The road south of here climbs along a cliff high above the Gulf, with very steep grades. This section should not be attempted except in a vehicle with extra-low gear and good brakes.
14.3	(3.4)	Juncalito. A subsistence farming and fishing settlement.
14.7	(0.4)	Chuenque. Ranch. This place was once an important Indian rancheria, and there are some stone foundations which are probably the ruins of a Jesuit visiting station.
17.2	(2.5)	Puerto Escondido. Cattle ranch. A branch road extends left 0.8 mi. to Puerto Escondido, a snug little harbor for small boats (see p. 208) and a good campsite.
18.0	(0.8)	Tripuí. Fishermen's shacks.
19.9	(1.9)	Tecomajá. Abandoned ranch. Very poor road to
22.9	(3.0)	Ligüí. Now a run-down cattle ranch, this place is the site of the mission of San Juan Bautista de Ligüí, founded in 1705 by the Jesuits. It was too exposed to raids of the hostile Pericú Indians, and too arid to be fit for a mission site, and was abandoned in 1721. The ruins of the chapel can scarcely be seen. There is a fairly good beach. Old mission trails go from here across the mountains to San Luis Gonzaga and along the coast to Los Dolores.

A road crosses the mountains from Loreto to the main highway near Santo Domingo del Pacífico.

Mi. from Loreto	Partial Mileage	
0.0	(0.0)	Loreto. Head past the church toward and into the mountains.
9.2	(9.2)	Cuevas Pintas. Ranch (uninhabited in 1961). Across the arroyo are some prehistoric rock paintings. The road climbs up the canyon (Arroyo de las Parras) with fairly steep grades.
9.6	(0.4)	La Venta. Goat ranch.
11.7	(2.1)	Las Parras. Attractive little farm in a steep canyon, with an orchard irrigated from a small spring.
13.0	(1.3)	Divide between the Gulf and Pacific drainage slopes, elev. 1,700 ft. Behind is a fine view of the Gulf, with Isla de Carmen directly opposite Loreto. To the north is a sugarloaf peak, Pilón de las Parras. The road descends gradually into the upper basin of Arroyo Santo Domingo.
16.7	(3.7)	Rancho Viejo, now a small cattle ranch, the original site of the mission of San Javier (see below).

Mi. from Loreto	Partial Mileage	
17.7	(1.0)	Side road goes via PUERTA VIEJA (ranch 10.4 mi.), a grade (summit 13.4 mi. from junction), and LLANO DE SAN JULIO (dry lake, 21.7 mi.) to SAN JOSÉ DE COMONDÚ (28.2 mi. from junction, see pp. 157-58).
19.3	(1.6)	EL HORNO. Cattle ranch.
22.2	(2.9)	SAN JAVIER. Elev. 1,020 ft. A small agricultural settlement dependent upon a tiny spring ½ mile above the town, which is used to irrigate several acres of fruit trees and vegetables. The mission of San Francisco Javier de Vigge was first founded at Rancho Viejo in 1699 by Padre Francisco María Piccolo, S.J. The present site was developed as a visiting station and garden by Padre Juan de Ugarte in 1707, and the mission headquarters was moved here about 1720.

The impressive stone church, of simple Moorish style, was begun in 1744 and finished in 1758. It is the best-preserved and finest Jesuit church in Baja California. To the left of the entrance is a baptistry, and to the right a spiral staircase to the choir loft and bell tower. Two of the bells bear the date of 1761, and the third 1803. The stone work and ornamentation is remarkable. There are two small lateral chapels. The gilded *altar mayor* with its statue of St. Francis was brought in 32 boxes from Mexico City. Behind the altar are four large rooms arranged in two stories, and off to one side are two more rooms intended for missionaries' quarters. Behind the church are extensive gardens and two stone reservoirs built by the Jesuits and still in use. Above looms a great black cliff dwarfing the tiny settlement (see illustration p. 163).

The houses are arranged in two neat rows before the church and between the dry arroyo and a single irrigation ditch. There are many kinds of fruit trees, but the chief harvest is of olives. There are several venerable old olive trees said to have been planted from seed by the Jesuits.

On the Saint's feast day (December 3) hundreds of ranchers come to San Javier, some of them traveling a week or more on muleback across rough mountain trails.

The road continues down Arroyo Santo Domingo:

	Partial Mileage	
23.6	(1.4)	SEGUNDO PASO. Ranch.
24.7	(1.1)	EL RANCHITO. Trail left to LOS DOLORES (1.5 mi.), formerly a visiting station of San Javier mission, now a small agricultural center producing wheat and figs.
26.9	(2.2)	PRESA VIEJA. Cattle ranch.
28.8	(1.9)	AGUA ESCONDIDA. Cattle ranch and garden.
32.5	(3.7)	SANTO DOMINGO. A pool of water surrounded by fan palms.
33.3	(0.8)	LA PRESENTACIÓN (uninhabited). Off the road to the right are the ruins of a stone chapel and a large stone reservoir, probably built by the Franciscan Fr. Palou about 1769.
35.3	(2.0)	POZA DE TERESA. Ranch.
41.2	(5.9)	PALO BLANCO. Ranch.
48.8	(7.6)	SAN IGNACIO. Cattle ranch.

Mi. from Loreto	Partial Mileage	
51.3	(2.5)	LA BAJADA. Ranch.
55.3	(4.0)	LAS PIEDRAS. Stone ruins of former ranch. A little beyond here the road enters the flat coastal plain.
67.5	(12.2)	Junction with main highway at M. 189.3, 1.7 mi. below Santo Domingo junction (see p. 166).

Leaving Canipolé (M. 100.0) the main road crosses a low divide (elev. 1,000 ft.) and enters the Pacific slope.

Mi. from Sta. Rosalía	Partial Mileage	
107.9	7.9	Road fork. The shortest route to La Paz, via Comondú, is to the left. An alternate route (11.7 mi. longer) via La Purísima is to the right. Both are bad roads, impassable after a heavy rain. That via Comondú is characterized by a surface of sharp lava rock, very hard on tires, while the Purísima road has some bad stream crossings. In spite of these drawbacks both roads offer some of the most pleasant scenery on the trip. See illustration page 164.

The route VIA COMONDÚ follows here: (For the route via La Purísima see page 159).

From Sta. Rosalía via Comondú	Partial Mileage	
115.4	7.5	SAN JUAN (COMONDÚ VIEJO). Cattle ranch to the right.
116.5	1.1	COMONDÚ VIEJO (uninhabited). Original site of the mission of San José de Comondú, founded by Padre Mayorga in 1708. It was moved 24 mi. south (see below) about 1737. Ruins of irrigation works and a stone chapel may be seen a few yards from the road.
117.0	0.5	LA PRESA. Ranch off road to left.
117.8	0.8	CAMBALAQUIÓ. Deserted ranch and a water hole, to right. The road crosses a broad plain and climbs the MEZQUITITO grade (summit elev. 1,900 ft.) to the great lava plateau which covers the central part of the peninsula.
123.7	5.9	SAN ANTONIO. Deserted corral and water hole in a steep canyon.
132.1	8.4	Landing strip for light planes, to left.
138.2	6.1	SAN JOSÉ COMONDÚ. Elev. 1,530 ft. Estimated pop.

in 1960: 350. An attractive subsistence farming community in the bottom of a precipitous canyon, surrounded by barren lava mesas. The valley floor is a narrow ribbon of verdure 7 mi. long fed by several springs, which provide enough water to irrigate some 700 acres of rich soil. Figs, raisins, dates, and sugar cane are the principal crops. The complete isolation of the place, and the friendly, easy-going attitude of its inhabitants, give it a sort of Shangri-La character, while the groves of date palms and the whitewashed adobe houses clustered at the foot of great frowning cliffs form a tremendously picturesque scene.

Travelers usually arrive at the home of Doña María de Verdugo, where cots and meals are available. Gasoline and supplies are sold at a general store.

Next to the tiny plaza is the site of Comondú mission, moved here from Comondú Viejo about 1737. The mission church, built in the 1750's, was torn down to make room for a school, but the missionaries' house is still standing and is now used as a chapel.

The road from San José de Comondú to San Javier, 32.7 mi. (see p. 156), leaves San José from the northeast and climbs out of the canyon to a mesa.

The main road follows the left side of the arroyo, past a continuous succession of small farms, to:

From Sta.
Rosalía via   Partial
Comondú   Mileage

140.0   1.8   SAN MIGUEL COMONDÚ, on a side road to the right, across the river. Estimated pop. in 1960: 370. Communications: Telephone to Loreto, La Purísima and Santa Rosalía; telegraph; mail 3 times a week to Santa Rosalía. A more compact and modern-looking town than its neighbor San José, but in fact an even older settlement, San Miguel was developed in 1714 by Padre Juan de Ugarte as a visiting station, cattle ranch, and garden of San Javier mission (see above). Ugarte brought 160,000 mule-loads of earth to fill in the Cañada de Aranjuez, which enters from the east opposite the town, and planted sugar cane, grapevines, and fruit trees. In 1730 San Miguel became a separate mission, and in 1737 it was annexed as a *pueblo* to the mission of Comondú. After the Indians disappeared the place was deserted until comparatively recent years, when it was resettled by mestizo colonists (see illustration page 163). There are several stores, a plaza, and a small chapel. The road continues down Arroyo Comondú, a spectacular drive with great cliffs towering above.

From Sta.
Rosalía via   Partial
Comondú   Mileage

140.8   0.8   CASAS VIEJAS. Ranch and garden.

141.7   0.9   SANTA BRÍGIDA. Ranch and garden. This is the last point where water is usually found flowing in the arroyo.

From Sta. Rosalía via Comondú	Partial Mileage	
146.1	4.4	PIEDRAS RODADAS. An old ranch with some adobe ruins and a good spring of water. The verdure of Comondú is left behind.
154.4	8.3	A branch right is short cut back to La Purísima.
158.1	3.7	Connection right with road via La Purísima.

The route from M. 107.9, VIA LA PURÍSIMA, as mentioned on page 157, follows here:

From Sta. Rosalía via Purísima	Partial Mileage	
107.9	0.0	Road follows Arroyo de la Purísima, here normally dry, past several occasionally inhabited goat ranch sites. Those listed below were the principal inhabited sites in 1961:
112.9	5.0	CORRAL DE DOS PUERTAS. Small ranch.
113.5	0.6	CALAGUÁ. Small ranch.
114.0	0.5	PALO VERDE. Small ranch.
123.5	9.5	EL GUARISMO. Ranch on side road left, ca. 2 mi. (not visited by authors).
124.6	1.1	OJO DE AGUA, large spring across canyon to left. It forms a stream which maintains a constant flow to below La Purísima, collecting at intervals in deep pools.
125.1	0.5	OJO DE AGUA. Group of ranches, with an adobe chapel.
125.6	0.5	LAS MOCHILLAS. First of three ranches so named, extending for 0.3 mi.
127.5	1.9	LOS PANALES. Another community of ranches.
128.3	0.8	The first of seven shallow fords across the flowing creek.
131.6	3.3	HUERTA VIEJA. Several springs coming out of the cliffside irrigate an old orchard of orange trees.
133.9	2.3	Seventh and last of the fords across the creek.
134.5	0.6	EL ZACATÓN. A dam, the beginning of San Isidro's irrigation system.
135.7	1.2	LAS PAREDES. Group of ranches.
136.8	1.1	EL CARAMBUCHE (EL CONCHAL). A suburb of San Isidro. School.
136.9	0.1	Branch road right across river, to PURÍSIMA VIEJA (16.0 mi., first site of mission of La Purísima); PASO HONDO

From Sta.
Rosalía via   Partial
Purísima   Mileage

(19.4 mi., collection of ranches); SAN JOSÉ DE LOS ARCE (22.3 mi., another small oasis of farms and goat ranches). From San José, the end of the road, a trail continues across the mountains to Mulegé.

138.1   1.2   SAN ISIDRO (LA COLONIA). Estimated pop. in 1960: 650. Communications: Government telephone to Comondú; mail weekly. A pleasant little farming community on the edge of a bluff overlooking the river. It is a new town which came into being in the 1930's as the result of a Government irrigation project. Here the valley of La Purísima spreads out to a width of ½ mile, intensely cultivated, with many varieties of fruit trees, date palms, etc. On the north side of the river, between San Isidro and La Purísima, is the conspicuous hat-shaped mountain of El Pilón, actually a piece of the surrounding mesa detached by erosion.

Gasoline is sold at a general store. Excellent meals may be obtained at the home of Doña Anicia de Meza, across from the school.

North of the river, on the road to Purísima Vieja, is a landing strip which can be used by light planes.

From Sta.
Rosalía via   Partial
Purísima   Mileage

140.6   2.5   LA PURÍSIMA. Elev. ca. 600 ft. Estimated pop. in 1960: 500. Communications: Government telephone to Comondú. Mail once a week to Santa Rosalía. Climate: cool in winter (average temperature Nov.-Apr., 65° F.; coldest months, Dec.-Mar.); pleasant in summer (average temperature May-Oct., 78° F.; warmest months, July-Sep.). Average annual rainfall: 1.9 in.

The town is on the left bank of the arroyo, opposite a dam. Just above the dam are the ruins of the mission of La Purísima Concepción de Cadegomo, an unrecognizable mound of adobe. The original site of the mission was Purísima Vieja (see above), but headquarters was moved here in the 1730's. The Indian population shrank from 2,000 in 1730, to 54 in 1800. In 1822 the last missionary died, and the place was deserted for several years before being repopulated by settlers from across the Gulf. La Purísima is not as attractive a town as San Isidro, and the water is bad. There are several stores, and gasoline is generally available.

Continuing down the arroyo, the road leaves the date groves and traverses a more familiar desert landscape. Water is not found except in scattered pools below La Purísima. There is a short airstrip just below the town, but the field near San Isidro is longer and in better condition.

From Sta. Rosalía via Purísima	Partial Mileage	
144.8	4.2	The road up the Pacific coast to San Ignacio via San Juanico (see pages 141-42) continues ahead down the arroyo. The main road turns left and climbs the canyon side to a broad mesa.
152.5	7.7	EL PORTÓN. The road passes through a conspicuous break in the plateau. A branch road right goes down to the sea at LAS BARRANCAS (8.8 mi.), where there is a fishing shack and a good beach.
160.9	8.4	EL PABELLÓN. Cattle ranch off the road to left.
167.8	6.9	Short cut left to road back through Comondú.
169.8	2.0	Connection with Comondú road at M. 158.1.

NOTE: TOTAL MILEAGES below are given VIA COMONDÚ. (If route was taken via La Purísima, add 11.7 mi.).

Mi. from Sta. Rosalía	Partial Mileage	
158.1	......	Junction of road via Comondú with that via La Purísima.
165.3	7.2	Fork in road. Straight ahead (right) is old main road:

Mi. from M. 165.3		
(2.7)	2.7	POZA GRANDE. A struggling little farming community. Meals can be obtained. From here to Santo Domingo the old road is a loose sandy type, difficult for narrow tread vehicles.
(0.3)	3.0	Branch road right to SAN JORGE (6.5 mi.), a fishing camp at the north end of a long lagoon running down to Magdalena Bay.
(6.1)	9.1	LOS ANGELES. Cattle ranch.
(3.7)	12.8	MÉDANO BLANCO. Cattle ranch.
(12.0)	24.8	SANTO DOMINGO (see below).

The left branch at M. 165.3 is the new highway being built from La Paz to the north. Just south of here this becomes a broad, crushed rock road, perfectly straight and well graded, but with a "wash-board" surface making it quite rough. This road is gradually being paved out of La Paz.

187.6   22.3   Junction for SANTO DOMINGO (DEL PACÍFICO). Village is 2.1 mi. to right. Estimated 1960 pop. 500. Communications: Air mail once a week to La Paz; Army radio. A dusty, windswept, bleak collection of shacks, Santo Domingo is at the northern edge of an important farming area developed since 1940. Several thousand acres are irrigated from wells and planted to wheat, alfalfa, cotton, and other crops. In 1942 the colony of MARÍA AUXILIADORA was established at Santo Domingo by the Sinarquistas, a militant religious (Roman Catholic) group allied with the Spanish Falange. Some 400 destitute peasants from central Mexico were brought here, but only a few families remain. Later other groups of colonists were brought over by the Government and a number of coöperative farming colonies have been formed, extending about 60 mi. south along the Magdalena Plain. The colonists are given land, water, farming implements, and government loans.

Gasoline, supplies, and meals are usually available in Santo Domingo.

The old highway leaves Santo Domingo from the south. In some ways it is a pleasanter and less monotonous route than the new road, but is considerably longer. There are several branch roads connecting the two roads. Inquiry should be made in Santo Domingo before using the old road, as there is little through traffic and parts may be impassable. Furthermore, as new land is cultivated, old roads are often rerouted or closed. The following log of the old road was made in 1953. (For the new highway see pages 165-68).

Old Road From Sto. Domingo	Partial Mileage	
0.0	(0.0)	Old road angles toward new highway and crosses to the east of it.
9.2	(9.2)	QUERÉTARO. Agricultural colony. A little south of here the old road recrosses to the west of the new highway.
30.2	(21.0)	BUENA VISTA. Formerly a cattle ranch, now a supply center for the colonists.
43.8	(13.6)	CERVATILLO. Abandoned ranch off to right. A branch road cuts back to the northwest to RAMADITA (18.1 mi. from fork), SANTA MARTA (18.8 mi.), and MATANCITA (21.4 mi.). The last place, now a nondescript group of shacks clustered around a garden and orchard, was once the headquarters of the Lower California Company, a group of American speculators who in 1866 obtained from the Mexican Government a grant of 46,800 sq. mi. (about 5/6 of the peninsula). In 1870-71 three shiploads of American colonists arrived in this area. They were inadequately prepared and the colony was a dismal failure. The grant was annulled in 1871, although an extension was allowed to collect orchilla, a parasitic plant from which dye was extracted. Later the company turned to cattle-raising, but the concession was finally expropriated during the Mexican Revolution.

Beyond Matancita two little-used roads run down to the shore of the lagoon north of Magdalena Bay, at SAN CARLOS (15.5

THE PERFECTLY PRESERVED JESUIT MISSION CHURCH AT SAN JAVIER
See text page 156.

CHILDREN OF COMONDÚ
Notice the variation in racial types. See text pages 157-158.

A SECTION OF LA PURÍSIMA CANYON
The road is rocky, with several stream crossings. See text pages 157, 159.

THE ATTRACTIVE LA PRESA RANCH
At the edge of the mountains north of La Paz. See text page 167.

Old Road From Sto. Domingo	Partial Mileage	
		mi.) and La Florida (12.0 mi.), fishing camps (deserted in 1952).
53.7	(9.9)	El Refugio. A collection of ranches. A branch road left to new highway at M. 233.5 (ca. 12 mi., see p. 167). Another road to the right goes to Médano Amarillo on the shore of Magdalena Bay (13.7 mi; see p. 200).
64.0	(10.3)	Side road right to Estero Salinas (9.5) mi.).
80.0	(16.0)	El Médano. A collection of cattle ranches.
81.0	(1.0)	Branch road right, to Bahía Almejas, an extension of Magdalena Bay:

Mi. from fork

0.2	Laguna Verde. Cattle ranch off road to right.
3.7	La Salada. There is a landing field suitable for medium planes, and a ruined adobe fort, built during World War II when a battalion of the Mexican Army was stationed here.
7.8	Side road left back to the main road (4.9 mi.).
8.0	Side road left to El Dátil (3.2 mi.), a fishing camp.
10.6	Puerto Chale. A fishing camp on a brackish estuary emptying into Almejas Bay.

83.9	(2.9)	Branch road right, connecting with the road to Puerto Chale.
105.5	(21.6)	Venancio. Ranch.
108.8	(3.3)	Santa Fe.
119.5	(10.7)	Guadalupe. Ranch. Just beyond Guadalupe the road reaches the coast, which it follows for the next 25 mi. There are several fine beaches near the road.
124.2	(4.7)	Datilar.
132.6	(8.4)	Punta Conejo.
135.4	(2.8)	Santa Ana (La Vieja).
138.7	(3.3)	La Ballena.
143.2	(4.5)	La Aguja, off road to left.
145.9	(2.7)	El Cedro.
147.7	(1.8)	Arroyo Seco. Here the road leaves the beach and turns inland across the low peninsular divide. A side road, very faint, runs down the beach to Cuñaño, a cattle ranch.
169.7	(22.0)	Junction with new highway, 21.7 mi. from La Paz.

The new highway from Santo Domingo to La Paz keeps farther inland than the old road just described. The first part of the trip on the new highway is very monotonous, a perfectly straight road across the flat Magdalena Plain. The last half is more interesting as the road passes through low hills forming a watershed between the Pacific and the Gulf.

187.6 ...... SANTO DOMINGO junction.

189.3 1.7 (Km. 265) Road left to Loreto (67.5 mi.) via San Javier (45.3 mi.). (See pp. 155-57).

The highway continues past many clearings and agricultural settlements on the broad desert plain, with many dirt roads branching off. Only the larger of these settlements are included below.

191.5 2.2 COLONIA PURÍSIMA. Store.

194.8 3.3 Road right to COLONIA MARÍA AUXILIADORA (see page 162).

197.5 2.7 COLONIA ALVAREZ. Store.

206.7 9.2 COLONIA DE LA TOBA. Store, wireless telegraph station, cotton gin.

218.0 11.3 In April, 1961, the pavement northward from La Paz had reached this point, ca. Km. 219 from La Paz.

218.2 0.2 Branch roads, west (not traveled by authors) to Matancita (see page 162), and east to San Luis Gonzaga. The latter rejoins the highway at Pénjamo. (A better way reach San Luis Gonzaga is from M. 234.5, see page 167). The following was logged in 1953:

Partial   Mi. from
Mileage   M. 218.2

(3.5) 3.5 (Approx. This stretch from the highway to Palo Bola has not been traveled by authors). PALO BOLA. Agricultural center. The road surface for some miles beyond here is a very fine, soft dust except after a rain, when it would be impassable.

(5.4) 8.9 LAS LAGUNITAS. Cattle ranch.

(3.5) 12.4 SAN BERNARDO. Small farm.

(2.0) 14.4 VELÁZQUEZ. Ranch.

(2.1) 16.5 LAS DELICIAS. Congregation of ranches and gardens.

(5.7) 22.2 EL IGUAJIL. Ranch.

(0.8) 23.0 EL TORRE. Ranch.

(3.9) 26.9 EL RANCHITO. Goat ranch.

(1.8) 28.7 A road right via EL TORO to new highway, 19.2 mi., at M. 234.5.

(4.8) 33.5 SAN LUIS GONZAGA. One of the original Jesuit missions; an attractive little oasis in the midst of some of the most barren and forbidding country in the peninsula. It consists of a grove of date and fan palms below a tiny spring. The mission garden, irrigated by a masonry dam, produces figs, oranges, grapes, mangos, and other fruits and vegetables. There is a small stone church built by Padre

Baegert in the 1750's, still in good condition. Behind is a churchyard, and about 200 yards farther on are some old Indian graves. San Luis, known to the Indians as *Chiriyaki*, was founded in 1737 to convert the tribes of the Magdalena Plain and establish a mission station near Magdalena Bay, intended as a port for the Manila galleon. There were once about 2,000 Indians in the area; when the mission was closed in 1768 only 300 Indians remained. In later years San Luis was a way-station for travelers on the trail from Loreto to the Cape Region, and it is still a supply point for the surrounding ranches. There is a large store and an abandoned barracks, later used as a school. On the north side of the arroyo is a landing field long enough for heavy planes.

Partial Mileage	Mi. from M. 218.2	
(5.7)	39.2	EL PLÁTANO. Another small oasis, with date and fan palms and a garden.
(6.6)	45.8	IRITÚ. An abandoned ranch off the road to left.
(0.7)	46.5	Road fork. The main road keeps to the right, while a little-used branch goes left up the Arroyo de la Pasión to LA PRESA (13.0 mi.), an attractive ranch with palm grove and about 15 acres planted to corn, beans and alfalfa (see illustration p. 164).
		A trail goes from here across the mountains to Los Dolores, on the Gulf. Two mi. above La Presa is the ruined stone chapel of LA PASIÓN, where the Jesuits founded a mission in 1737. There are several springs in the arroyo, which is dammed to form a small pond. The mission was closed in 1768 and its Indians moved to Todos Santos.
(0.4)	46.9	A side road left connects with the La Presa road. The main road heads south along the base of the mountains.
(2.4)	49.3	LAS TINAJITAS. Goat ranch and landing field.
(4.2)	53.5	EL OBISPO. Cattle and goat ranch.
(6.5)	60.0	LA PUNTA DEL CERRO. Goat ranch, off to left.
(13.1)	73.1	EL PILAR. A congregation of houses in an oasis with a palm grove. A vineyard is irrigated from a small spring.
(10.8)	83.9	Joins main highway near PÉNJAMO, at M. 284.9.

On main highway below M. 218.2:

New Road Mi. from Sta. Rosalía	Partial Mileage	
223.3	5.1	EL CRUCERO (VILLA CONSTITUCIÓN). Estimated pop. in 1960: 2,000. A bustling new supply center for the agricultural colonies in the vicinity. There are numerous stores and restaurants, a hotel (III), two gasoline pumps, and a paved airstrip.
233.5	10.2	Side road right to El Refugio, ca. 12 mi. (see p. 165).
234.5	1.0	Road left is most direct route to old mission San Luis Gonzaga. This goes via COLONIA SANTA FE (3.2 mi.)

New Road Mi. from Sta. Rosalía	Partial Mileage	
		and EL TORO (ranch, 4.9 mi., take right branch) to SAN LUIS GONZAGA (24.0 mi., see pp. 166-67).
238.9	4.4	EL COYOTE, ranch. Here the cultivated fields, irrigated from deep wells in the Magdalena Plain, are replaced by arid country which extends to La Paz.
240.7	1.8	EL IMPOSIBLE. Ranch.
256.2	15.5	SANTA RITA. A group of ranches and a restaurant.
274.9	18.7	BUENAVENTURA. Ranch.
283.6	8.7	LAS POCITAS, cattle ranch.
284.8	1.2	PÉNJAMO. There is a restaurant with kerosene refrigerator (cold beer). Gasoline is sometimes available. Side road right (not traveled by authors) to Santa Fe and the beach. Ahead 0.1 mi. is connecting road from left via San Luis Gonzaga (see page 167). The highway now begins to wind through hills.
291.5	6.7	KM. 100. There is a house built by the Government to accommodate travelers but it is not so used. A side road goes left to the old farming community of SAN HILARIO, developed as a mission garden by the Jesuits.
303.7	12.2	Side road right (not traveled by authors) to the beach at Punta Conejo.
306.1	2.4	SAN AGUSTÍN (Km. 77). Roadside store.
332.3	26.2	VIRGEN MARÍA, restaurant. The old highway (see page 165) comes in from the right. Just beyond here the highway begins dropping down to the Gulf, with spectacular views of La Paz Bay, offshore islands, and the Cape Region mountains.
337.3	5.0	Side road left (not traveled by authors) said to reach San Juan ranch on the Gulf coast.
344.7	7.4	LAS HAMACAS (LOS ARIPES). Ranch on the shore of Ensenada de los Aripes, a shallow extension of La Paz Bay. To the left a side road comes in from Rodríguez (see page 174). From here into La Paz the highway follows the shore.
354.0	9.3	LA PAZ. Sea level. Population in 1960: 23,324.

Climate: Cool and windy in winter (average temperature, Dec.-Apr., 66.4° F.; coldest months, Dec.-Feb.); warm in summer (average temperature, May-Nov., 78.7° F.; hottest months, July-Sep.). Average rainfall: 5.5 in., most of which falls from Aug. to Dec. During the winter there are periods of two or three cloudy days in a row, with cold north winds blowing off the Gulf. Summer days are warm, sometimes oppressively so, but there is nearly always a cool evening breeze (known locally as the *coromuel*) off the land. July to October is the season for tropical hurricanes *(chubascos)* from the south, but these are usually confined to September, and sometimes several years go by without a hurricane. The weather is most apt to be perfect in November, April, and May. The best time for deep-sea fishing is spring and summer.

Communications: There is direct radio-phone and radio-telegraph service between La Paz and the United States and elsewhere. Government telephone to all the towns in the Cape Region south of La Paz. Daily air mail service.

Hotels: Los Cocos (I-A), 1½ mi. from town, swimming pool, boat jetty. Guaycura (I-B), at the edge of town on main road to north, swimming pool. Los Arcos (I-B), on the waterfront, pleasant patio. Perla (II-A), large and modern, outdoor dining terrace facing the sunsets. Misión (II-A), on the waterfront. Quinta Dorita (II-B), on a hill above the bay. Yéneka (II-B), in center of town.

The best restaurants are in the hotels; also Flamingo's Drive-in, Bahía, Intimo.

"El Bucanero" is a night club in a palm grove on the beach just southwest of town. Music and sea food are the attractions.

Banks: Banco Nacional de México and Banco de Londres y México have branches in La Paz. "La Perla de la Paz" (Ruffo's store) also has banking facilities.

Hospitals: There is a fairly well-equipped municipal hospital, Hospital Salvatierra. There are several doctors, dentists, etc. Fees are substantially less than in the United States.

The principal merchants are the Ruffo brothers, owners of "La Perla de la Paz," a combination of a department store, bank, garage, and other facilities. Librería Arámburo, on the plaza, carries most American and Mexican magazines. San Diego and Mexico City newspapers are brought in daily by plane. There are several local newspapers.

La Paz is the capital and largest town of the Territorio Sur, comprising the southern half of Baja California. It is attractively spread out on a series of low bluffs along the shallow Ensenada de los Aripes, protected from the open Gulf by a long sandspit known as El Mogote, which comes to an end just opposite the town.

Although in a way it is a typical Mexican provincial capital, La Paz has an atmosphere all its own. The older part of the town, at the mouth of an arroyo (now a street, Avenida 16 de Septiembre), is a hodgepodge of crooked lanes covered by graceful shade trees. The favorite promenade is the *malecón,* a concrete walk along the beach lined with coconut palms (see illustration p. 181). Above the arroyo on a low hill is the plaza, with the Government Palace on one side and the Church (built 1861-65) opposite. Everywhere are countless windmills and attractive patios.

The town of La Paz is not very old, but its site was one of the first places visited by Spaniards. Fortún Ximénez, a pilot of one of Hernán Cortés' ships, was killed by Indians at or near La Paz about 1533. Cortés himself spent some time on the shore of La Paz Bay in 1535 trying to found a colony. For the next 185 years the place was visited many times by Spanish pearl-hunters and expeditions sent out by the viceroy to colonize California, but none of these colonies lasted more than a few months. It was not until 1720 that a mission, Nuestra Señora del Pilar de la Paz, was founded here by the Jesuit Padres Jaime Bravo and Juan de Ugarte. The site of the mission church, of which no trace remains, was probably near the present Government Palace overlooking the bay. The Indians were practically wiped out in a series of epidemics, and the mission was abandoned about 1749. Later the harbor was used as a supply point for the missions and mines farther south, but La Paz remained without permanent inhabitants until 1811, when a retired soldier named Juan José Espinoza settled here. Other colonists came after the War of Independence. There were about 400 inhabitants in 1830 when the territorial government was moved from Loreto to La Paz. The town was occupied by American troops during the Mexican War, and again by the filibuster William Walker in 1853.

The famous pearl fisheries of La Paz have been exploited for over 400 years. Until 1874 the oysters were brought up by naked Indian divers, but in that year diving suits were introduced and the industry began to assume considerable proportions. La Paz has long been noted for its black (actually a translucent gray) and other colored pearls, some of which are among the crown jewels of Europe. After 1884 the fisheries were developed along capitalistic lines and great quantities of pearl shell were exported, the pearls themselves taking second place in importance. The disturbances of the Mexican Revolution put an end to the industry in 1914, since which time there has been only slight activity by individual divers. Pearls, occasionally a really beautiful and valuable one, can still be seen, but the visitor is advised to use caution in making purchases. Not long ago an American paid a generous price for a large black "pearl" which, on closer inspection, turned out to be a ball bearing!

In recent years La Paz has been emerging from a long period of

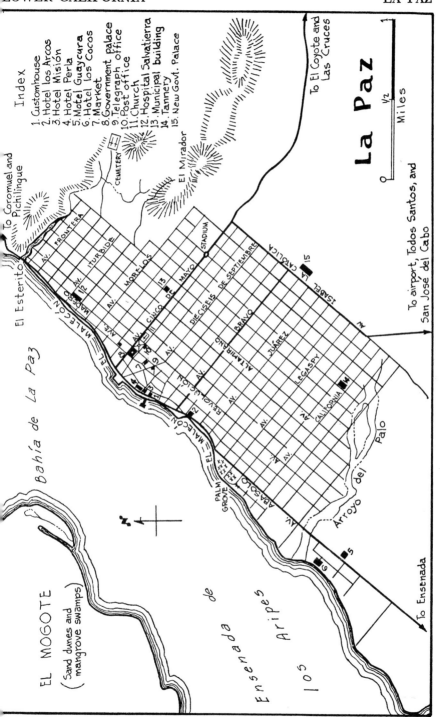

La Paz

Index

1. Customhouse
2. Hotel los Arcos
3. Hotel Misión
4. Hotel Perla
5. Motel Guaycura
6. Hotel los Cocos
7. Market
8. Government palace
9. Telegraph office
10. Post office
11. Church
12. Hospital Salvatierra
13. Municipal building
14. Tannery
15. New Govt. Palace

To Coromuel and Pichilingue

El Esterito

Bahía de La Paz

EL MOGOTE
(Sand dunes and
mangrove swamps)

Ensenada de Aripes

105

Arroyo del Palo

To El Coyote and Las Cruces

To airport, Todos Santos, and San José del Cabo

To Ensenada

Miles
0   ½   1

economic depression. Experiments in cotton raising have led to the establishment of a cotton mill which promises to be of some importance. Winter vegetables, both fresh and canned, are exported to the United States, and wheat raising has been currently successful. An older industry is the tannery on the outskirts of town, which processes hides and produces leather used throughout Mexico.

The excellent deep-sea fishing in La Paz Bay attracts a steadily growing number of enthusiasts from the United States. Many world's record fish have been landed at La Paz. Practically every known type of game fish is found in the waters of the Gulf, including marlin, sailfish, swordfish, tuna, dolphin, yellowtail, roosterfish, cabrilla, sierra, giant manta ray, shark,and even an occasional tarpon. Launches especially equipped for deep-sea fishing are available for $45 to $60 U.S. cy. a day, including tackle, bait, and expert advice (cold beer is extra). Smaller boats with outboard motors may be rented for $2.50 an hour. The best season for deep-sea fishing is from March to September. Marlin are caught from March through July, sailfish from June to October.

Taxis can be rented (about $250 pesos a day) for excursions in the vicinity. The trip to San José del Cabo and return normally takes two days and the usual rate is $50 U.S. cy. For trips within the city limits taxis charge $3 pesos; to Coromuel, $12 pesos round trip; to airport, $10 pesos.

ROUTE 7

EXCURSIONS NEAR LA PAZ

Mi. from La Paz	Partial Mileage	
0.0	0.0	A road extends from La Paz northeast along the shore to Pichilingue Bay. It is paved as far as Punta Prieta.
2.7	2.7	COROMUEL. A shallow white-sand beach with a bathing pavilion, much frequented by the residents of La Paz on Sundays. Bar service, juke box, etc. Water skiing is a favorite sport. From here the road continues past EL CAIMANCITO, a palatial residence intended for use of the president of Mexico on his official visits.
5.5	2.8	PUNTA PRIETA. Pemex oil dock and storage tanks. The road follows the shore past a lighthouse to a salt flat, detours around a mangrove swamp, and turns inland. It comes back to the coast at BAHÍA FALSA, a long shallow indentation with several nice beaches some distance off the road. Then it continues over a hill to
13.5	8.0	BAHÍA PICHILINGUE. A beautiful deep harbor sheltered by Pichilingue Island. For full description see p. 203 and p. 13. The road goes down to the shore of the bay and ends in a mangrove swamp. There is reason to believe that this was the site of the first Spanish settlement in California, founded by Hernán Cortés in 1535.

0.0	0.0	Another road leaves La Paz as a continuation of Avenida Cinco de Mayo and crosses to El Coyote and Las Cruces, northeast of La Paz on the Gulf:
4.2	4.2	Fork in road. The left branch goes to El Coyote (see below). The right fork crosses the mountains to the Gulf shore, past LA SORPRESA (good beach) and EL SALTITO, to LAS CRUCES (22.5 mi. from La Paz), a luxurious resort hotel which in early 1962 was converted into a private club.
4.9	0.7	Side road left to LA LAGUNA, an abandoned ranch.
6.5	1.6	CALMALLÍ. Ranch.
7.3	0.8	SAN LUIS. Ranch.

Mi. from La Paz	Partial Mileage	
7.6	0.3	La Fortuna. Ranch with a small chapel.
8.3	0.7	Buenavista. Ranch.
10.0	1.7	Santa María. Ranch.
11.4	1.4	Santa Victoria. Ranch off road to left.
13.0	1.6	El Coyote. A collection of ranches and small farms. The road continues across a salt flat to the beach, at Bahía Coyote. Excellent swimming and a good camp site.

0.0	0.0	There is another road around Ensenada de los Aripes to Rodríguez, on the Gulf shore west of La Paz. The main highway to the north, described in Route 6, is followed as far as Los Aripes:
9.3	9.3	Las Hamacas (Los Aripes). A ranch and palm grove on the shore of the bay. Here the Rodríguez road leaves the main highway and turns northwest through a thick growth of desert vegetation. Several side roads branch off to the right and run down to the shore of Ensenada de los Aripes. There is a fairly nice beach about a mile north of Los Aripes, on a low sandy point.
13.1	3.8	El Salvioso. Cattle ranch.
14.1	1.0	Datilito. Cattle ranch off road to right.
16.3	2.2	San Julián. Ranch.
16.8	0.5	El Quelele. Ranch.
18.8	2.0	Rodríguez. Cattle ranch at the end of the road, on the shore of La Paz Bay with Espíritu Santo Island in the distance. Currents make the beach dirty and not too pleasant for swimming, but there are some good camping places east of here towards El Mogote. There is an old mission trail, still used by pack trains, running northwest from Rodríguez to San Luis Gonzaga (ca. 90 mi.) and beyond.

ROUTE 8

LA PAZ TO SAN JOSÉ DEL CABO
VIA SANTIAGO

Motorists visiting the southern tip of the peninsula usually go down by this route and come back by Route 9 through Todos Santos. Both roads are for the most part rough unimproved tracks, although a new highway is now (1961) graded as far as El Triunfo and being continued southward. It still takes a day, however, to reach San José del Cabo. The Cape Region, as this section is called, is the only part of Baja California within the Tropics. There are many attractive towns and good camping spots. (See also Preface page 13.)

Mi. from La Paz	Partial Mileage	
0.0	0.0	LA PAZ. The road leaves town on Avenida Isabel la Católica, then turns south.
3.2	3.2	Road junction. The main road continues straight ahead, while an alternate route via Los Planes (5 mi. longer) goes to the left:

Mi. from
La Paz
(Alt. route)

(11.8)   15.0   LA HUERTA, off road to right. An old ranch dating from the 18th century, with a garden irrigated from a tiny spring. There is a brick chapel and an old churchyard. From here the road crosses the barren Cacachilas Mountains, reaching a height of 2,000 ft. before descending in a straight line to the broad valley of Los Planes.

(14.6)   29.6   Crossroads. The left branch goes to EL SARGENTO (8.0 mi.), a fishing village on the shore of Ventana Bay. The road straight ahead goes to LOS PLANES (33.2 mi. from La Paz), a center of recent agricultural activity. About 4,000 acres in the broad valley are planted to cotton and winter vegetables, irrigated from wells. This was the site of an unsuccessful colonizing attempt by an American land company in 1863. Beyond Los Planes the road continues to another fork at 37.3. The right branch is a little-used road back to San Antonio. The left branch goes on to BAHÍA DE LOS MUERTOS (44.4 mi. from La Paz). This port, consisting of an old ruined pier and a few shacks, was developed by the Boleo Company in 1924 as a shipping point for the silver ore from El Triunfo (see below). More recently it was used for shipping vegetables from Los Planes. A fair beach.

The right fork of the crossroads at 29.6 mi. from La Paz goes south to San Antonio:

Mi. from La Paz	Partial Mileage	Mi. from La Paz (Alt. route)	
	(0.2)	29.8	LA MISERIA. Cattle ranch.
	(1.6)	31.4	SOLEDAD. Cattle ranch.
	(8.8)	40.2	TESCALAMA. An old silver mine, of some importance in the late 18th century. It is now a collection of ranches. The arroyo is lined with fan palms.
	(0.9)	41.1	EL ZAPOTE. Ranch.
	(0.5)	41.6	EL ALAMO. Ranch.
	(0.4)	42.0	LA POSTA. Goat ranch, with an old smelter.
	(0.1)	42.1	Junction with main road from La Paz. San Antonio is 2.4 mi. to the right (44.5 mi. from La Paz by the Los Planes road, compared to 39.6 mi. via El Triunfo).

From the Los Planes road junction at M. 3.2, the main road continues to

3.5	0.3	La Paz airport, to right. Pavement ends after two miles.
18.0	14.5	SAN PEDRO. A small ranching community. Rainfall here is three times as heavy as at La Paz and there is a thick growth of desert and semi-tropical vegetation. A side road goes left 2.8 mi. to EL NOVILLO, a cattle ranch dating from about 1770 at the foot of the Trinchera Mountains, with a small garden and a ruined chapel.
18.5	0.5	Fork in road. The right branch goes via Todos Santos to San José del Cabo (see below, Route 9). The new road to El Triunfo keeps to left.
25.5	7.0	Side road to left:

	Mi. from junction	
(2.2)	2.2	EL SALTO (La Casa Blanca). An old cattle ranch at the foot of the Trinchera Mountains. There is a cement dam across the arroyo, intended to store water for irrigation. The road continues up the arroyo.
(0.2)	2.4	EL LLANO. Cattle ranch.
(1.5)	3.9	Branch road right to the ranches of EL CIRUELITO and EL COAVE.
(1.2)	5.1	SAN BLAS. All that remains of this old ranching community, founded about 1760, is a stone chapel. There are some old bells on the roof. A side road goes right 1.0 mi. to LOS DIVISADEROS, a large ranch.
(1.0)	6.1	ESTRELLA DEL NORTE. Ranch. Just before reaching this place there is a trail to the left which climbs about 500 ft. up the mountain to the site of ANGEL DE LA GUARDA (El Zalate), established in 1721 by Padre Bravo as a cattle ranch and visiting station of La Paz mission. It is

Mi. from La Paz	Partial Mileage	Mi. from junction	

a pretty oasis (now uninhabited) near the summit of the Trinchera range, with a palm grove and fruit trees watered from a tiny spring.

(0.4)   6.5   LA TRINCHERA. End of road. A collection of ranches which existed before the town of La Paz began.

The main road from M. 25.5 continues through sandy, rolling country:

31.8   6.3   Side road right to Las Gallinas, Valle Perdido, etc. (see below, p. 191).

34.8   3.0   EL TRIUNFO. Elev. 1,850 ft. Estimated pop. in 1960: 500. Climate: Considerably cooler than in La Paz. Communications: Government telephone to La Paz.

At one time an important silver mining center and the largest city in the south, El Triunfo is now pretty much of a ghost town. The site is first mentioned in records of the Jesuit era as a mission cattle ranch. In 1862 the Triunfo Gold and Silver Mining Co. was organized and a mining town came into existence. Within a few years El Triunfo had taken the place of San Antonio (see below) as the center of mining activity and had a population of about 10,000, mostly Yaqui Indians from Sonora. In 1874, with a 36-stamp mill in operation, silver to the value of $50,000 a month was being shipped to La Paz. Gradually the ore declined in quality, and a hurricane flooded the mines in 1918. After this the Boleo Company from Santa Rosalía tried to rehabilitate the mines, but they abandoned them in 1926. Since then most of the people have left, but mining is still carried on on a limited scale.

A visit to the old smelter and mine workings is of interest. There are several stores and a modern church. Gasoline pump.

The new road between El Triunfo and San Antonio was almost ready for traffic in April, 1961. Leaving El Triunfo the *old* road winds through the mountains to:

Mi. from La Paz	Partial Mileage	

39.6   4.8   SAN ANTONIO. Elev. 1,350 ft. Estimated pop. in 1960: 800. Communications: Government telephone to La Paz.

An old silver mining town, for a short period the capital of Baja California, San Antonio is now a pleasant, sleepy little village of merchants and cattle ranchers. Mining activity in this area began in 1748 when a retired soldier of the Loreto garrison, Manuel de Osio, moved to Santa Ana (reached by trail), about 5 mi. south of here. San Antonio was founded as a rival mining venture by another Spaniard, Gaspar Pisón, in 1756. The two towns were the first non-Indian communities in California (the natives were not permitted to work in the mines). In the colonial period the mines were not very successful but a group of foreign capitalists became interested in them in 1861. For a few years San Antonio flourished, until it was outdistanced by El Triunfo.

The town is in a basin surrounded by low hills. It is a pleasant-looking place, with the old adobe houses, palm trees, and cobblestone streets. The church, on one side of the plaza, was built about 1825 but has been completely remodeled in recent years, in simple colonial style.

Several stores and bars. Gasoline is usually available.

Leaving San Antonio the road follows a dry arroyo.

Mi. from La Paz	Partial Mileage	
42.0	2.4	Fork in road. The Los Planes road turns left down the arroyo (see p. 176). The main road keeps right and leaves the arroyo.
50.0	8.0	AGUA CALIENTE. Palm grove and ranch off road, right.
50.9	0.9	LA VENTA. Cattle ranch.
61.5	10.6	SAN BARTOLO. Elev. 1,180 ft. 1950 pop. 316. Communications: Government telephone to La Paz. A pretty little farming village in a very narrow canyon, forming a ribbon of green surrounded by barren hills. The water from a large spring is retained by a concrete dam to irrigate the fields for about 5 miles below. Sugar cane is the principal crop. There is a store and a small inn where travelers can spend the night. On the far side of the arroyo is an old stone chapel.
		The road leaves San Bartolo along the edge of a cliff, then drops down to the sandy arroyo bottom.
70.8	9.3	Side road left to AGUA DE LA COSTA (1.2 mi.), a ranch on the beach. The main road reaches the sea at the mouth of Arroyo San Bartolo and follows the shore.
72.2	1.4	BUENOS AIRES. Cattle ranch.
72.9	0.7	ENSENADA DE PALMAS. A collection of fishermen's shacks on the Bahía de Las Palmas.
73.6	0.7	LOS BARRILES. A small village of ranchers and fishermen, with a store and gasoline pump. Hotel Bahía de Palmas (I-B) has a fine beach, fishing boats for rent, etc. New airstrip.
74.1	0.5	PIEDRAS GORDAS. Ranch.
75.7	1.6	BUENA VISTA. A fishing resort, Rancho Buena Vista

(1-B). Several bungalows have been built for visitors, and launches are available. There is an excellent bathing beach. Just above the ranch is a small landing strip.

76.4   0.7   AGUA CALIENTE. A large house on the beach belonging to General Agustín Olachea. The main road leaves the coast here and goes inland to Santiago. A side road keeps left and continues down the coast to Los Frailes:

Mi. from
Agua Caliente

(1.3)   1.3   LA CAPILLA. Ranch. Here the road leaves the coast, to to return below Los Mártires.

(1.0)   2.3   EL ANHELO. Ranch off road to left.

(0.5)   2.8   LOS MÁRTIRES. School and collection of ranches. This place was an Indian ranchería and visiting station of Santiago mission.

(3.0)   5.8   SURGIDERO. Ranch.

(1.7)   7.5   EUREKA. Ranch.

(0.5)   8.0   LA RIBERA. A village of farmers and fishermen on the beach at the mouth of Arroyo Santiago. There is a store where supplies and gasoline may be purchased.

A side road turns right up the arroyo past POZA COLORADA (4.3 mi. from La Ribera) and LAS CUEVAS (7.5 mi., off road to left), and joins the main road (10.2 mi. from La Ribera, M. 85.4 from La Paz; see below).

(0.7)   8.7   Side road left to a fresh-water pond (estero) on the beach. All these esteros, of which there are many at the mouths of arroyos in the Cape Region, offer good duck hunting during the fall and winter months. This is a good camping spot.

(0.2)   8.9   LA BOCA. Ranch.

(0.7)   9.6   Side road right to LAS DELICIAS, ranch.

(1.4)   11.0   Side road left to LA CALERA and CABO DE HORNOS. The road turns inland.

(5.6)   16.6   LAS LAGUNAS. Ranch.

(3.4)   20.0   Here the road returns to the coast, to an excellent bathing beach.

(0.3)   20.3   BOCA DE LOS TESOS. Ranch.

(1.0)   21.3   MIRAMAR. Ranch.

(1.7)   23.0   LAS BARRACAS. Ranch.

(2.8)   25.8   EL PULMO. Ranch, landing strip. There are several good camp sites along the coast, with perfect beaches.

(2.9)   28.7   EL ZALATITO. Ranch. Los Frailes, an impressive cluster of rocks over 400 ft. high, is the easternmost point in Baja California. Good beach.

Mi. from La Paz	Partial Mileage	Mi. from Ag. Caliente	
	(1.6)	30.3	Los Frailes, ranch just south of the point. The road, now very little used, continues south along the shore to the mouth of Arroyo Salado. From here a poor road, passable to 4-wheel-drive vehicles, is said to be open, following the coast to San José del Cabo.

The main road turns inland from Agua Caliente, at M. 76.4:

85.4	9.0		Junction of La Ribera road, from left (see above). The main road crosses Arroyo Santiago and continues up the right side. The approach to Santiago is through palm groves and fields of sugar cane.
89.2	3.8		San Isidro. A suburb of Santiago. A side road to Las Cuevas cuts off to the left. The main road recrosses the arroyo to Santiago, on the left bank.

89.8   0.6   SANTIAGO. Elev. 450 ft. Estimated pop. in 1960: 600. Climate: cool in winter (average temperature Nov.-Apr., 66.0° F.; coldest months, Dec.-Feb.); warm in summer (average temperature May-Oct., 80.8° F.; warmest months, June-Sep.). Average annual rainfall: 10.2 in., nearly all in Aug. and Sep. Communications: Government telephone to La Paz and San José del Cabo. There is a landing strip long enough for medium planes on the mesa above the town.

One of the most attractive towns in the peninsula, Santiago is divided in two sections, on hills a half mile apart on the west side of a broad, sandy arroyo. On the north hill (Loma Norte) are several stores grouped around a plaza. Supplies, meals and gasoline may be purchased. On the top of the hill is the town hall (Casa del Pueblo), a large unfurnished house where travelers who wish to spend the night are usually accommodated. The south hill (Loma Sur) is occupied by a new brick church and government offices.

Water enough to irrigate about 1,500 acres comes from several springs. Between the two hills and the west side of the canyon is a former lake, now partially drained and planted almost entirely to sugar cane.

Santiago was first visited by the Jesuit Padre Napoli in 1721, although a mission was not established here until three years later. The original site was on the right bank of the arroyo about two miles north of the town, but all traces of the mission church have disappeared. It was here that the Pericú Indian revolt began in 1734 with the murder of the missionary, Padre Carranco. According to a legend, Carranco was describing to his flock the eternal fires of hell. Since it was a cold

COWBOYS OF THE SOUTH
Displaying their typical leather trappings

THE MALECÓN, OR SEA WALK, AT LA PAZ
See text page 170.

CAPE SAN LUCAS
Southern tip of the peninsula. See text page 187.

A TRAPICHE, OR SUGAR MILL, IN TODOS SANTOS
For making of panocha from sugar cane. See text page 190.

winter's day and the Indians were naked, they asked the Padre to lead them to this warm place. When he indignantly refused they rose in rebellion. Whether or not this legend is true, as a matter of historical fact many lives were lost before the Jesuits regained control of the southern missions. Soon afterward an epidemic practically wiped out the Santiago tribes, and when the mission was abandoned in 1795 only 40 Indians, out of an original population of about 1,100, remained alive. The place was repopulated by mestizos from the mainland.

Leaving Santiago the road crosses to the right bank of the arroyo. Ahead are the rugged Cape Region mountains, which reach a height of about 7,000 ft.

Mi. from La Paz	Partial Mileage	
93.2	3.4	LAS CABRAS. Ranch almost exactly on the Tropic of Cancer, northern limit of the Torrid Zone.
95.1	1.9	AGUA CALIENTE. A small farming village at the foot of the mountains. A side road right goes up the arroyo to EL CHORRO (2.4 mi.), a concrete dam and reservoir filled from hot springs in the cliffside. From Agua Caliente the road leaves Arroyo Santiago and turns south across a low divide to the upper valley of Arroyo San José.
100.0	4.9	EL CHINAL. Ranch.
100.3	0.3	Side road right to BOCA DE LA SIERRA (2.8 mi.), a farming community on Arroyo San Bernardo. Water for irrigation comes from a concrete dam about a mile up the arroyo. This is a good starting point for an excursion on horse or muleback into the mountains. Above the dam the arroyo becomes a stream of clear, cold running water forming deep pools in the rocks, for ideal swimming holes. Farther above are forests of oak, and near the summit are cool groves of piñon pine. There is good hunting for deer, mountain lion, wild pigs, and smaller game. It is possible to go from Boca de la Sierra to Todos Santos by way of LA LAGUNA, a beautiful meadow at an elevation of almost 6,000 ft. The trip (not made by authors) takes about four days. Guides and animals can be hired either at Boca de la Sierra or Miraflores.
100.8	0.5	MIRAFLORES. 1950 pop. 550. A farming, stock-raising village, locally famous for the fine leather work turned out in several shops. Saddles, belts, shoes and huar-

Mi. from La Paz	Partial Mileage	
		aches, gun holsters, and other articles are made to order at prices considerably lower than in La Paz. Most of the saddles and *cueras* (leather armor) used by the cowboys of Baja California come from Miraflores. There is an interesting old church. Meals can be obtained, and gasoline is usually available.
103.7	2.9	CADUAÑO. An attractive little farming town on the left bank of Arroyo San Pablo, just off the road to the left. Six springs, rising in a beautiful grove of *guamúchil* trees, irrigate about 65 acres of sugar cane. There is a schoolhouse and a new brick chapel. Caduaño was developed as a mission garden by the Dominicans, and was the final site of Santiago mission, from about 1790 to 1795.
109.2	5.5	LA PALMA. Cattle ranch on Arroyo de la Palma. After leaving this arroyo the road traverses a sandy stretch and joins the main Arroyo San José at Santa Anita.
117.1	7.9	Side road left across the arroyo to LOS POTREROS and SAN PEDRO, farming communities.
117.4	0.3	SANTA ANITA. A little farming village on the right bank of Arroyo San José, a broad sandy wash which is followed from here to San José del Cabo.
118.6	1.2	Side road left to SAN PEDRO (1.3 mi.).
119.9	1.3	Side road left to SAN BERNABÉ and SANTA CATARINA (1.5 mi., a farming town). A large spring in the arroyo provides the drinking water for San José del Cabo.
121.4	1.5	Another side road left to San Bernabé and Santa Catarina (3.6 mi.).
121.9	0.5	SAN JOSÉ VIEJO. A collection of ranches and farms, one of the early sites (1730-34) of the Jesuit mission of San José del Cabo. A ranch house on the edge of the bluff overlooking the arroyo is pointed out as the site of the mission chapel. The landing strip for San José del Cabo, long enough for medium planes, is just north of here.
123.9	2.0	SANTA ROSA. An attractive little ranching and subsistence farming community. It was founded in 1730 as a visiting station of San José del Cabo mission. Here the Jesuit Padre Tamaral was murdered by Indians in the rebellion of 1734.

Mi. from La Paz	Partial Mileage
124.9	1.0

124.9 1.0 ROSARITO. A suburb of San José.

126.2 1.3 SAN JOSÉ DEL CABO. Elev. 75 ft. Estimated pop. in 1960: 2,000. Climate: cool in winter (average temperature Nov.-Apr., 68° F.; coldest months, Dec.-Feb.); warm in summer (average temperature May-Oct., 79° F.; warmest months, July-Sep., tempered by sea breezes). Average annual rainfall: 8.0 in., nearly all of which falls in September. San José is exposed to tropical hurricanes (*chubascos*), most apt to occur in September. However, sometimes several years go by without a hurricane. Communications: Government telephone to La Paz. Mail three times a week.

The guest house of Señora de Fisher has clean accommodations (III). Hotel La Palmilla (I-A) is five miles out on the way to San Lucas (see below).

The principal store is that of González Canseco Hermanos. All kinds of supplies, gasoline, minor repairs, and some spare parts are available.

There is a new, well-equipped municipal hospital. Malaria, once a problem, is no longer a danger to the visitor since the anopheles mosquito has been destroyed.

There is an agency of Banco Nacional de México.

San José, with its mild climate, somnolent atmosphere and beautiful surroundings, is certainly one of the most attractive towns in Baja California. It is situated about a mile from the beach on a low hill dominating the broad valley, with cultivated lands on three sides. The principal crop is sugar cane, but many other kinds of fruits and vegetables are grown, including papayas, mangos, and bananas.

At the mouth of the arroyo below the town is a large fresh-water pond (*estero*) which drains into the sea. There is a clean white sand beach with ideal bathing, since the warm waters of the Gulf and the cold waters of the Pacific join here in just the right combination.

The waters off San José are teeming with a great many kinds of fish. Launches are available to go out after the big game fish, which are found here even during the cold months when they desert the area around La Paz. There is excellent surf-fishing along the shore, and the favorite activity of the boys of San José is to wander along the beach with fishing spears, collecting their dinner.

The original site of the Jesuit mission of San José, founded in 1730, was on the beach at the west end of the *estero*, adjacent to the cemetery. The site was changed several times, until in 1753 it was moved to where the church is today, next to the plaza. The Indian population, decimated by a series of epidemics, dropped from an original 1,500 to 100 in 1750. Gradually the town was resettled by whites and mestizos.

In mission times San José was important as a refitting point for the Manila galleon, which crossed each year from the Philippines to Acapulco. The eastbound voyage sometimes lasted seven or eight months. The galleon often called here to take on water and supplies, and to give its scurvy-ridden sailors a few days on shore.

In 1847-48, during the Mexican War, San José was occupied by a small garrison of U.S. marines. They were besieged for two months by Mexican troops, and were almost annihilated before reinforcements came. The Mexicans occupied the mission church, while the marines converted the missionary's house (*casa cural*, present site of the electric plant) into a fortress. Both buildings were demolished during the siege. The death of a Mexican naval lieutenant, José Antonio Mijares, who was killed in an attempt to rush the American positions, is commemorated in the name of the main street and a monument.

The present church was built in the 1940's. A mosaic above the entrance represents the martyrdom of the Jesuit Tamaral at the hands of the Indians in 1734.

ROUTE 9

SAN JOSÉ DEL CABO TO LA PAZ
VIA TODOS SANTOS

Most of this road is within sight of the sea, with numerous fine beaches and camping places. (See also Preface page 13.)

Mi. from San José	Partial Mileage	
0.0	0.0	SAN JOSÉ DEL CABO. The road leaves town as a continuation of the street on the church side of the plaza, branching off to the right just before reaching the cemetery and an abandoned airstrip. Between here and Cabo San Lucas the road follows the coast, along which there are many sheltered coves ideal for swimming and camping.
3.6	3.6	COSTA AZUL. A large house here is often occupied by seasonal American visitors.
5.0	1.4	Branch road left 0.9 mi. to Hotel La Palmilla (I-A), a luxurious resort with a good airstrip, fishing boats, etc., at PUNTA PALMILLA.
11.2	6.2	EL BLEDITO, ranch.
14.0	2.8	EL TULE, ranch. Hotel Cabo San Lucas (I-A) is on a promontory off to the left; a large luxurious resort hotel completed early in 1962. Airstrip.
15.3	1.3	PUERTO CHILENO, cove and stone house to left.
23.8	8.5	Branch road left to SAN LUCAS (0.5 mi.). 1950 pop.

548. Communications: Government telephone to La Paz; radio station at the cannery which may be used in emergencies. Gasoline is sold at the cannery. San Lucas has a good landing strip for large aircraft.

The Cape of San Lucas, a cluster of huge, weird-shaped rocks one mile south of the town, is the southernmost point in California. It was first sighted by Francisco de Ulloa, Cortés' pilot, in 1537. For 250 years the bay was an occasional port of call for the Manila galleon, an annual trading ship which brought the silks, wax, spices, and other fineries of the Orient from the Philippines to Mexico. The galleon hugged the California coast on its return voyage, then rounded the Cape and crossed the mouth of the Gulf to Colima. During the long passage, which took the better part of a year, nearly everyone aboard became ill with scurvy and beri-beri. It was not unusual for half the crew to die before reaching Acapulco, and for this reason the galleon sometimes stopped for a few days at San Lucas to take on water and allow the sailors to recuperate. It was also a favorite place for pirates to lie in wait for Spanish ships. In 1587 the English sea rover Thomas Cavendish captured a galleon here called the "Santa Ana," with 122,000 gold pesos and a great quantity of silks, satins, damasks, musk, wines, and other booty. The prize was towed into San Lucas Bay and divided between Cavendish's two ships, one of which sailed across the Pacific, while the other headed north and was never seen again. This treasure probably still lies on the bottom some place along the coast north of here.

The town of San Lucas was completely destroyed by a flood in 1941, and rebuilt in a slightly more sheltered location. It is a frequent port of call for fishing boats from San Pedro, California, and elsewhere. There are several nice beaches and camping spots nearby. Deep sea fishing is excellent. See illustration page 182.

From San Lucas turnoff the road heads inland up the arroyo:

Mi. from San José	Partial Mileage	
33.8	10.0	Los Pozos. A collection of cattle ranches in the foothills of the Cape Region mountains. The vegetation is heavy, of semi-tropical and desert plants.
34.8	1.0	Saucito. Cattle ranch.
38.9	4.1	Buenavista. Cattle ranch. The road climbs down a steep arroyo and crosses a mesa to the Pacific coast.
45.4	6.5	Chula Vista, ranch near the sea.
46.0	0.6	Migriño. Ranch near the mouth of Arroyo Candelaria. There is a side road right almost to La Candelaria, a little farming town in the foothills. North of Migriño there are several good camping spots along the beach, but the big breakers are only for strong swimmers.
52.2	6.2	La Tinaja. Ranch off road to right. The road continues parallel to but some distance from the coast, across barren mesas with many cross-washes. This section is impassable after a heavy rain.
54.6	2.4	Branch road right to La Matancita (4.1 mi.), a ranching community.
59.9	5.3	Las Piedritas. Ranch on the beach.
60.8	0.9	San Juan de los Lagos, an attractive ranch between the road and the sea.
62.1	1.3	Colonia Calles. An agricultural colony at the mouth of Arroyo San Jacinto.

Mi. from San José	Partial Mileage	
67.1	5.0	Branch road right to EL PALMAR (2.4 mi.), SAN RAFAEL (6.6 mi.), SAN VENANCIO, EL POTRERO, SAN JACINTO, EL SALTITO, ranches in the foothills of the Cape Region mountains. From here the road goes around a lagoon and follows along the beach for a few miles.
68.4	1.3	The road leaves the beach and goes inland.
70.8	2.4	CUATRO VIENTOS. Ranch. Side road right to AGUA DE LOS COCHIS and EL REFUGIO, ranching communities (not visited by authors).
72.1	1.3	PESCADERO. 1950 pop. 600. Communications: Government telephone to Todos Santos and La Paz. An agricultural village about three miles from the sea. Some 500 acres of sugar cane, vegetables and fruit trees are irrigated from a spring. The town is divided between two low hills, with a plaza, church, school, stores, etc. Side road inland to LOS HORCONSITOS (see below).
76.0	3.9	Side road left to SAN PEDRITO (1.4 mi.), a prosperous ranch on the beach. It is a favorite bathing and picnicking place for the local residents. There is a palm grove and lagoon immediately behind the beach.
76.7	0.7	Side road right to SAUCITO (13.5 mi.) and LOS HORCONSITOS (17.6 mi.), ranches at the foot of the mountains. A branch of this road goes to LA BURRERA. Horses or mules can be hired for a trip up the steep eastern side of the mountains to La Laguna and across to Miraflores, south of Santiago (see p. 183).
78.6	1.9	Side road left to PUNTA LOBOS, a bluff almost 700 ft. high forming a small and ill-protected harbor with a fine sand beach. It is a favorite fishing place for the residents of Todos Santos. To the south of Punta Lobos is a rocky cove known as PUERTO CAMPECHANO (reached by trail), where a concrete pier was built in 1935.

79.7   1.1   TODOS SANTOS. Elev. 45 ft. Estimated pop. in 1960: 2,000. Climate cool in winter and spring (average temperature Dec.-June, 69.7° F.; coldest months, Jan.-May); warm in summer, tempered by constant breezes from the sea (average temperature July-Nov., 80.0° F.; warmest months, July-Oct.). Average annual rainfall, 5.1 in., from July to Jan. Communications: Government telephone to La Paz.

A farming village attractively situated on a hill on the east side of a broad arroyo, one mile from the Pacific. Water from a small dam irrigates the lower valley, almost entirely planted to sugar cane. The juice from the cane is processed in several mills *(trapiches)* and made into small cones of almost black sugar called *panocha* (see illustration p. 182). Todos Santos is also renowned for its delicious mangos. Farther above, the water comes from the springs of San Juan (see p. 191) which periodically dry up, making it necessary to abandon the fields above the dam. Canals carry the precious liquid for several miles northeast along the coast to irrigate fields in adjacent arroyos. Everywhere are graceful fan-palms, fruit trees, and waving sugar cane.

The town itself is a neat collection of one-story adobe houses dominated by the church, a large whitewashed building originally built about 1840, but completely remodeled since 1941 when it was wrecked in a hurricane. On the arroyo side of the plaza is a large movie theater. There are a number of stores where supplies may be purchased. On the south edge of town is a new government hospital. Travelers may spend the night at Hotel California (III), which has a bar, restaurant, and gasoline pump.

The site of Todos Santos was discovered by Padre Jaime Bravo, the missionary of La Paz, who developed it as a farm and visiting station of that mission in 1724. Ten years later it became a separate mission, but it was completely ruined during the Indian rebellion of 1734-36. The Indians, originally about 1,100, were wiped out in an epidemic in 1742-44, and the mission was repopulated twice, first with the Indians of La Paz and later with those of San Luis Gonzaga and La Pasión missions, which were all abandoned. Further epidemics killed off these Indians, and Todos Santos was settled by mestizos during the 19th century. The original site of the mission church was about a mile above the town at Misión Vieja. A few stones are pointed out as the ruins.

A side road branches off on the south edge of town and goes down to the fresh-water *estero*. Beyond is the beach, which has excellent surf bathing for those who can handle the great breakers.

Another road crosses to the right bank of the arroyo and continues north along the coast:

Mi. from San José	Partial Mileage	Mi. from Todos Santos	
	(0.5)	0.5	SAN IGNACIO. A suburb of Todos Santos, with a small chapel, store, etc. A branch road runs up the right bank past a cane mill to EL RINCONCITO and PRESA JUÁREZ, the source of irrigation water. The main road keeps left.
	(0.9)	1.4	SAN JUAN DEL LLANO. Ranch near the sea.
	(1.8)	3.2	CAÑADA HONDA. A prosperous sugar cane farm, off road to right.
	(0.8)	4.0	Fresh water pond *(estero)* at the mouth of an arroyo.
	(1.0)	5.0	SANTA CRUZ. Ranch.
	(0.5)	5.5	ESTEROS DEL BATEQUI. A palm-grove on the beach (excellent bathing) with two fresh-water *esteros*.

Mi. from San José	Partial Mileage	Mi. from Todos Santos	
	(0.3)	5.8	LA PASTORA. Ranch. From here a little-used track continues northwest along the coast to Arroyo Carrizal.

The main road to La Paz leaves Todos Santos on the north edge of town; it follows the arroyo's left bank:

80.6	0.9		MISIÓN VIEJA. A shack now covers the original site of the mission church of Todos Santos (see above).
81.7	1.1		Branch road right to SAN JUAN (0.4 mi.). Three springs furnish water enough to irrigate the upper part of Todos Santos valley. Periodically they dry up, and the fields above Misión Vieja must be abandoned. The road continues up the arroyo past a new airfield.
85.3	3.6		Side road right to EL MANGLITO (2.5 mi.), LA REFORMA (3.4 mi.), and EL SALTO (7.6 mi.), cattle ranches. Horses or mules can be hired for excursions across the mountains. However, La Burrera is a better place to start such an excursion (see p. 189).
101.0	15.7		Side road right to VALLE PERDIDO and LAS GALLINAS, with a short cut to El Triunfo:

	Mi. from M. 101.0	
(2.2)	2.2	Branch road right to BAJADA DEL MOLINO (3.8 mi.) and VALLE PERDIDO (7.5 mi.). The latter is a mining camp in the foothills. A road goes north from Valle Perdido to El Triunfo (see below).
(0.4)	2.6	LAS TRES PACHITAS. Cattle ranch.
(3.9)	6.5	Crossroads. The right branch goes to VALLE PERDIDO (3.5 mi.), the left branch to EL TRIUNFO. Straight ahead to Las Gallinas:
(1.8)	8.3	LAS GALLINAS (El Rosario). Elev. 1,540 ft. A tiny village in a basin in the foothills, with a population of cattlemen and miners. It was founded as a cattle *estancia* of Todos Santos mission in the 1730's. There is a small chapel, built during a mining boom in 1863.

102.4	1.4	ARROYO HONDO, a broad sandy wash, difficult to cross after a rain.
108.6	6.2	Branch road left to EL CARRIZAL (6.4 mi. from junction), JUAN MÁRQUEZ (9.8 mi.) and other ranches.
112.5	3.9	Junction with old El Triunfo road.
114.9	2.4	Junction with new road to El Triunfo, right (see Route 8, page 176).
115.4	0.5	SAN PEDRO.
133.4	18.0	LA PAZ (for description, see pp. 168-72).

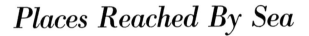

Places Reached By Sea

ROUTE 10
PLACES REACHED BY SEA

Baja California has a long coastline on both the Pacific and Gulf sides, with many offshore islands. Six of these islands (Cedros, Magdalena, Margarita, Pichilingue, San José, and Carmen) have landing fields and can be reached by plane; the others are accessible only by boat. As a rule the roads keep inland and avoid stretches of barren waterless coast, with the result that the yachtsman sees an entirely different picture from that seen by the motorist. Although there are few settlements along the coast, there are many harbors and remote and beautiful beaches which can be reached only by sea. For navigation purposes, the sailing directions (see page 54) and charts published by the Hydrographic Office, U.S. Navy Department, Washington, D.C., are recommended. Most of the charts are considerably out-of-date and inaccurate as to inland features, but the sailing directions are constantly revised with supplements. Following is a general description of the places of interest to yachtsmen along the coast and outlying islands. This list is arranged geographically, from north to south on the Pacific side, then up the Gulf from south to north.[1]

ISLA GUADALUPE (SEE MAP 16)

Mexico's westernmost possession, Guadalupe Island, is far out in the Pacific, 220 miles southwest of Ensenada. It is 98 square miles in area, 22 miles long from north to south, with a maximum width of 6 miles. It is of volcanic origin with great lava-covered mountains, precipitous canyons, and massive cliffs on all sides, but particularly in the north. The highest point, in the northern part of the island, is 4,257 ft. above sea level. The population is about 40 or 50, consisting of a few Mexican officials and their families at the south end of the island. The waters abound in tuna and yellowtail and are much frequented by fishermen from San Diego and elsewhere.

The southern end of the island is almost devoid of vegetation, but the northwest slopes have several forests of pines and cypresses, a few oaks, and groves of fan palms. Fresh water is found only in the north, where there are some little springs among the palms.

---

[1] Of the places described, the authors have not visited I. Guadalupe, I. Cerralvo, Los Dolores, I. Catalina, I. Monserrate, B. Agua Verde, B. San Nicolás, I. San Marcos, I. Tortuga, nor I. Angel de la Guarda.

The climate is very similar to that of Ensenada. Rain is practically confined to the winter months (November to March), but fogs are more frequent during the summer. The wooded northwest corner of the island is almost constantly shrouded in fog and has a much more humid atmosphere than the south end. Near the top of the island frosts are common, and even snow sometimes occurs.

Guadalupe was probably discovered by one of Sebastián Vizcaíno's ships in 1602. It was often sighted by the Manila galleons, though they seldom put ashore there. In the early days the island was the home of large herds of fur seal and elephant seal. The fur seals were killed in such numbers by American hunters in the 19th century that they disappeared, though recently they have been seen here again. Later visitors were whalers who killed great numbers of elephant seals for their valuable oil. These strange mammals (also referred to as sea elephants) were once abundant in the Antarctic but were exterminated except on Guadalupe Island. Several decades ago they reappeared on the nearby San Benito Islands, and now they are thriving to such an extent that small colonies are found on several other islands off the California coast. A recent estimate of the number of elephant seals on Guadalupe is 13,000. They may be seen at several sheltered beaches around the north end of the island. Perhaps the most accessible rookery is a beach on the east coast, just south of Pilot Rock. The males sometimes reach a length of 16 or 17 feet. In spite of their size and ferocious appearance they are quite harmless, and sleep so soundly that they may be approached within a few feet.

Permission of the Mexican government is required for landing on Guadalupe, which is a wild life preserve.

The only land mammals on Guadalupe are several thousand wild goats and quantities of cats and rats, all introduced by whalers around the middle of the last century. These destructive newcomers have multiplied to such an extent that practically nothing remains of the original flora and fauna. There has not been a single sapling of pine, oak or cypress for over 50 years. The goats are said to have learned to drink sea water, but there is so little plant life that many of them die each year.

The principal anchorage is Melpómene Bay, at the south end of the island, partly sheltered by a string of islets. An international weather station has been in operation here since 1946. The personnel consists of several Mexican officials and their families. There is a radio station which communicates daily with Ensenada. Drinking water is brought from the mainland. Adjacent to this settlement are remains of an old seal hunters' camp, and elsewhere along the coast are stone ruins of these camps.

Near the north end of Guadalupe, on the east side, is another anchorage protected from the prevailing winds. Here at the foot of a precipitous canyon are some conspicuous white buildings formerly used by a detachment of the Mexican Army, which periodically stationed troops on Guadalupe. Nearby are the ruins of a goat meat cannery, established by an American company in the early 1900's but soon abandoned. Near the beach is a well of salty water. A trail runs up the canyon behind the houses to a tiny spring of fresh water and the pine and cypress forests at the top of the island.

BAHÍA DE TODOS SANTOS, the port of Ensenada, see pages 90-92.

BAHÍA DE SAN QUINTÍN. See page 110.

BAHÍA ROSARIO. See page 112.

PUERTO SAN CARLOS. See page 113.

SANTA CATARINA LANDING. See page 116.

BLACK WARRIOR LAGOON. See page 129.

SCAMMON'S LAGOON (OJO DE LIEBRE).

An extensive arm of the sea, running back about 40 miles into the Desert of Sebastián Vizcaíno. The bay is locally known as Laguna Ojo de Liebre (Jack Rabbit Spring Lagoon) after a tiny water hole near its eastern end. It is sometimes visited by fishermen in search of sea turtles *(caguamas)*. The shores are low, sandy and barren, and the lagoon is studded with low islands and sand bars. Game is scarce, consisting of jack rabbits and a few deer and pronghorn antelope. The lagoon has not been accurately charted and many wrecks have occurred in the vicinity. The entrance should not be attempted without a good local pilot.

The east arm of the lagoon is connected by a poor motor road to the north with the salt works of Guerrero Negro (see page 129). Further to the east a ruined causeway from the shore connects with a road to the ranch of El Huisache, on the "coastal route" (see page 130).

Although known to earlier navigators, such as the crew of the "Tower Castle," a British whaler shipwrecked in 1836 near the entrance, Scammon's Lagoon was first visited for commercial reasons in 1858 by the brig "Boston," which entered in search of whales. The lagoon was then, as now, a favorite breeding ground of the California gray whale. For the next few years many American ships came to Scammon's and by 1861 the whales had practically disappeared. Since then the only visitors have been ships coming to load salt, and an occasional fisherman, with the result that the lagoon has again become the biggest whale calving nursery on the west coast.

Between Scammon's Lagoon and Cedros Island the mainland coast makes a long sweep to the westward, backed by the arid SIERRA PINTADA (see page 131). Because of the currents and the prevailing wind this coast, known as MALARRIMO, is a depository of maritime refuse and an ideal place for beachcombing. There are tales, some of them probably true, of treasure-laden galleons being washed up along here.

ISLA DE CEDROS (SEE MAP 16)

Cedros is a large, barren, mountainous island off the west coast of Baja California. It has an area of 135 square miles, a greatest length of 23 miles, with a width varying from 4 to 11 miles, and a population of 1,003 (in 1950). Its economic importance is due to a large fish cannery on the east side. It is of interest to yachtsmen, hunters, and fishermen.

The coasts of the island are formed by high cliffs occasionally broken by arroyo mouths with rocky beaches. The west side has very heavy surf, but the south and east coasts are sheltered from the prevailing northwest winds. The highest point is Monte Cedros (known locally as Cerro Cenizo), immediately behind the cannery, 3,950 feet above sea level. Monte Gill, near the north end, reaches a height of 3,488 feet. The mountains are separated by deeply eroded canyons.

The climate is temperate, slightly warmer than that of Ensenada, with very little rainfall. Sometimes a year goes by with no rain at all. In the summertime there is usually a fog in the evening which clears off before noon.

The "Ariel," a motor launch belonging to the cannery, makes frequent trips between Ensenada and Cedros Island and carries mail and passengers. During the summer many other boats from Ensenada and elsewhere call at the island. The run from Ensenada takes anywhere from 24 to 36 hours. Sometimes it is possible to get passage on one of the planes which fly lobster from Cedros to San Diego. There is a Mexican Army radio telegraph station which accepts messages to Ensenada and beyond. The cannery has a private radio telephone.

Practically the entire population is concentrated at the cannery of "Pesquera del Pacífico" near the southeast corner of the island. Above the cannery along the hillside is a sizeable village of wooden houses. There is good anchorage in a sandy bottom about ½ mile off the town. Boats can tie up to the cannery pier, which has a depth of 15 feet at the end, to take on water and fuel. There is a half-ton electric crane on the pier, and a fairly well-equipped machine shop. Supplies, mostly fish and canned goods, are available at high prices. Cattle are scarce, but pigs are fairly abundant. There is a small dispensary with a male nurse in attendance. The cannery, which owns everything on the island, has its head office in El Sauzal, near Ensenada. It has a capacity of 100 tons of abalone per day; sardines and mackerel are canned in lesser quantities. Most of the abalone divers were formerly employed in the pearl fisheries near La Paz. The best place to watch the divers at work is around the southwest corner of Cedros Island (Cabo San Agustín) and off the adjoining island of Natividad. The sardines and mackerel are caught from May to September, from small boats in the waters near the cannery. The fishing is done at night when the schools of mackerel are easily seen because of their phosphorescence. If the visitor is fortunate enough to be taken out by the fishermen he will see an expert demonstration in the handling of the nets, which requires great skill. Lobster are also caught, particularly on the west shore of the island, and flown to San Diego.

The only automobile road on Cedros runs from the cannery about five miles south to a landing field near the southeast tip of the island.

An interesting excursion can be made on foot from the village to a spring about 1,300 feet up the southeast side of Cerro Cenizo, from which water is piped to the cannery. The place is a pretty oasis with a grove of cedars (from which the island gets its name) and palm trees.

Two miles north of the town on the beach is another spring in a palm grove, known as LA PALMITA. This spring has been used by navigators from the time of the Manila galleons (see below). It is now a favorite anchorage for American tuna boats in search of live bait. About 8 miles north of La Palmita is a beach at the mouth of a long canyon which forms a pass across the island north of Cerro Cenizo. A trail runs across this divide to the abandoned ranch of SAN LUIS, where there are some ruined houses and a tiny spring.

The ridge of mountains at the north end of the island has two small forests of pine trees, some of which reach a height of 70 feet. They are rather hard to reach, on the northwest slope at an elevation of 1,500-3,000 feet. This area is much more humid than the rest of the island and is the refuge of mule deer and wild goats, the latter descended from a few pairs left by whalers many years ago to provide a meat supply.

Along the whole eastern shore of Cedros there is good fishing (during the summer) for yellowtail, barracuda, cabrilla, tuna, albacore, and bonito. Around the north end (Cabo Norte) and along the western shore are rookeries of harbor seals. Formerly there were large herds of fur seal, sea otter, and sea elephant. Sea elephants are still found on the adjacent San Benito Islands, and on Guadalupe Island (see p. 196).

Originally Cedros was inhabited by a tribe of Cochimí Indians, who called it Amalguá, or Isle of Fogs. It was discovered in 1540 by Francisco de Ulloa, who had been sent out by Hernán Cortés to explore the coasts of California. After spending three months on the island Ulloa sent one of his ships back to Mexico and himself sailed north, never to be seen again. Beginning in 1565, and for the next 250 years, Cedros Island was sighted almost every year by the Manila galleon on its long eastward voyage from the Orient to Acapulco. Occasionally the galleon called at La Palmita or one of the other springs to take on water. There are several reports of scrapes with the Indians. Ulloa managed to frighten them away with dogs, and Sebastián Vizcaíno, who visited Cedros in 1602-03, also had his troubles with them. In 1732 the Jesuit Padre Taraval had the entire population of the island moved across to the mainland mission of San Ignacio. From that year until about 1920, when the cannery was started, Cedros was without permanent inhabitants, although it was frequently visited by American ships looking for fur seals and sea otters, until these animals disappeared about 1850. Around the middle of the last century the island was much frequented by whalers. Early in the 1900's an American company began exploiting a gold and copper mine near the north end of the island, but this enterprise was abandoned during the Mexican Revolution.

BAHÍA TORTUGAS. Excellent harbor for vessels of any size. See page 131.

PUNTA ABREOJOS. See page 140.

LAGUNA DE SAN IGNACIO (LA LAGUNA)

A large inlet of the same type as Scammon's Lagoon, surrounded by flat sandy country with very little vegetation. The entrance is easier to negotiate than that of Scammon's, and once inside there is a fine, smooth deep-water harbor. On the east side is a fishing settlement connected by motor road with San Ignacio (see page 141). The lagoon is a good place for catching *caguamas* (giant sea turtles). A large salt flat extends northward to San Angel.

The entrance to San Ignacio Lagoon was discovered by Rodríguez Cabrillo in 1542. Sebastián Vizcaíno, who visited this coast in 1602, called the outer bay Ballenas because of the large number of whales which used the lagoon as a breeding place. From 1859 to 1867 the lagoon was visited by many American ships and practically all the whales were killed.

BAHÍA SAN JUANICO. See page 142.

ESTERO DE SAN GREGORIO. See page 142.

BAHÍA MAGDALENA

Magdalena Bay is one of the finest natural harbors in the world. It is a very large deep-water bay formed by a series of mountainous islands which protect it from all winds. The entrance channel is 2½ miles wide and 10 to 20 fathoms deep. North of the main part of the bay is a long shallow lagoon navigable to small vessels for about 70 miles. To the south is a connecting bay, Bahía Almejas. The mainland is extremely flat and barren, with mangrove swamps along the shore. It is uninhabited except for temporary fishing camps. There are three small settlements on the islands: BAHÍA MAGDALENA, on Magdalena Island, and PUERTO CORTÉS and PUERTO ALCATRAZ, on Margarita Island. Fairly good fresh water is found on Margarita. There are some brackish wells on the mainland, and water is taken to the village of Bahía Magdalena in barrels. Tracks connecting with the main highway to La Paz (see p. 165) run to the bay at La Florida, San Carlos, Médano Amarillo, Estero Salinas, and Puerto Chale (the latter on Almejas Bay).

There is good sport fishing in the waters of the bay, particularly during the summer months. It is a good place to catch *caguamas* (sea turtles), the favorite dish of Baja California.

ISLA MAGDALENA is a narrow irregular-shaped island with a length of more than 50 miles. The southern part is mountainous, while the rest of the island is a succession of sand dunes and mangrove swamps. Its southern point forms the north entrance to Magdalena Bay. Twelve miles north of here on the east side of the island is Caleta del Navío (Man-of-War Cove), the best anchorage, where the village of Bahía Magdalena is located. It had a population of 100 in 1950, mostly government officials and fishermen, living in a cluster of frame houses. There is a Government radio station, and a customhouse where foreign vessels are expected to show their papers. Only very limited supplies are available. There is a landing field suitable for light aircraft 1½ miles west of the village.

ISLA MARGARITA is 21 miles long, 4½ miles wide, and has an area of 85 square miles. The whole island is mountainous except in the center, where a low pass divides the two ranges. The greatest elevation is Cerro Margarita, 1,860 feet high, near the southeast end. On the north side, on the connecting channel between Magdalena and Almejas bays, is the Mexican naval base of Puerto Cortés, which had a population of 390 in 1950. It is a new settlement, begun in 1934, and is the headquarters of the Third Naval Zone. There is a post and telegraph office, a government radio station, and an excellent airport. A road runs from Puerto Cortés north to a small and declining fishing village, Puerto Alcatraz.

Magdalena Bay was discovered by Francisco de Ulloa, the pilot of Hernán Cortés, in 1539. Ulloa baptized the bay San Abad. While the Spaniards were looking for fresh water they were attacked by Indians, and Ulloa was wounded. The bay received its present name from Sebastián Vizcaíno, who stopped here in 1602. Vizcaíno and his men camped on the shore for several days and were visited by many Indians, who had canoes and built fish traps along the beach. The Jesuit missionary Padre Guillén made an overland expedition to Magdalena Bay in 1719, with the idea of developing a port of refuge for the Manila galleons. A visiting station was founded about 1734 near the shore of the bay, probably in the vicinity of Laguna Verde, and the galleons occasionally entered and traded with the missionaries. About the middle of the last century Magdalena was a favorite port-of-call for American whalers. Later, in the 1870's, the great plains stretching north of the bay were the scene of an unsuccessful attempt at colonization by an American land company. In the early 1900's another company was organized to exploit the magnesite deposits on Margarita Island. Every effort to colonize the shores of the bay, from the earliest times, failed because of the extreme shortage of fresh water. In spite of this, Magdalena has great strategic importance and was coveted by the United States, Japan, and other countries long before Mexico decided to develop it herself as a naval base.

PUNTA LOBOS. The landing place for Todos Santos. See page 189.

CABO SAN LUCAS, at the tip of the peninsula. The bay is protected from the northwest winds, but is dangerous during the summer months. See page 187.

SAN JOSÉ DEL CABO. See page 185.

BAHÍA DE LAS PALMAS. See page 178.

BAHA DE LOS MUERTOS. See page 175.

ISLA CERRALVO

Cerralvo is the southernmost island on the Gulf side of Baja California. It is 18 miles long and has a greatest width of 4¼ miles and an area of 50 square miles. With the exception of the southwest end, which is low and sandy, the island is very rugged and mountainous. There is a ridge of mountains about 2,000 feet high, reaching a peak of 2,520 feet near the center of the island. The shoreline on both sides is an alternation of steep rocky cliffs and small stretches of gravel beach, with deep water close inshore. The best anchorage is at the south end where there is a well of brackish water near the beach. There are two other small bays with sandy beaches on the west shore. The whole island is barren and covered with a dense growth of cactus.

The waters around Cerralvo are good fishing grounds, particularly during the summer months. Formerly the west side of the island was an important pearl-diving area. The only game consists of a herd of goats.

Cerralvo, at first known as Isla Santiago, was discovered by Hernán Cortés in 1535. At that time the island was inhabited by Indians of the Pericú tribe. A Spanish pearler, Francisco de Ortega, called here in 1632 and gave Cerralvo its present name in honor of his patron the viceroy of New Spain. The island was visited by many other pearling expeditions during the 17th and 18th centuries. In 1721 a party of Cerralvo Indians raided the newly-founded mission of La Paz. To punish them the missionaries sent some soldiers across, but they were unable to do very much as the Indians escaped to the hills. Soon afterward the Cerralvo tribe was Christianized and moved to the mainland, since which time the island has remained without permanent inhabitants.

LAS CRUCES. See page 173.

BAHÍA COYOTE. See page 174.

BAHÍA PICHILINGUE. See page 173.

This is a small, well-protected harbor between Pichilingue Island (called on the chart Isla San Juan Nepomuceno) and the mainland, 8 miles north of La Paz. There is a road passable to automobiles from La Paz. It is a beautiful calm bay, deep enough for the largest vessels. The north entrance is rather tricky, even for small boats, but the south entrance has a depth of 5 fathoms. The surrounding country is extremely barren, with mangrove swamps along the mainland shore. To the east is a mountain range of jagged black peaks, looking like a weird landscape on the moon. The warm waters of the bay are a good place to catch the smaller varieties of game fish. There are several white sand beaches at the north end, perfect for bathing.

At the south end of Pichilingue Island is a salt deposit, used to supply La Paz, and a Mexican naval storage base cared for by a few sailors. This was originally (1866 to 1925) a coaling station of the U.S. Navy. Fresh water is brought from La Paz. Above the naval base on the flat top of the island is a landing field.

There is good reason to believe that Pichilingue Bay was the site of Hernán Cortés' colony of Santa Cruz, the first Spanish settlement in California, which lasted from 1535 to 1536. Sebastián Vizcaíno called here in 1596 and named the place Puerto del Marqués (in honor of Cortés, who was Marqués del Valle), because there were some ruins which he assumed to be those of Santa Cruz. At that time there was a village of Indian fishermen on the shore. The place was visited many times during the following years by Spanish pearling expeditions. The name Pichilingue was given to the bay after the visit of some French buccaneers ("Pichilingue" is a corruption of Vlissingen, or Flushing, in Holland, the home port of Dutch freebooters; the term came to be applied to buccaneers of any nationality). The pirates in question raided the coast of Nueva Galicia from 1687 to 1691, carrying off a large quantity of silver. Altogether they spent seven months at Pichilingue Bay, on three different occasions, careening their ship and trading with the Indians for pearls. Inevitably the legend arose that they had buried their treasure on Pichilingue Island, but it is likely that they took it with them when they left.

In 1768 the *visitador general* Gálvez established this bay as the official port for the south and ordered its name changed to Puerto de Cortés, "its honorable and former title," but the more romantic name of Pichilingue has prevailed.

LA PAZ. See pages 168-72.

ISLA DEL ESPÍRITU SANTO (SEE MAP 16)

Espíritu Santo Island lies about 5 miles off the mainland, 18 miles north of La Paz. It is 14 miles long, 5 miles at its widest point, with an area of 42 square miles. On the east side it drops down to the Gulf in steep cliffs from a few hundred to almost 2,000 feet high. From the top of this main ridge a series of mesas and lower ridges slope gradually down to the west. The dry gullies that separate these ridges form a number of deep bays cutting far into the west shore, snug little harbors protected from prevailing winds. Each bay has a small tidal estuary partly covered with mangrove, and many of them have beautiful white sand beaches. The water is perfectly clear, ideal for bathing. There are three small islets off the west side, the largest of which is called Ballena (whale) Island. The northern end of Espíritu Santo is detached from the rest of the island and is called on some maps Isla Partida. The two sections are sometimes joined by a low isthmus.

Espíritu Santo gets only about 5 inches of rain a year, resulting in a sparse desert vegetation. The only permanent fresh water occurs in underground seepages in some of the longer canyons on the west side, although it can be found in *tinajas,* or natural rock reservoirs, after a rain. Generally the climate is similar to that of La Paz.

The island is uninhabited, although it is visited by fishermen and an occasional American yacht. Many big game fish have been caught off the west shore. Peculiar to this island is a species of black jack rabbit which makes excellent eating. About the only other game are a few ring-tailed cats.

When it was discovered by the Spaniards (probably in 1533) Espíritu

Santo supported a population of several hundred Indians who lived from fishing. Cortés, the conqueror of Mexico, visited the island and called it ISLA DE PERLAS. The pearl beds off the west shore are frequently mentioned in early manuscript accounts, and they were much visited by Spanish pearlers in the 16th, 17th, and 18th centuries. Francisco de Ortega, who gave the island its present name, spent several days here in 1632 with a wooden diving bell weighted with lead and big enough for two people, and heavy iron drags for scraping oysters from the sea floor. He reported that the Indian men went entirely naked and did nothing but fish and hunt, while the women, who brought water and wood to the camp and did the cooking, wore a buckskin covering below the waist. Admiral Atondo spent a week at Espíritu Santo in 1685. He gave the Indians one knife for each 50 oysters, and also distributed sandals and rattles which were much appreciated. In one day 500 oysters were brought up.

In 1720 the Indians of Espíritu Santo were assigned to the newly-founded mission of La Paz, but they continued to live on their island, visiting the mission periodically to attend mass and learn the catechism. Pearlers still arrived and traded with the islanders, although the missionaries discouraged their visits. After the Pericú rebellion of 1734-36 the Espíritu Santo Indians disappeared; some were killed, others moved to the mainland, and the rest died from disease.

Near the southern end of the island at the head of San Gabriel Bay are some old stone ruins, all that remains of an interesting experiment in pearl-raising. In the early 1900's a French resident of La Paz, Gaston Vives, built a number of stone corrals along the edge of the tidal estuary. Here young pearl oysters were kept protected from their natural enemies until they were large enough to be planted in private beds in the Gulf. No effort was made to produce *cultured* pearls by inserting artificial irritants, the idea being that, through protection, the number of oysters and pearls would be increased. The experiment was wrecked during the Mexican Revolution before it had time to prove its worth.

ISLA SAN JOSÉ (SEE MAP 16)

San José is a large rugged island, 78 square miles in area, with a length of 19 miles and a greatest width of 6½ miles. The highest point, near the center, is 2,080 feet above sea level. The mountains drop steeply off to the Gulf on the east, while there is a more gradual slope on the west. The coast along the east side is a succession of steep cliffs with few beaches. The southern and western shores are much lower with frequent sand beaches, perfect for bathing. Fresh water is found at the head of Bahía Amortajada, at the settlement at Punta Salinas, and near the mouths of the longer arroyos on the west side. The canyons are filled with many varieties of cactus, while the higher slopes are almost devoid of vegetation.

There is a very fine snug harbor at Bahía Amortajada, protected by a long sand-spit and the islet of El Cayo. Five miles up the coast at Punta Salinas is an extensive salt deposit, a tiny settlement (8 people in 1950), and a landing strip. The salt is taken by launch to La Paz.

During the summer the waters around San José are teeming with all kinds of fish, including the big game varieties. There is good hunting in the northern part of the island for mule deer. Wild goats, rabbits, and ring-tailed cats are also found.

The west side of San José was a favorite haunt of Spanish pearlers in the 16th and 17th centuries. The island was named by Francisco de Ortega in 1633. The San José Indians, a branch of the Pericú tribe, caused the Jesuit missionaries a good deal of trouble by raiding the mission settlements on the mainland until they were pacified by Padre Bravo in 1720. Many of them were killed by punitive expeditions, and the rest died from disease, so that the island was depopulated by 1750.

On the mainland opposite the south end of San José is a great rocky cliff known as EL MECHUDO (the long-haired man). According to a legend, many years ago some Indians were diving for pearls in the rich oyster beds nearby. Most of them were good Christians and invoked the protection of the Virgin before diving, promising Her the finest pearl of the day's catch. However, there was a bad Indian among them who said that he cared nothing for the Virgin but would rely on the protection of the devil, and would keep his pearls for himself. He soon came up with a tremendous black pearl, the finest that had ever been seen. Intoxicated with his success he dived again, but this time did not return to the surface. His companions went down to see what was the matter and found the wicked diver with his leg caught in a giant clam, his long black hair waving about, and the terror of eternal damnation in his eyes. The black pearl was given to the Virgin through her legitimate representative, the missionary, and the divers even to the present day give a wide berth to El Mechudo.

Los Dolores

A small ranching community on the mainland shore opposite the north end of San José Island. The inhabitants (pop. 31 in 1950) live from fishing, cattle-raising, and subsistence farming. Vegetables, grapes, and many kinds of fruits are irrigated from several springs and wells in the arroyo. The bay, a rather exposed anchorage, is a port-of-call for small coasting vessels from La Paz, and a shipping and supply point for ranches in the interior. A trail runs up the canyon and across a pass to La Presa, 20 miles inland, which can be reached by automobile from La Paz (see p. 167).

About three miles up the arroyo from the beach are a ruined dam and irrigation ditch and an old orchard of orange and lemon trees, all that remains of the mission of Nuestra Señora de los Dolores. The Jesuit Padre Guillén founded this mission in 1721 on a site known to the Indians as Apate. Originally the territory assigned to Los Dolores extended across the peninsula to Magdalena Bay, but in 1737 separate missions were founded at La Pasión (near La Presa) and San Luis Gonzaga, and a few years later Los Dolores was reduced to the status of a visiting station. It was reestablished as a private ranch early in the 19th century.

This is a good place to get guides and animals for hunting trips in the interior. Mountain sheep are found on the higher slopes of the coast range about a day's ride above Los Dolores.

Isla Catalina

A barren island, probably without fresh water, 15 miles out in the Gulf. It is 7½ miles long, 3 miles wide, and has an area of 16 square miles. The coast is a succession of steep cliffs, although there is reported to be a landing place with a sand beach on the east side. The mountains reach a height of 1,540 feet above sea level in the south. Very little is known about this island, although it is occasionally visited by fishermen.

The original name given to this island by the pearler Ortega in 1633 was San Diego, but later this name was shifted to another island farther to the south. On most early maps it appears as Isla Catalán or Catalana. When the U.S. Navy charted the coast they changed the name again to Santa Catalina. There is no record that it was ever inhabited, and it was only rarely visited by the pearlers.

Isla Monserrate

Monserrate is another rugged, waterless, treeless island, 8 miles from shore. It is 4½ miles long, 2 miles wide, and 7 square miles in area. There are low mountains which reach a height of 730 feet, falling off on the east and south shores in steep cliffs. The western shore is low and rocky, and there is a sand beach on the north side.

At one time Monserrate must have had fresh water, as it was inhabited by Indians as late as 1717. During colonial times it was occasionally visited by Spanish pearling expeditions. It was baptized Santa Cruz by Ortega in 1633, but Atondo in 1683 renamed it Monserrate.

Bahía Agua Verde

A small bay on the Gulf side south of Isla Monserrate. It is a snug harbor protected against the usual winds by the tall bluff of Punta San Pascual on the north and another cliff on the east. At the entrance is a precipitous white rock called Solitaria on the chart. There is an inner harbor at the end of the bay, protected by another islet. At the south end is a sand beach and the small fishing and ranching village of Agua Verde (pop. 51 in 1950). Brackish but drinkable water is obtained from a shallow well. A trail runs along the coast connecting the settlement with Ligüí, 22 miles north, accessible by car from Loreto.

Agua Verde Bay was visited and named by one of Vizcaíno's captains on a pearling expedition in 1596. Ortega called here in 1633 and saw many mountain sheep (they are still found in the mountains above the bay). Atondo, who visited Agua Verde in 1685, reported that there was a ranchería of friendly Indians on the shore.

Puerto Escondido

A beautiful and well-protected little harbor for small boats, 17 miles south of Loreto by motor road. There is an outer bay which offers good enough protection from most winds, but the inner harbor is perfectly still and almost completely landlocked. The entrance channel is only 75 feet wide and has a depth of 9 feet, while inside the water is 4 to 7 fathoms deep. At the entrance is an abandoned white house. A road leads ½ mile inland to the ranch of Puerto Escondido, where good water can be obtained. There is excellent fishing in the port, and good hunting in the mountains, which come very close to the shore at this point.

Puerto Escondido seems to have been first visited by the Spanish pearling captain Ortega in 1633. At that time the entrance channel was on the north, through Bahía Chuenque. Ortega called it Bahía de los Danzantes (Bay of Dancers), because the Indians received him dancing and playing flutes. Atondo in 1685 renamed the harbor San Ignacio de Loyola. The Jesuits built a warehouse at the entrance and used Puerto Escondido as a harbor of refuge and a supply point for the missions. They were probably responsible for blocking off the north entrance and opening the present southern channel.

Isla de Carmen (see map 16)

A large, bare, mountainous island opposite the town of Loreto. It is 20 miles long, with a maximum width of 7 miles, tapering to a point in the south. The area is 55 square miles. A chain of mountains extends the entire length reaching a peak of 1,570 feet above sea level near the north end. There are several small ports and harbors. Near the northwest corner is Puerto Balandra, a fine inlet with a narow entrance; it is connected with Bahía Salinas, on the east side, by a trail across the mountains. Salinas Bay, used by large ships, is open to the south but protected from the usual winds. Bahía Marqués, on the southwest side of the island, is rather open with a sandy beach.

Behind Salinas Bay, in the sunken crater of an extinct volcano, is one of the finest salt deposits in the world. The salt, 99.6% pure, has been the principal supply of Mexico since colonial times, although now most of the production goes to the United States. Large scale exploitation began in the 1850's and is now in the hands of Salinas del Pacífico, S.A., a Mexican company. About 40,000 tons are taken out each year. The company settlement, between the salt lagoon and the bay, had a population of 400 in 1950. A narrow gauge railway runs from the salt works to a pier extending into the bay, where lighters transfer the salt to ships. There is a radio station and a landing field occasionally used by the planes of commercial air lines.

During the summer months there is excellent deep-sea fishing in the waters around Carmen Island. Fresh water is found at several places along the shore.

The coasts of Isla de Carmen were a favorite diving area of the Spanish pearlers in the 17th and 18th centuries. The island was baptized Nuestra Señora del Carmen by Francisco de Ortega, who called here in 1633 and found it inhabited. The Jesuit missionaries used the island as a grazing area for cattle, and tried without success to get a monopoly of the salt production.

LORETO. See page 154.

ISLA CORONADOS

A small, barren island near the mainland northeast of Loreto. It is 2 miles in length, with an average width of 1½ miles and an area of 3½ square miles. The highest point is a volcanic cone near the north end, 930 feet above sea level. The coast is composed of steep cliffs except at the southwest corner, where there is a long sandy peninsula. There is no fresh water on the island.

Ortega visited this island on his 1633 pearling expedition and named it Isla de los Coronados. The limestone deposits were used by the Jesuit missionaries in constructing the church and other buildings in Loreto.

BAHÍA SAN NICOLÁS

A large open bay on the Gulf side, reportedly connected by a road (ca. 12 mi.) with the transpeninsular highway. The shore is low on the south, with bluffs and mountains on the west. Near the center of the bay is the small settlement of San Nicolás, at the mouth of a broad arroyo. It consists of four or five families of fishermen, and some gardens irrigated from wells.

This bay is shown on early maps as *Bahía de Comondú*. It was probably the site of a visiting station of Comondú mission.

At the entrance to San Nicolás Bay is the small (one square mile) island of SAN ILDEFONSO, a barren piece of land reaching 390 feet above sea level. Apparently this island has been sinking into the sea, as Ortega describes it as being considerably larger in 1636. At that time San Ildefonso was inhabited by Indians and had some wells of brackish water on the beach.

BAHÍA CONCEPCIÓN

A deep indentation in the Gulf coast south of Mulegé. It is about 25 miles long and from 2½ to 6 miles wide. Most of the bay is unprotected from the northwesterly winds, but there is a fine sheltered anchorage on the west side in Bahía Coyote. This is a beautiful harbor with deep water and many little islands and sandy beaches. The main transpeninsular road runs along the west and south shores, and there are several little fishing settlements along the road (see page 152). There is an old road, no longer used, on the east shore of the bay running out to Punta Concepción, where there is an abandoned manganese mine. Fishing is good, particularly during the summer months.

Concepción Bay was probably discovered by Ulloa during his exploration of the Gulf in 1539. Sebastián Vizcaíno took refuge from a storm in Bahía Coyote in 1596. Another pearling captain, Lucenilla, visited the bay in 1668 and reported that the shores were peopled with white-skinned Indians who lived from fruits and shellfish. These Indians were Christianized and gathered into the mission of Mulegé by the Jesuit Padre Basaldúa, who opened the first trail along the west shore in 1705.

MULEGÉ. See page 151.

ISLA SAN MARCOS

The barren, mountainous island of San Marcos is six miles long with a maximum width of 2½ miles and an area of 12 square miles. The highest elevation, near the center, is 890 feet above sea level. The coast is a series of rugged cliffs, broken occasionally by sand and gravel beaches. At the southern tip is a long sandspit. There are several brackish wells, but drinking water is brought from the mainland. About the only animals on the island are a few goats. The population in 1950 was 268, all employees of the gypsum company and their families.

San Marcos is a concession originally operated by the Compañía Occidental Mexicana to exploit the large gypsum deposits. The settlement is near the southwest end of the island, where there is a long T-shaped pier with a depth alongside of 35 feet. The gypsum is quarried both from the surface and from an intricate system of tunnels, moved to the pier by means of a narrow gauge railroad, and loaded onto vessels by a belt conveyor and chutes. Most of it goes to the United States for use in building materials. The company began operations in 1925. There is a launch which goes to Santa Rosalía (15 miles away) about once a week for supplies and mail.

When San Marcos was discovered by the Spaniards it was inhabited by a small tribe of fishermen Indians. The original name was ISLA TORTUGAS, or GALÁPAGOS (Turtle Island), but this name has been transferred to another island (see below). One of the Jesuit missionaries used gypsum from San Marcos to make glass windows for the church at Mulegé.

ISLA TORTUGA

Tortuga, 22 miles off the coast of Santa Rosalía, is the protruding top of a volcano which erupted in fairly recent geological times from the floor of the Gulf, 5,000 feet below the surface. It is considered by geologists to be the youngest island in the Gulf. The highest point is 1,020 feet above sea level. It is about 3½ miles long, slightly over a mile wide, and has an area of three square miles. The center is occupied by the broad crater of the volcano, and the whole island is covered with dark lava rocks making it difficult to climb. There is no fresh water, and very little vegetation.

SANTA ROSALÍA. See page 143.

EL BARRIL. See page 136.

ISLA ANGEL DE LA GUARDA

The largest island of Baja California, Angel de la Guarda is 45 miles long and has a greatest width of 12 miles, with an area of 350 square miles. It is extremely barren and mountainous, with several peaks over 3,000 feet high. The east shore has bold rocky bluffs alternating with open bays and gravel beaches. A spur from the main mountain range runs out to Punta Rocosa, consisting of high steep peaks. The west shore is abrupt, and the channel between the island and the mainland (8 miles wide) is very deep with a swift current. The best harbor is Puerto Refugio, formed by several offshore islands at the north end of Angel de la Guarda, with good shelter and sandy beaches. There is excellent fishing during the summer months.

As far as is known there is no fresh water on the island except that found in *tinajas*, or natural tanks in the mountains. Rainfall is very slight, and consequently plant life is restricted to a thin covering of cactus. The island is chiefly inhabited by *iguanas* (large lizards) and black rattlesnakes. There is no large game.

Angel de la Guarda Island was discovered by Francisco de Ulloa in his exploration of the upper Gulf in 1539. Apparently it has never been inhabited, and only rarely visited. In 1765, on the strength of a rumor that some fires had been seen on Angel de la Guarda, the Jesuit Padre Link crossed over from Los Angeles Bay and explored most of the island, but he found no Indians, animals, nor fresh water.

BAHÍA DE LOS ANGELES. See pages 123-24.

PUERTO DE CALAMAJUÉ. See page 86.

BAHÍA SAN LUIS GONZAGA. See page 84.

This is a small deep harbor shown on the H. O. chart as Willard Bay, at the northwest end of Ensenada de San Francisquito (which in turn is erroneously called Gonzaga, or San Luis Gonzales, Bay on the chart). It is sheltered from all winds, with low sandy shores.

PUERTECITOS. See page 83.

SAN FELIPE. See pages 81-82.

THE MAPS

In the following atlas of maps the roads of the Lower California peninsula are shown on fifteen detailed sections, and a sixteenth section covers some of the more important islands.

The larger folding map is the key to locating the individual section maps as well as the routes described in the text.

Topography shown on the maps, with some exceptions, is as depicted on aeronautical charts published by the United States Government. Except where stated to the contrary in the text description, all roads shown have been traveled by one or both of the authors, and their locations, together with the place names shown are taken from their personal observations. This information has been supplemented and verified by first hand information from other travelers and residents.

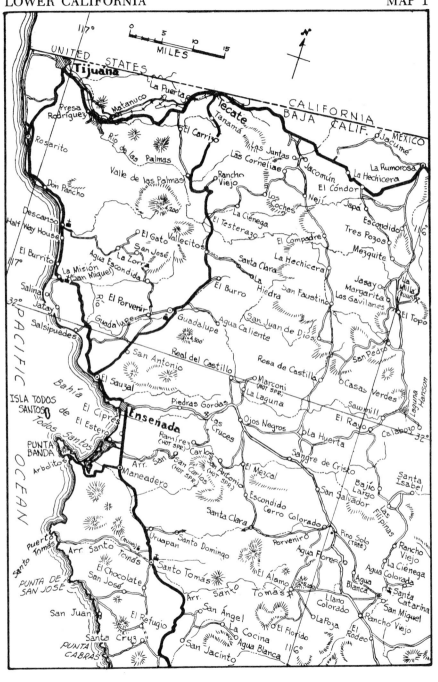

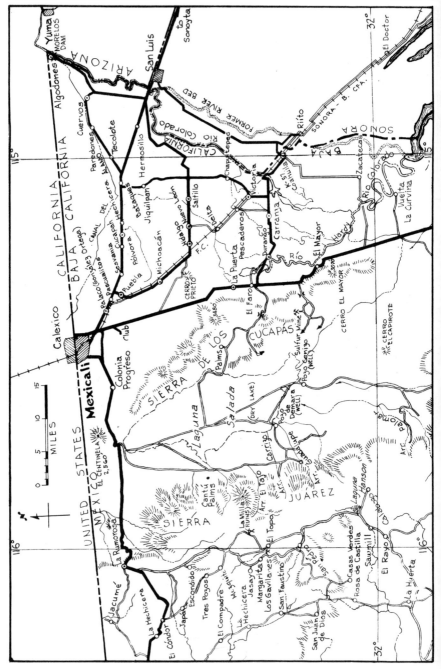

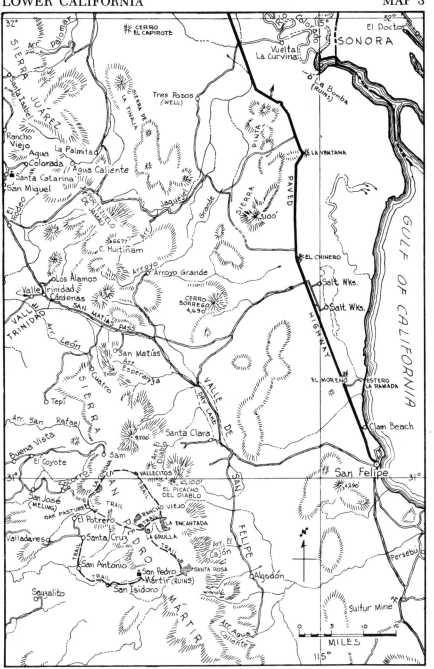

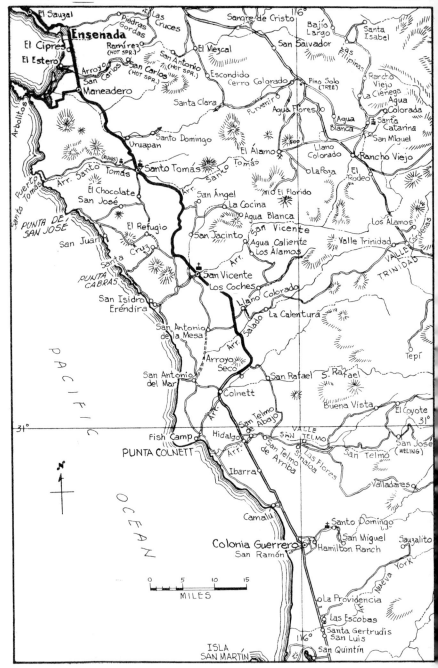

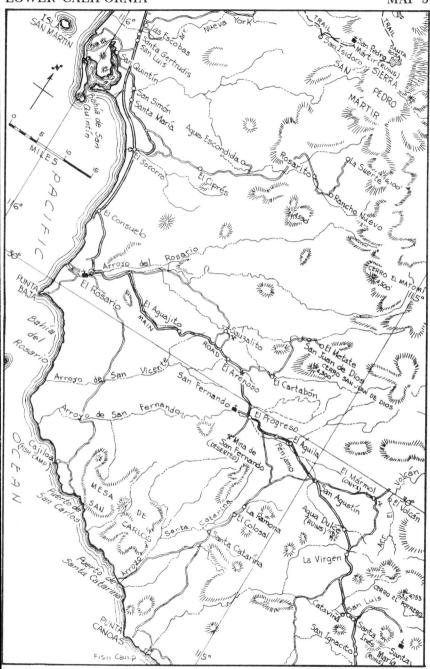

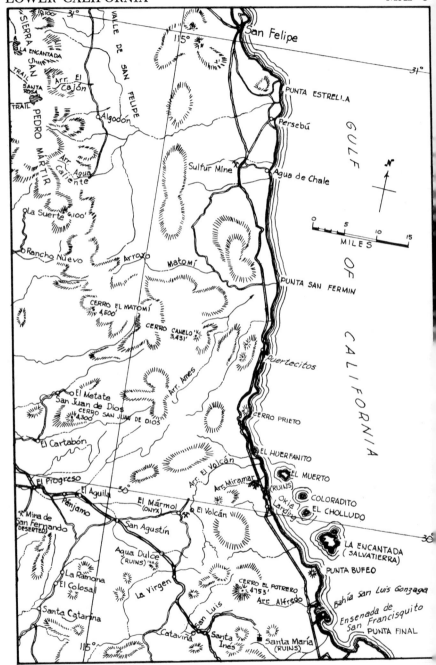

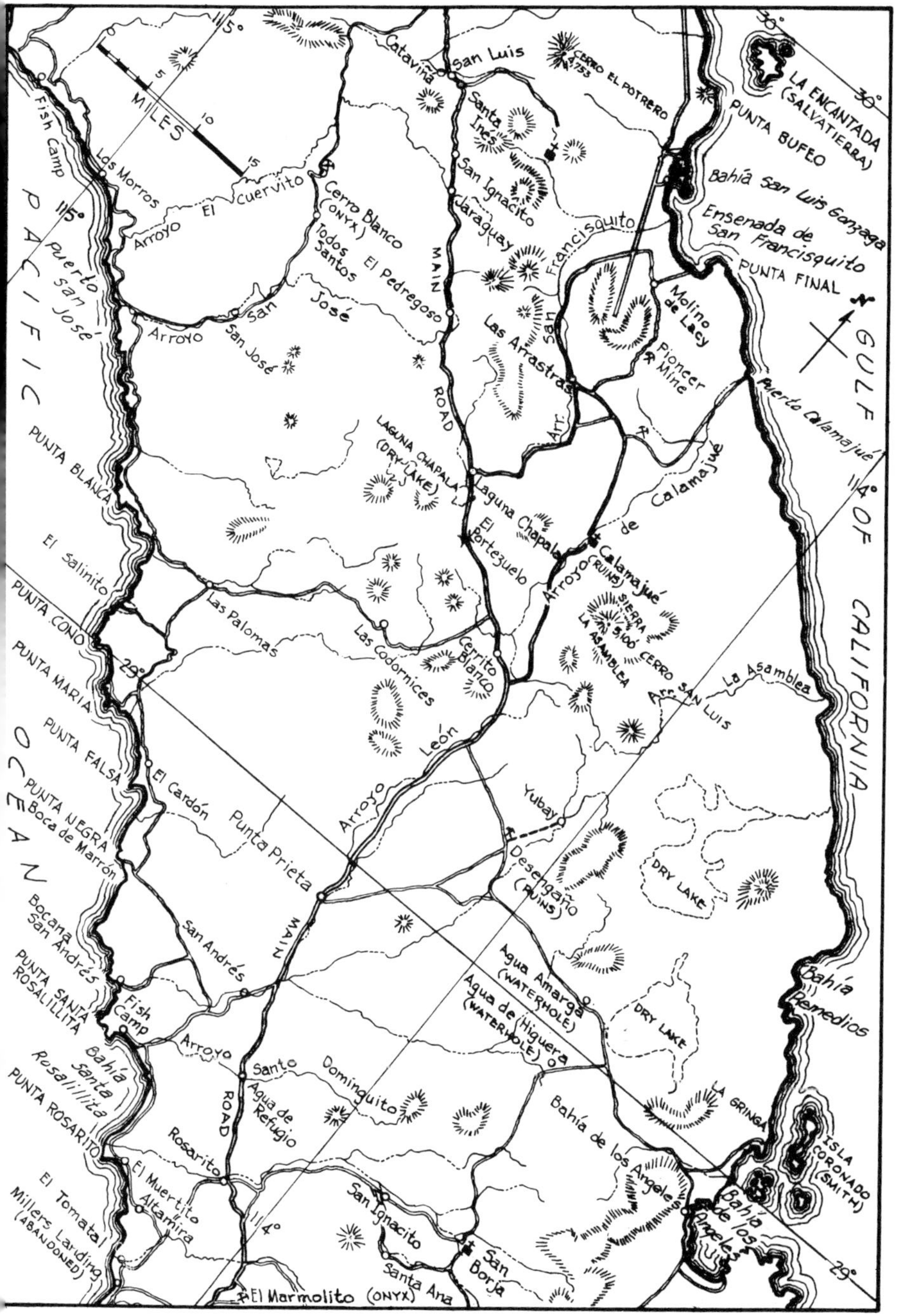
MILES
PACIFIC OCEAN
GULF OF CALIFORNIA
Cataviña
San Luis
CERRO EL POTRERO
Santa Inés
San Ignacito
Jaraguay
MAIN ROAD
Cerro Blanco (ONYX)
Todos Santos
El Pedregoso
Arroyo El Cuervito
Los Morros
Fish Camp
Puerto San José
Arroyo San José
LA ENCANTADA (SALVATIERRA)
PUNTA BUFEO
Bahía San Luis Gonzaga
Ensenada de San Francisquito
San Francisquito
PUNTA FINAL
Molino de Lacy
Pioneer Mine
Las Arrastras
Puerto Calamajué
LAGUNA CHAPALA (DRY LAKE)
Laguna Chapala
El Portezuelo
Arroyo de Calamajué
Calamajué (RUINS)
PUNTA BLANCA
El Salinito
PUNTA CONO
PUNTA MARIA
PUNTA FALSA
PUNTA NEGRA
Boca de Marrón
Las Palomas
Las Codornices
Cerrito Blanco
SIERRA LA ASAMBLEA
CERRO SAN LUIS
La Asamblea
Arroyo León
El Cardón
Punta Prieta
Yubay
Desengaño (RUINS)
DRY LAKE
Bocana San Andrés
San Andrés
PUNTA SANTA ROSALILLITA
Fish Camp
Agua Amarga (WATERHOLE)
Agua de Higuera (WATERHOLE)
Bahía Remedios
Bahía Santa Rosalillita
Arroyo Santo Domingo
Dominguito
Agua de Refugio
PUNTA ROSARITO
Rosarito
El Muertito
Altamira
El Tomatal
Millers Landing (ABANDONED)
LA GRINGA
ISLA CORONADO (SMITH)
Bahía de los Angeles
San Ignacito
San Borja
Santa Ana
El Marmolito (ONYX)

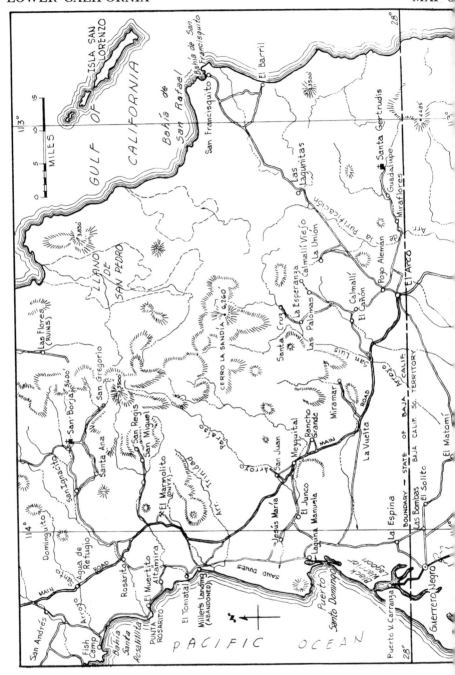

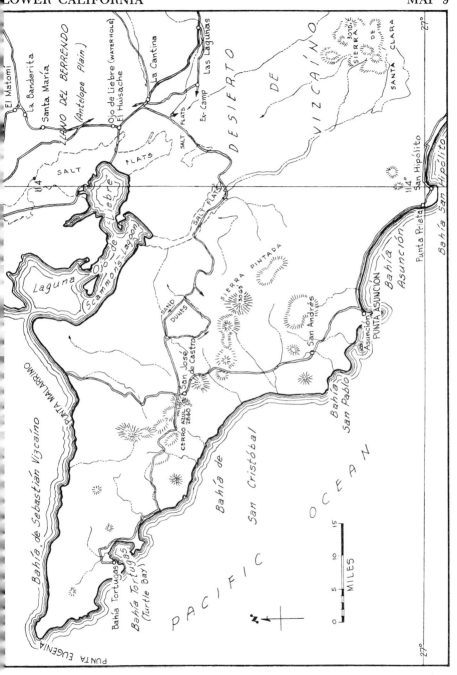

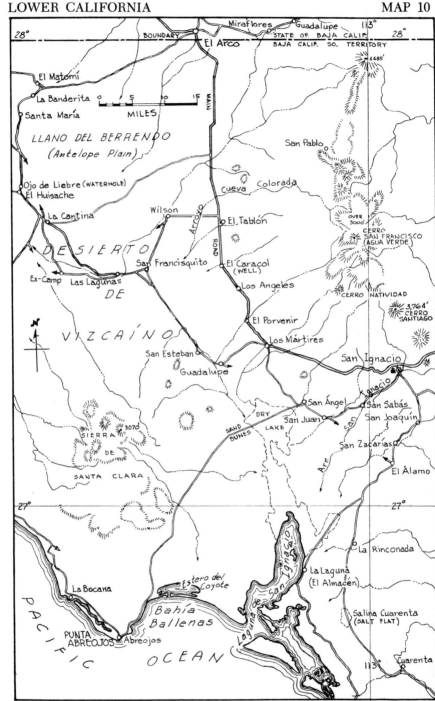

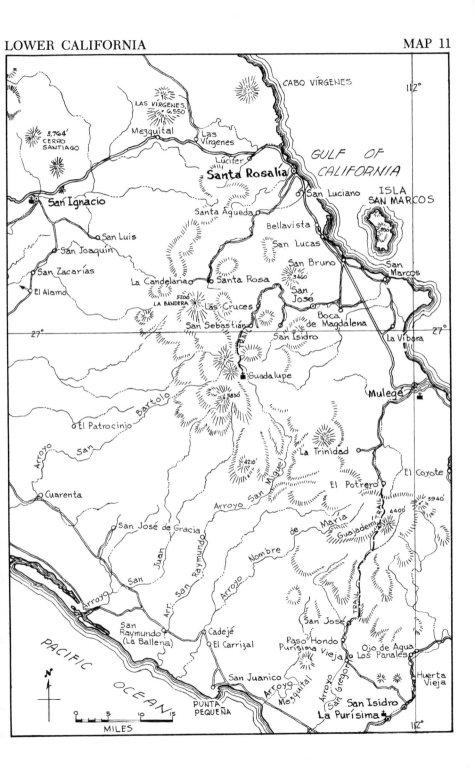

CABO VÍRGENES

LAS VÍRGENES, 6,550

Mezquital

Las Vírgenes

3,764' CERRO SANTIAGO

Lúcifer

Santa Rosalía

GULF OF CALIFORNIA

San Ignacio

San Luciano

ISLA SAN MARCOS

Santa Águeda

Bellavista

5,550

San Luis

San Lucas

San Joaquín

San Bruno

San Marcos

San Zacarías

3460

El Alamo

La Candelaria

Santa Rosa

San José

5200

LA BANDERA

Las Cruces

San Sebastián

Boca de Magdalena

La Víbora

San Isidro

27°   27°

Guadalupe

Mulegé

5830

El Patrocinio

La Trinidad

El Coyote

4210'

El Potrero

3940'

Cuarenta

Arroyo San Miguel

4400'

San José de Gracia

María Guajademi

Nombre

de

San Raymundo

San José

San Raymundo (La Ballena)

Cadejé

Paso Hondo

El Carrizal

Purísima Vieja

Ojo de Agua Los Panales

San Juanico

Huerta Vieja

PACIFIC OCEAN

PUNTA PEQUEÑA

Arroyo Mezquital

San Gregorio

San Isidro

La Purísima

Bartolo

San Juan

Arr.

N

5   10   15

MILES

112°

112°

MAP 12

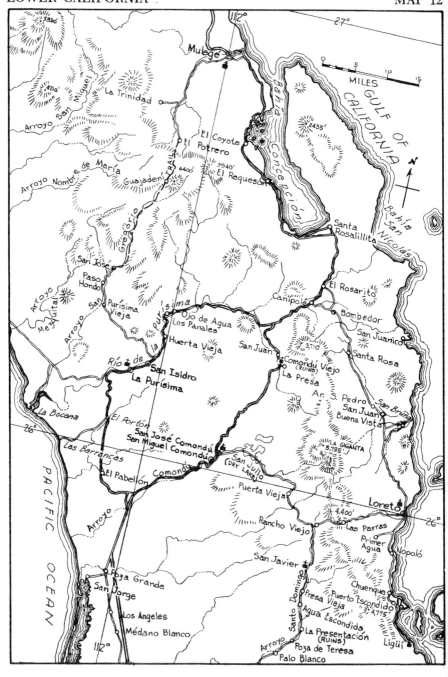

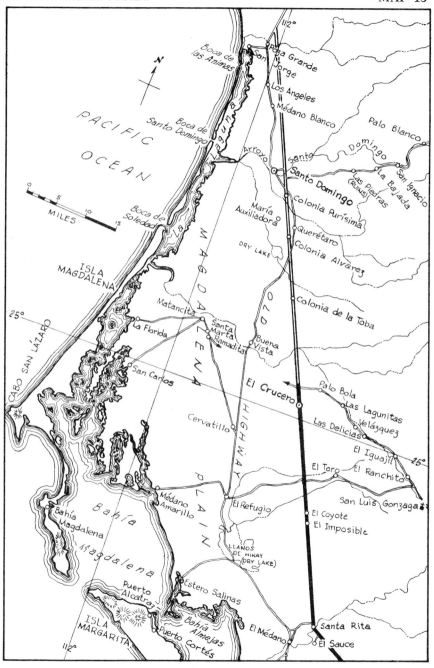

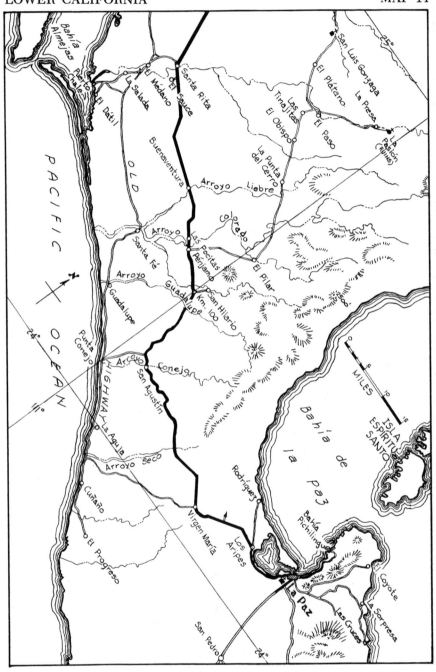

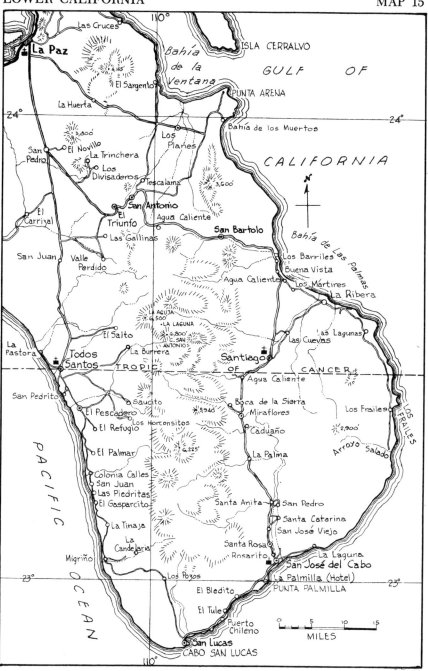

Las Cruces

La Paz

Bahía
de la
Ventana

ISLA CERRALVO

GULF   OF

PUNTA ARENA

La Huerta

24°   24°

Bahía de los Muertos

3,000'
San
Pedro   El Novillo   La Trinchera

Los
Planes

CALIFORNIA

Los
Divisaderos   Tescalama

3,600'

El
Carrizal

San Antonio

El
Triunfo   Agua Caliente

Las Gallinas

San Bartolo

Bahía de Las Palmas

San Juan   Valle
Perdido

Los Barriles
Buena Vista

Agua Caliente   Los Mártires

La Ribera

LA AGUJA
6,500'
LA LAGUNA
El Salto   6,800'
C. SAN
ANTONIO
La Burrera

Las Lagunas

Las Cuevas

La
Pastora   Todos
Santos   Santiago

TROPIC   OF   CANCER

San Pedrito

Saucito   Agua Caliente

El Pescadero   Los Horconsitos   Boca de la Sierra
El Refugio   Miraflores

Los Frailes

LOS
FRAILES

5,940'

2,900'

Arroyo   Salado

El Palmar   6,225'   Caduaño

La Palma

Colonia Calles
San Juan
Las Piedritas
El Gasparcito

Santa Anita   San Pedro

Santa Catarina
San José Viejo

La Tinaja

La
Candelaria

Santa Rosa
Rosarito

La Laguna

Migriño

Los Pozos

San José del Cabo
La Palmilla (Hotel)

23°   PUNTA PALMILLA   23°

El Bledito

El Tule

Puerto
Chileno

0   5   10   15

MILES

San Lucas
CABO SAN LUCAS

PACIFIC

OCEAN

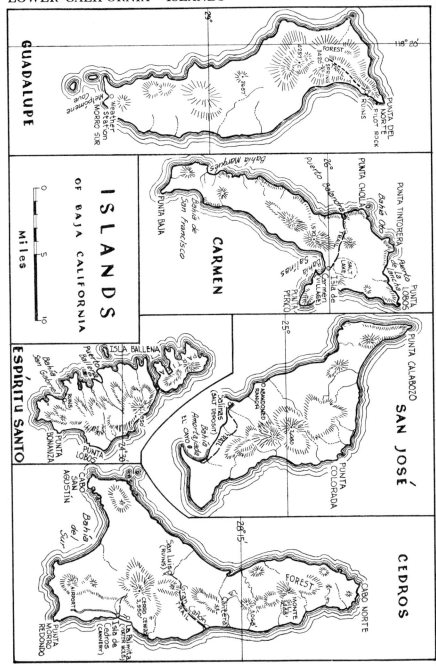

ISLANDS
OF BAJA CALIFORNIA

GUADALUPE

CARMEN

ESPÍRITU SANTO

SAN JOSÉ

CEDROS

INDEX

ABREOJOS: 140
Agriculture: 15-16, 72-73, 103, 109, 110, 162, 166, 172, 175, 189, 190
Agua Amarga: 123; 133
Agua Blanca: 96
Agua Caliente: 62; 68; 77; 106; 178; 179; Arroyo: 102
Agua Caliente (race track): 58, 59, 60
Agua Caliente (village): 183
Agua Caliente de Marconi: 94
Agua Caliente de Ramírez: 93
Agua Caliente de San Antonio: 95
Agua Caliente de San Carlos: 103
Agua de ——: see under rest of name
Agua Dulce: 120
Agua Escondida: 62, 88; 111; 156
Agua Flores: 97
Agua Verde, Bahía: 208
Aguajito: 114
Aguila, El: 115
Aguja, La: 165
Ahumada, (Padre) Tomás: 88
Air lines: 36-37
Ajusco, Ejido: 104
Alamito: 81
Alamo, El (ranches): 138, 141; 176
Alamo, El (village): 96-97
Alamos, Los: 106
Alaska: 66
Alcatraz, Puerto: 201
Alfredo, Arroyo: 84
Algodón: 102
Algodones: 76
All-American Canal: 73
Almacén, El: 84; 141
Almejas, Bahía: 165, 201
Almejas, Playa: 81
Altamira: 126
Alvarez, Colonia: 166
Amortajada, Bahía: 205, 206
Angel de la Guarda: 176
Angel de la Guarda, Isla: 124, 211-212

Angeles, Los (ranches): 138; 161
Angeles, Bahía de los: 123-124
Anhelo, El: 179
Animals: 40-42
Antelope: 41, 197
Año Nuevo: 153
Arbolitos: 103
Arco, El: 12, 130, 135, 136, 137
Arenoso, El: 114
Aripes, Los: 168, 169, 174
Armenta: 152
Arnés (Padre) Victoriano: 85, 121
Arquitos, Los: 84
Arrastras, Las: 85
Arroyo ——: see under name of arroyo
Arroyo Grande: 80, 101
Arroyo de San Pedro (ranch): 153
Arroyo Hondo: 191
Arroyo Salado: 106; 180
Arroyo Seco: 106; 165
Aserradero (sawmill) de Sierra Juárez: 95
Asunción: 140
Atondo y Antillón, Isidro: 24, 153, 205, 207
Azufre: Cañón de, 143; Puerto de, 78

BACHANDRES: 12, 126
Bachata, La: 133
Baegert, (Padre) Juan Jacobo: 52, 166-167
Bahía ——: see under name of bay
Baja, Punta: 112
Bajada: La, 157; del Molino, 191
Bajío Largo del Sur: 95
Balandra, Puerto: 209
Ballena: La, 142, 165; Bahía, 140; Isla, 204
Banda, Punta: 10, 90-92, 103-104
Banderita, La: 130
Bandini, Juan: 61
Barracas, Las: 179

Barrancas, Las: 161
Barril, El: 93; 136
Barriles, Los: 178
Basaldúa, (Padre) Juan Manuel: 210
Bataques: 76
Becerra, Diego de: 23
Beer: 33, 61, 72
Bellavista: 147
Berrendo, Llano del: 137
Biarritz: 143
Bibliography: 52-54
Birds: 42-43
Black Warrior Lagoon: see Guerrero
 Negro
Bledito, El: 187
Boca, La: 179
Boca de ——: see also rest of name
Boca de la Sierra: 183
Bocana, La: 112; 140; 142; (de Santo
 Tomás): 104
Boleo Mining Company: 144, 175, 177
Bomba, La: 79
Bombas, Las: 129, 130
Bombedor: 153
Bonó: 155
Bravo, Nicolás, Colonia: 116
Bravo, (Padre) Jaime: 170, 176, 190,
 206
Brillante, El: 94
Buenaventura: 168
Buenavista: 174; 188
Buena Vista: 107; 153; 162; 178; Paso
 de: 102
Buenos Aires: 106; 178; Llano de: 115
Bufadora, La: 10
Bule, El: 147
Bullfights: 59, 87
Buried treasure: 25, 67, 121-122, 125,
 140, 198, 204
Burrera, La: 189, 191
Burro, El: 62, 94
Bus lines: 38-39, 57, 69-70

CABALLERO, (Padre) Félix: 62
Caballo, El: 153
Cabo de Hornos: 179
Cabras, Las: 108; 183; Punta: 105
Cabrillo: see Rodríguez Cabrillo
Cacachilas Mountains: 175
Cachanilla: 144
Cadejé: 142, 152

Caduaño: 184
Caimancito, El: 173
Cajiloa: 113
Cajón, Cañón el: 102
Calabazas, Puente: 76
Calabozo, El: 95
Calaguá: 159
Calamajué (mission): 25, 86
Calamajué: 85, 86; Puerto de: 86; Mo-
 lino de: 86
Calaveras, Punta: 105
Calentura, La: 98, 106
Calera, La: 179
Caleta del Navío: 201
Calexico (California): 72
Calles, Colonia: 188
Calmallí: 129, 134, 135; (ranch): 173
Calmallí Viejo: 135
Camalú: 109
Cambalaquió: 157
Campechano, Puerto: 189
Cañada Ancha: 98
Cañada Honda: 190
Candelaria, La: 147; 188
Canipolé: 153, 157
Canoas, Punta: 116
Cañón de Calmallí, El (ranch): 134
Cantina, La: 132, 137
Cantú, Esteban: 72
Cantú Palms: 67
Capilla, La: 179
Caracol, El: 137
Carambuche, El: 159
Cárdenas, Lázaro, Colonia: 98
Cardón (cactus): 47, 114, 120, 151,
 153
Cardón, El: 119
Cardonal, El: 133
Carmen, Isla de: 155, 208-209
Carranco, (Padre) Lorenzo: 180, 183
Carranza, Colonia: 78
Carranza, Venustiano, Puerto de: 129
Carrizal, El: 142; 191
Carrizo, El: ranch, 60; Cañón, 67
Cartabón, El: 114
Casa Blanca, La: 176
Casas Verdes: 64
Casas Viejas: 158
Castillo, El: 113
Catalina, Isla: 207
Cataviñá: 120

Cataviñacito: 11, 120
Cavendish, Thomas: 188
Cayo, El: 206
Cedro, El: 165
Cedros, Isla de: 198-200
Cenizo, Pozo: 68; Cerro: 198
Centinela, El: 69
Cerralvo, Isla: 202-203
Cerrito Blanco: 123
Cerro Blanco: 116, 120
Cerro Colorado: 96
Cerro de Costilla: 108
Cerro Prieto: 75, 77; 83; (ranch): 95
Cerros Cuates: 98
Cervatillo: 162
Chale: Agua de, 83; Puerto, 165, 201
Chapala, Laguna (ranch and dry lake): 85, 122-123
Chávez, Rancho de: 151
Chileno: El, 116; Puerto, 13, 187
Chinal, El: 183
Chinero, El: 81
Chocolate, El: 105
Chorro, El: 183
Chuenque: 155, 208
Chula Vista: 188
Ciénega, La: 61, 63; 95
Ciprés, El: airport, 90, 103; ranch, 111
Cirio: 47, 114, 120, 124
Ciruelito, El: 176
Clam Beach: 81
Climate: 15
Coahuila, Colonia: 78
Coave, El: 176
Coches, Los: 63; 106
Cochimí Indians: 199-200
Cochis, Agua de los: 189
Cócopa Indians: 79
Codornices, Las: 119, 123
Colnett: Punta, 106, 107; Colonia, 107
Colonia ——: see under name of colony
Colonia, La: 160
Colorado River: 9, 59, 66, 72-73, 75-76, 78, 79; picture: 99
Colosal, El: 115
Compadre, El: 63
Comondú: 12, 25, 161; description: 157-158; picture: 163
Comondú Viejo: 157
Concepción: Bahía, 152, 210; picture, 146; Calera, 67

Conchal, El: 159
Cóndor, El: 65
Conejo, Punta: 165, 168
Conejos, Los: 106
Cono, Punta: 119
Consag, (Padre) Fernando: 84, 86, 124, 136
Constitución, Villa: 167
Consuelo, El: 111
Copper mining: 144, 147
Cornelias, Las: 63
Coromuel: 173
Corona, La (in San Pedro Mártir): 108, 109; picture: 100
Coronados, Isla: 209
Corral de dos Puertas: 159
Cortés, Hernán: 23, 24, 170, 173, 201, 203, 205
Cortés, Puerto: 201; 204
Costa Azul: 187
Costa, Agua de la: 178
Cotton: 16, 69, 72-73, 162, 172, 175
Coyote, El (on Concepción Bay): 12, 152, 210
Coyote, El: ranches, 107, 108, 168; settlement, 173, 174
Coyote, Estero del: 140
Crucero, El: 167
Cruces, Las: mine, 93; ranch, 150; club, 173
Cuarenta: 142; Salina: 142
Cuatro: 98
Cuatro Vientos: 189
Cucapá Indians: 79
Cucapás, Sierra: 66-67, 69, 72, 77, 78
Cucapah: 76
Cuervos: 76
Cueva Colorada: 137
Cuevas, Las: 179, 180
Cuevas Pintas, 155
Cuevitas, Las: 95
Cuñaño, 165
Customs regulations: 27

Daggett, Dick: 85
Danzantes, Bahía de los: 208
Dates: 139, 151, 158, 160
Dátil, El: 165; Estero, 141
Datilar: 165
Datilito: 174
David, Cañón de: 78

Deer: 41, 108, 111, 124, 197, 199, 206
Delgadito, El: 141
Delicias, Las: 166; 179
Demara, Pozo: 68
Descanso: 26, 88, 153
Desengaño: 123
Diablito, Cañón el: 102
Diablo: Picacho del, 101, 108; Cañón el, 102
Díez, (Padre) Juan José: 85
Divisaderos, Los: 176
Dolores, Los: 25, 167, 207; (near San Javier): 156
Dominicans: 25-26
Don Pancho: 88
Durango, Ejido: 78

Ejido ——: see under second word
Ejidos: 73, 75-76
El ——: see under second word
Elephant seals: 42, 196, 199
Elephant trees: 48, 51, 120, 123
Encantada, La: 108
Encinal, El: 63
Encino, El: 98
Encino Solo: 94
Encinos, Los: 108
Ensenada: 10, 26, 90-93, 103; map: 91
Ensenada de Palmas: 178
Envidia, La: 153
Eréndira, Ejido: 10, 11, 105
Escalante, (Padre) Francisco: 151
Escondido: 66; 95
Espantado: 93
Esperanza, Cañón de la: 101
Esperanza, La: 135; 143
Espiga de Oro: 61
Espina, La: 129
Espinosa, Santiago: 11
Espinoza, Juan José: 170
Espíritu Santo, Isla: 174, 204-205
Estero, El: 103
Estero Salinas: 201
Esteros del Batequi: 190
Estrella, Punta: 82
Estrella del Norte: 176
Estrellita, La: rancho, 11
Eureka: 179

Falsa, Bahía: 173
Faro, El: 77

Felicidad, Mina de la: 93
Fenómeno, El: 64
Ferryboat: 8-9, 13
Fiestas: 20-22
Filipinas, Las: 95
Fishing: 43-45, 82, 84, 92, 124, 172, 199
Fish packing plants: 89, 92, 131, 132, 142, 187, 198-199
Flores, Las: 107; 124
Florida, La: 165, 201
Florido, El: 60
Fonseca: 102
Food and drink: 32-33
Fortuna, La: 174
Frailes, Los: 179, 180; Pozo de: 84
Franciscans: 25, 115, 154
Freeway: 10
Frijol, El: 152
Fruit: 33, 160, 185, 189, 190

Gallinas, Las: 191
Gálvez, José de: 25, 204
Gandul, El: 60
Gardner, Erle Stanley: 12, 53
Gavilanes, Los: 65
Giganta, La: 153
Gill, Monte: 198
Gold mining: 65, 83, 85, 93, 94, 96-97, 135, 140
Golfo, El (Sonora): 9, 78
Gómez, (Padre): 139
Gonzaga: see under San Luis Gonzaga
González Ortega: 75
Grande, Arroyo: 80, 101
Gringa, La: 123
Grulla, La: meadow, 108; gun club, 103
Guadalupe (missions): del Sur, 25, 49, 150; del Norte, 26, 62, 63
Guadalupe: village, 62; ranches, 61, 132, 136, 138, 165
Guadalupe, Cañón de: 68
Guadalupe, Isla: 195-197
Guarismo, El: 159
Guatamote: 80
Güérivo: 49, 150
Guerrero, Colonia: 109-110
Guerrero Negro: 12, 129-130, 134, 137, 197
Guillén, (Padre) Clemente: 202, 207
Gypsum: 210-211

HALF WAY HOUSE: 88
Hamacas, Las: 168, 174
Hamilton Ranch: 109, 110
Hanson, Laguna: 9, 66, 95
Hardy, Rio: 79
Hechicera: 76; La: 63; 65
Hermosillo, Ejido: 76
Hidalgo: Ejido, 75; Villa, 109
Hiedra, La: 62
Higuera, Agua de: 11, 124
History: 23-26
Horconsitos, Los: 189
Horno, El: 156
Huerfanito, El: 10, 83
Hotels: 31
Huerta, La: 64, 94; 175
Huerta Vieja: 159
Huisache, El: 130, 197
Hunting: 40-43, 108, 111, 124, 179, 206
Hurricanes: 154, 169, 185, 190

IBARRA, Rancho: 109
Iguajil, El: 166
Immigration: 27
Imposible, El: 168
Indians: 12, 23, 24, 26, 63, 64, 68, 79, 88, 98, 203, 205, 206; see also under names of missions listed pp. 25-26
Industries: 16
Infiernillo, Cuesta del: 143
Iritú: 167

JACOMÚN: 63
Jacumé: 64
Jamau: 9, 80, 97
Japá: 65
Japón, El: 147
Jaquejel: 9, 80
Jaraguay: 11, 122
Jasay: 65
Jatay: 89
Jatñil (Indian chief): 63
Jesuits: 24-25, 120-121, 154
Jesús María: 129, 134
Jiquilpan, Ejido: 76
Johnson, Harry: 108
Johnson Ranch: 106-107
Josefina, La (mine): 85
Juan Márquez: 191
Juárez, Sierra: 65-68, 79, 95

Juárez: Villa, 63; Presa, 190
Juncalito: 155
Junco, El: 129, 134
Juntas, Las: 63

KILÓMETRO 57: 78
Kilómetro 100: 168
Kiliwa Indians: 98
King Richard Mine: 85
Kino, (Padre) Eusebio Fco: 24, 153

LA ——: see under second word
Lacy, Molino de: 85
Laguna ——: see also under name of laguna
Laguna, La: 94; 141, 200; 173; 183, 189
Laguna Campestre (subdivision): 77
Laguna Salada: 9, 66-69, 78, 79, 80
Laguna Seca: 122
Laguna Verde: 165, 202
Lagunas, Las: 132; 179
Lagunitas, Las: 136; 166
Las ——: see under second word
Lasuén, (Padre) Fermín: 125
Lázaro Cárdenas, Colonia: 98
Leather work: 183, 184; picture: 181
Leñeros: 68-69
León, Arroyo: 98
Leona, Cuesta la: 83
Ley, Cuesta la: 136
Ligüí: 25, 155
Link, (Padre) Wenceslao: 115, 125, 212
Llano, El: 176
Llano Colorado: 97; 106
Lobera, La: 116
Lobos, Punta: 189
Loma Amarilla: 12, 129
Londó, San Juan Bautista: 153
Loreto: 12, 13, 21, 24, 25, 154-155
Loriente, (Padre) José: 104
Los ——: see under second word
Lost missions: 25, 121-122, 140
Lucenilla, Francisco de: 210
Lúcifer: 143
Lulesal, Rancho: 93
Luz, La: 153

MAGDALENA, Bahía: 161, 162, 165, 167, 200-202

Magdalena: Boca de (ranches, chapel), 150; Arroyo, 149, 150
Magdalena, Isla: 201
Magdalena Plain: 162-167, 202
Magdalena, Santa María de: 140
Malarrimo: 131, 198
Maneadero: 10, 27, 103-104
Manglito, El: 191
Manila galleon: 167, 186, 187-188, 196, 199, 200, 202
Manuela, Laguna: 129
Margarita: Isla, 201; mine, 65
Margaritas, Las: 109
María Auxiliadora: 162, 166
María Eugenia: 64
María, Punta: 119
Mariana, La: 78
Mariolas, Las: 150
Marítimo, Ejido: 79
Mármol, El: 119
Marmolito, El: 133
Marqués: Puerto del, 203; Bahía: 209
Marrón, Boca de: 119
Mártires, Los: 132, 138; 179
Matancita: 162; 188
Matanuco: 60
Matomí, El: Arroyo, 83; ranch, 130
Matomí, El (peak): 114; picture: 117
Mayor, El: 79; Sierra: 79
Mayorga, (Padre) Julián de: 157
Mazatlán, Puerto de (restaurant): 77
Mechudo, El: 206
Médano, El: 165
Médano Amarillo: 165, 201
Médano Blanco: 161
Medio Camino: 88
Meling Ranch: 108-109
Melpómene Bay: 196
Metate, El: 114
Mexicali: 26, 69-75; map: 71
México, Ejido: 107
Mezcal, El: 95
Mezquital: El, 134, 143, 150; Arroyo del, 142
Mezquite, El: 65
Mezquitito: Agua del, 84; grade, 157
Michoacán, Ejido: 75
Midriff, the: 42
Migriño: 188
Mijares, José Antonio: 186
Milla, La: 65

Miller's Landing: 126, 133
Mining: see copper, gold, silver
Miraflores: town, 183-184; ranch, 136
Miramar: 83; 134; 179
Miseria, La: 176
Misión, La: 9, 10, 59, 88-89
Misión Vieja: 190, 191
Missions: 24-26; also see under individual mission names, listed pp. 25-26
Mochillas, Las: 159
Mogote, El: 169, 174
Molino, El: 110, 111
Money: 29
Monserrate, Isla: 207
Morelos Dam: 76
Morros, Los: 116
Muertito, El: 126
Muertos, Bahía de los: 175
Mulegé: 21, 25, 26, 151, 210, 211

Napoli, (Padre) Ignacio María: 180
Natividad, Isla: 199
Nejí: 63
Nelson, Rancho: 93
Nopoló: 155
Notrí: 155
Novillo, El: 176
Nueva York: 110
Nuevo León, Ejido: 75, 76

Obispo, El: 167
Ojo de Agua: 159
Ojo de Liebre: water hole, 130, 197; Laguna, 130, 197; Salina, 130
Ojos Negros: 10, 66, 93, 94
Okie Landing: 84
Olivares Mexicanos: 62
Onyx: 116, 119, 133
Ortega, Francisco de: 24, 203, 205, 206, 207, 208, 209, 210
Osio, Manuel de: 177

Pabellón, El: 161
Paipai Indians: 68, 97, 98
Palaco: 75-76
Palma, La: 143; 184
Palmar, El: 189
Palmarito, El: 111
Palmas, Agua de las (in Cucapás mountains): 78
Palmas, Bahía de las: 178

Palmas, Valle de las: 60, 61
Palmilla, La: 13, 187
Palmita, La: 68; 199, 200
Palms (native): 49, 67, 68, 120, 156, 166, 195
Palo Blanco: 156
Palo Bola: 166
Palomar, El: 68
Palomas, Las: 116, 123; 135
Palou, (Padre) Francisco: 156
Palo Verde: 159
Panales, Los: 159
Paraíso: Arroyo, 133, 134; Boca de, 134
Paredes, Las: 159
Paredones: 76
Parra, La: 98
Parras, Las: 155; Arroyo de: 154, 155; Pilón de: 155
Partida, Isla: 204
Pascualitos: 75
Pasión, La: 25, 167, 207
Paso Hondo: 159-160
Pastora, La: 191
Patrocinio: 142
Pavillion Beach: 111
Paz, La: 8, 9, 13, 17, 23, 25, 26; description: 168-173; picture, 181; map, 171
"Paz, La," ferryboat: 8, 9, 13
Pearls: 170, 202-203, 204, 205, 206, 207, 208, 209
Pedregoso, El: 11, 122
Pemex: 130, 132, 173
Pénjamo: ranch, 115; restaurant, 167, 168
Pequeña, Punta: 142
Persebú: 82, 83
Pericú Indians: 180, 203, 206
Pescadero: 180
Pescaderos: 78
Petroglyphs: 11, 152
Piccolo, (Padre) Fco. María: 139, 156
Pichilingue, Bahía: 13, 173, 203-204
Piedras, Las: 157
Piedras Gordas: 10, 93; 178
Piedras Rodadas: 159
Piedritas, Las: 188
Pilar, El: 167
Pino Solo: 96
Piñón, Cerro el: 96

Pinta, Sierra: 80
Pintada, Sierra: 131, 140, 198
Pioneer Gold Mine: 85
Pirates: 188, 204
Pisón, Gaspar: 177
Pitahaya (cactus): 23, 33, 50
Planes, Los: 175
Plants: 46-51
Plátano, El: 167
Platero, El: 63
Playas de Tijuana: 87
Pleito, Arroyo el: 98
Pocitas, Las: 168
Pólvora: 76
Population: 15-16
Porter Casanate, Pedro: 24
Portezuelo, El: 123
Portón, El: 161
Porvenir, Ejido: 62, 88, 89
Porvenir, El (ranches): 96; 138
Posta, La: 176
Potrero, El: 107; 152; 189
Potreros, Los: 184
Poza Colorada: 179
Poza Grande: 161
Poza de Teresa: 156
Pozo Alemán: 135
Pozo Cenizo: 68
Pozo de la Brecha: 150
Pozos, Los: 188
Presa, La: 157; 167, 207; picture: 164
Presa Vieja: 156
Presentación, La: 156
Primer Agua: 154
Principio, Arroyo el: 124
Progreso: El, 65, 115; Colonia, 69
Providencia: Cañón la, 102; mine, 147
Puebla, Ejido: 75
Puerta, La: 60; 77
Puerta Vieja: 156
Puertecitos: 83
Puerto ——: see also under name of puerto
Puerto Escondido: 155, 208
Puerto Nuevo: 88
Pulmo, El: 179
Punta ——: see under name of point
Punta Piedra: 89
Punta del Cerro, La: 167
Punta Prieta (village): 12, 125-126, 132

Punta Prieta: 140; 173
Purísima, Colonia: 166
Purísima, La: 12, 25, 142, 157, 159-160
Purísima Vieja: 159, 160

QUELELE, El: 174
Querétaro: 162

RÁBICH, El: 140
Railways: 36, 69-70, 75
Ramadita: 162
Ramona, La: 115
Ranchito, El: 147; 156; 166
Rancho Alegre: 134
Rancho Grande: 106; 134
Rancho Nuevo: 98; 111
Rancho Viejo: 61; 95; 97; 155, 156
Rayo, El: 95
Real del Castillo: 92, 93-94
Recreo, El: 96
Reforma, El: 191
Refugio: El, 105, 165, 189; Agua de,
    133; Puerto, 211
Religion: 19
Rentoy: 153
Requesón, El: 152
Retiro, El: 134
Retz, (Padre) Jorge: 125, 136
Ribera, La: 179
Riíto (Sonora): 9, 78
Rincón, El: 147
Rincón de Guadalupe: 106
Rinconada, La: 142
Rinconcito, El: 190
Rio Grande: 134
Roads: 34-36
Rocosa, Punta: 211
Rodeo, El: 81, 97
Rodríguez: 168, 174
Rodríguez, Abelardo: 89
Rodríguez Cabrillo, Juan: 92, 132, 200
Rodríguez Dam: 9, 59, 60
Rosa de Castilla: 64
Rosario, El: 11, 25, 112-113; 191
Rosarito: 111; 12, 125, 133; 185; El:
    153
Rosarito Beach: 9, 10, 59, 88
Ruiz, José Manuel: 92
Rumorosa, La: 66
Russian colony: 62

SÁIZ, Arroyo el: 68, 80
Salada, La: 165
Salada, Laguna: see Laguna Salada
Salado, Arroyo: 106; 180
Sales, (Padre) Luis: 89
Salina Beach: 10, 89
Salinas: Estero, 201; Punta, 205, 206;
    Bahía, 209
Salinito: El, 119; Arroyo, 133
Salsipuedes: 89
Saltillo, Ejido: 75
Saltito, El: 173; 189
Salto, El: 111; 176; 191
Salvatierra, (Padre) Juan María: 24,
    153, 154
Salvioso, El: 174
Sam, Corral de: 108
San Agustín: 119; 168; Cabo: 199
San Andrés: 126; 140; Bocana de: 119
San Angel: 138
San Antonio: 63; 157
San Antonio (town): 177-178
San Antonio de la Mesa: 106
San Antonio del Mar: 105, 107
San Antonio de los Buenos: 87
San Bartolo: 178
San Bartolomé: 131, 132
San Benito, Islas: 196, 199
San Bernabé: 184
San Bernardo: 166; Arroyo: 183
San Blas: 176
San Borja: 12, 21, 25, 26, 124-125; pic-
    ture: 127
San Bruno: 149; 153
San Carlos: arroyo, 95; hot spring, 103;
    Puerto de, 113; ranch, 143; fishing
    camp, 162, 201
San Esteban: 132
San Faustino: 64
San Felipe: 81-82; 102
San Felipe: Sierra de, 102; Valle de,
    101-102
San Fernando (mission): 25, 115
San Fernando: Arroyo, 113; Cañada,
    113
San Francisco: peak and village, 12
San Francisquito (ranch): 132, 137
San Francisquito, Bahía: 136
San Francisquito: Ensenada de, 84, 85,
    212; Puerto de, 10, 85

San Gabriel: 205
San Gregorio: 125, (picture) 127; 142
San Hilario: 168
San Hipólito: 140
San Ignacio (town and mission): 21, 25, 26, 138-139, 141, 142-143; picture, *frontispiece*
San Ignacio, Laguna de: 141, 200; picture: 145
San Ignacio (ranches): 156; 190
San Ignacito: 11, 122; 12, 125
San Ildefonso, Isla: 210
San Isidro: Puerto de, 105; ranch, 150; town, 160; suburb of Santiago, 180
San Jacinto: 105; 189
San Javier (mission): 21, 25, 156; picture: 163
San Javier: canyon, 126; ranch, 147
San Jerónimo: 133; 150
San Joaquín: 141
San Jorge: 161
San José: ranches, 63, 105, 120; arroyo, 116, 120
San José, Isla: 205-206
San José de Castro: 131, 140
San José de Comondú: 156, 157-158
San José de Gracia: 142
San José de la Zorra: 88
San José del Cabo: 13, 25, 26, 185-187
San José de los Arce: 160
San José de Magdalena: 150
San José (Meling Ranch): 107, 108-109
San José Viejo: 184
San Juan: ranches, 105, 134, 138, 157, 168, 190, 191; mine, 124; Arroyo de, 125, 141, 142
San Juan Bautista Londó: 153
San Juan de Dios: 64; 114; (peak): 114
San Juan de los Lagos: 188
San Juan del Llano: 190
San Juan Nepomuceno: 203
San Juanico: 142
San Julián: 174
San Julio, Llano de: 156
San Lino: 138, 143
San Lorenzo, Isla: 136
San Lucas (cape, town, bay, hotels): 13, 187-188, 202

San Lucas: 149
San Luciano: 147
San Luis: ranches, 110, 141, 173, 199; Arroyo, 134
San Luis (de Cataviñá): 11, 120
San Luis Gonzaga (mission): 22, 25, 166-167, 168, 207
San Luis Gonzaga, Bahía: 84, 212
San Luis (Sonora): 77
San Marcos: 149; Isla: 149, 210-211
San Martín, Isla: 110
San Matías: 98-100
San Miguel (ranches): 97; 109; 133
San Miguel Comondú: 25, 158
San Miguel de la Frontera (mission): 25, 88, 89
San Miguel Village (resort): 10, 89
San Nicolás: 209-210
San Pablo: 137
San Pascual: 208
San Pedrito: 189
San Pedro: ranches, 65, 184; village, 176, 191
San Pedro, Arroyo de (ranch): 153
San Pedro Mártir (mission): 26, 108-109
San Pedro Mártir, Sierra: 101, 102, 108-109, 111, 114
San Quintín: 11, 110, 111
San Rafael: valley, 93; ranches, 106, 189
San Rafael, Arroyo de: 98, 106, 108, 109
San Ramón: 110
San Raymundo: 142
San Regis: 133; 143
San Sabás: 138
San Salvador: 96
San Sebastián: 150
San Simón: 11, 111; 11, 120
San Telmo: 106, 107, 109
San Valentín: 63
San Venancio: 189
San Vicente: mission and settlement, 10, 11, 25, 105-106; Valle de, 113
San Zacarías: 141
Sangre de Cristo: 96
Santa Agueda: 144, 147
Santa Ana: 125; 165; 177
Santa Ana, Llanos de: 123

Santa Anita: 184
Santa Brígida: 141; 158
Santa Catalina (mission): 26, 97
Santa Catarina: 95, 97; 115-116, 119; 184
Santa Clara: 62; 95, 96; 101; (Sonora): 9, 78
Santa Clara, Sierra: 140
Santa Cruz: 105; 107; 135; 190; 203
Santa Fe: 165; Colonia: 167
Santa Gertrudis (mission): 21, 25, 26, 136-137
Santa Gertrudis (ranch): 110
Santa Inés: ranch, 11, 120; bay, 12
Santa Isabel (lost mission): 121-122
Santa Isabel: 68, 95
Santa María: village, 11, 111; beaches, 111, 143; mine, 116; ranches, 130, 174
Santa María (mission): 25, 84, 120-121
Santa María Magdalena: 140
Santa María Sky Ranch: 111
Santa Marta: 124; 162
Santa Rita: 168
Santa Rosa: 76; (village): 184; (ranches): 147, 153
Santa Rosalía: 143-149; picture: 145
Santa Rosalillita: fishing camp, 126; ranch, 152
Santa Teresa: 136
Santa Victoria: 174
Santiago: 22, 25, 180-183
Santispac: 152
Santo Domingo (mission and settlement): 25, 109-110
Santo Domingo (landing): 129
Santo Domingo: ranch, 104; arroyo, 155, 156
Santo Domingo del Pacífico: 161-162, 166
Santo Dominguito, Arroyo de: 133
Santo Tomás: 26, 104-105; Puerto de: 104
Sargento, El: 175
Saucito: 188; 189; El: 84
Sauzal, El: 89-90; 141
Sauzalito: 113, 114
Scammon's Lagoon: 129, 130, 131, 197-198
Sea elephants: see Elephant seals

Sebastián Vizcaíno Desert: 129, 130, 137, 197; picture: 128
Segundo Paso: 156
Serra, (Padre) Junípero: 25, 107, 114, 115
Sesvania: 76
Sheep, mountain: 41, 86, 207, 208
Silver mining: 124, 176, 177-178
Sinaloa, Hacienda: 107
Sinarquistas: 162
Socorro, El: 111
Socorro (former mine): 108, 109
Soledad: 176
Solito, El: 130
Sonora Café: 11
Sorpresa, La: 173
Steamships: 37-38
Suerte, La: 111
Sulfur mine: 83
Surgidero: 179

TABLÓN, El: 12, 137
Tajo, El: 65, 67; 147
Tamaral, (Padre) Nicolás: 184, 186
Tanamá: 61
Taraval, (Padre) Sigismundo: 200
Taxis: 29, 57, 172
Tecate: 60-61
Tecolote: 76
Tecomajá: 155
Tepí: 98
Teraizo, Arroyo: 101
Tescalama: 176
Tesos, Boca de los: 179
Testerazo, El: 61, 63
Tiburón Island: 43, 136
Tijuana: 9, 10, 57-60, 87; map: 56
Tinaja, La: 188
Tinajitas, Las: 167
Tipping: 29
Toba, Colonia de la: 166
Todos Santos: mission and town, 13, 25, 26, 189-191; ranch, 120
Todos Santos Bay: 90-92
Tomatal, El: 126
Topo, El: 65
Toro, El: 168
Torote, El: 126
Torre, El: 166
Tortuga: Isla, 211; Valle, 142

Tortugas, Bahía: 131-132, 140; picture: 128
Transportation: 34-39
Travesía, La: 153
Tres Enriques: 120
Tres Pachitas, Las: 191
Tres Pozos: 65; 80
Tres Vírgenes, Las: 143
Trinchera: La, 177; Sierra, 176
Trinidad, Valle: 98, 106
Tripuí: 155
Triunfo, El: town, 13, 177; ranch, 93
Tule, El: 93; 187
Tungsten: 64, 65
Torquesa, La: 114
Turtle Bay: see Tortugas
Turtles: 33, 124, 131, 197, 200, 201

UGARTE, (Padre) Juan de: 150, 156, 158, 170
Ulloa, Francisco de: 187, 199-200, 201, 210, 212
Unión, La: 136
Uruapan, Ejido: 103

VALLADARES, 107
Vallecitos: 61; 108
Valle de: see under name of valley
Valle Perdido: 191
Valle Redondo: 60
Valle Seco: 62, 94
Velázquez: 166
Venancio: 169
Venta, La: 155; 178
Ventana: La, 68, 80, 81; bay, 175
Víbora, La: 133; 150, 151

Victoria: 75, 76, 78
Vieja, La: 165
Virgen, La: 120; Cuesta, 83
Virgen María: 168
Vírgenes, Las: 143
Vives, Gastón: 205
Vizcaíno Desert: see Sebastián Vizcaíno Desert
Vizcaíno, Salina: 129
Vizcaíno, Sebastián: 24, 132, 196, 200, 202, 203, 208, 210
Voladores, Los: 131
Volcán, El: 119
Volcano: 76; Laguna: 77
Volcanoes: 15, 77, 143, 209, 211
Vuelta, La: 134
Vuelta La Curvina: 9, 79

WALKER, William: 26, 170
Weights and measures: 30
Whales: 42, 197, 200
Willard Bay: 212
Wilson, Rancho de: 132, 137

XIMÉNEZ, Fortún: 23, 170

YUBAY, Tinaja de: 123

ZACATAL: 155
Zacatecas, Colonia: 78
Zacatón, El: 159
Zalate, El: 176
Zalatito, El: 179
Zapote, El: 176
Zaragoza, Colonia: 69
Zorra, La: 62, 88

The CLARK GUIDEBOOK Series . . .

I — Lower California Guidebook
by Peter Gerhard and Howard E. Gulick

II — Discovering Mayaland: a Guide to Yucatan
by Allen R. and Phyllis T. Ellis

III — Nayarit, Mexico: a Traveler's Guidebook
by Howard E. Gulick